DRILLED TO WRITE

DRILLED TO WRITE

Becoming a Cadet Writer at a Senior Military College

J. MICHAEL RIFENBURG

UTAH STATE UNIVERSITY PRESS
Logan

© 2022 by University Press of Colorado

Published by Utah State University Press
An imprint of University Press of Colorado
245 Century Circle, Suite 202
Louisville, Colorado 80027

All rights reserved

 The University Press of Colorado is a proud member of the Association of University Presses.

The University Press of Colorado is a cooperative publishing enterprise supported, in part, by Adams State University, Colorado State University, Fort Lewis College, Metropolitan State University of Denver, Regis University, University of Alaska Fairbanks, University of Colorado, University of Denver, University of Northern Colorado, University of Wyoming, Utah State University, and Western Colorado University.

ISBN: 978-1-64642-277-7 (paperback)
ISBN: 978-1-64642-278-4 (ebook)
https://doi.org/10.7330/9781646422784

Library of Congress Cataloging-in-Publication Data

Names: Rifenburg, J. Michael, 1982– author.
Title: Drilled to write : becoming a cadet writer at a senior military college / J. Michael Rifenburg.
Description: Logan : Utah State University Press, [2022] | Includes bibliographical references and index.
Identifiers: LCCN 2022017934 (print) | LCCN 2022017935 (ebook) | ISBN 9781646422777 (paperback) | ISBN 9781646422784 (ebook)
Subjects: LCSH: Academic writing—Study and teaching (Higher)—United States—Case studies. | Military cadets—Education (Higher)—United States—Case studies. | Military cadets—Education (Higher)—United States—Anecdotes. | English language—Rhetoric—Study and teaching (Higher)—United States.
Classification: LCC P301.5.A27 R54 2022 (print) | LCC P301.5.A27 (ebook) | DDC 808.06/6378—dc23/eng/20220520
LC record available at https://lccn.loc.gov/2022017934
LC ebook record available at https://lccn.loc.gov/2022017935

Cover illustration by Bradley Huff

to Amy

CONTENTS

Reveille: A General, a Howitzer, and a Cadet   1

**SECTION 1: BECOMING A CADET:
A TEXTWORLD IN PREPARATION FOR YEAR ONE**   25

1   ROTC, Higher Education, and Citizen-Soldiers   27

2   This Study, Longitudinal Research, and Rhetorical Genre Studies   39

3   The Army's Version of the First-Year Experience: FROGs, Hills, and Haircuts   59

   Intersection 1: Getting There: Stepping into Longitudinal Research   71

SECTION 2: YEAR 1, CADET PRIVATE   81

4   Finding 1: What Writing Is Not   83

5   Banned Books, Anne Bradstreet, and First-Year Composition   87

6   Operations Orders as a Beginnings of Army Writing   108

SECTION 3: YEAR 2, CADET SERGEANT FIRST CLASS   115

7   Finding 2: The Lamination of Literate Activity   117

8   Flipped Classroom and Increased Morale   119

9   Dancing with Extracurricular Literate Activity   127

   Intersection 2: Staying There: Storying Our Data Collection and Analysis in Longitudinal Research   134

SECTION 4: YEAR 3, CADET SECOND LIEUTENANT   137

10   Finding 3: Offloading Cognitive Tasks   139

11   "A little field book," OPORDs, and Cordon and Search Tactical Techniques   142

12   Self-Sponsored Writing and a Presidential Election   160

SECTION 5: YEAR 4, CADET SECOND LIEUTENANT 171

13 Finding 4: The Military Decision-Making Process 173

14 The MDMP as a Critical-Thinking Heuristic 175

15 Drawing the Spaces of Writing and Then Graduating 191

Intersection 3: Leaving There: Articulating Our Longitudinal Research Findings and Implications 197

Retreat: A Researcher in Poland and an Officer at Fort Stewart 209

Appendix A: US Army echelons 219

Appendix B: US Army officer ranks from highest to lowest 220

Appendix C: US Army cadet ranks from highest to lowest 221

Appendix D: Abbreviations 222

Appendix E: Interview transcript with General Stephen J. Townsend, commander, United States Africa Command 223

References 233

Index 245

About the Author 259

Effective Army writing is understood by the reader in a single rapid reading and is clear, concise, and well-organized.
—*Preparing and Managing Correspondence,*
US Army Regulation 25-50

Writing occurs in almost all spheres of action and in many moments, each with separate demands and opportunities. Trajectories of writing development are intertwined with trajectories of intellectual, professional, and personal development, such that writing development contributes to personal uniqueness.
—Charles Bazerman, Arthur N. Applebee,
Virginia W. Berninger, Deborah Brandt,
Steve Graham, Paul Kei Matsuda, Sandra Murphy,
Deborah Wells Rowe, and Mary Schleppegrell

REVEILLE
A General, a Howitzer, and a Cadet

I'm sitting alone in the executive conference room on the fifth floor of US Army Training and Doctrine Command (TRADOC) headquarters at Fort Eustis, Virginia. Building 950. My hand reaches to feel my smoothly shaven cheek, an odd feeling after years of facial hair. I tug awkwardly at the suit jacket I put on for the occasion. Nine black leather chairs surround the brown rectangular conference table, four on each side and one at the head. Mics are scattered around the middle of the table, and a large camera sits above the LG flat-screen television that faces the head of the table, with two desktop monitors off to the side. The blinds are shut tight.

I'm seven hundred miles from home, waiting to interview General Stephen J. Townsend. He is one of just eighteen four-star generals in the US Army, a military branch with over one million active-duty, reserve, and national-guard soldiers. He serves as commanding general of TRADOC, which, in a talk at the American Association of Colleges and Universities (AAC&U) annual meeting, he described as being "the president of the Army's university." Townsend oversees the training of over five hundred thousand servicemembers each year. He oversees US Army Cadet Command (USACC). The Reserve Officers' Training Corps (ROTC) falls under USACC. ROTC operates with an $800 million annual budget for the training and support of roughly thirty thousand senior (i.e., college-level) cadets. Outside the TRADOC headquarters sits a large rubber mat on which TRADOC's logo is spelled out in white letters against the black background: Victory Starts Here!

Back in the executive conference room, a red LCD displays different time zones: Hawai'ian, Pacific, Central, Eastern, Zulu, German, Iraqi, Korean. In the television's reflection, I see myself at the head of the table and the display behind me. The TRADOC insignia, the descriptor (Headquarters US Army Training and Doctrine Command), and the motto again, Victory Starts Here. This time the logo comes sans an exclamation mark.

A dry-erase board hangs on the wall perpendicular to me. A doodle—maybe the floor plan of a room?—is in green marker. An orange marker sits in the tray on the board. The space reminds me of the many video-teleconference rooms I have sat in for department meetings at my five-campus home institution. But the different time zones remind me of the global focus of this space, and the large padlock on the door, accompanied by an emergency alarm button, reminds me of the security of the space.

The interview was to begin two hours ago. In the days leading up to the interview, Townsend's executive scheduler changed the time of the interview three times. I wonder whether this interview will be cancelled. Last evening, I received a text from the executive scheduler with another change to the start time.

I wait, checking and double-checking my digital recorder and the recording app I downloaded as back-up. I wait, fidgeting with my suit jacket and wondering whether I should ask for the Wi-Fi password. I wait, checking my interview transcript, IRB consent document.

A GENERAL...

Two men enter the room dressed in the occupational camouflage pattern (OCPs): Colonel Adam Nestor, executive officer to the commanding general, and Colonel Michael Indovina, chief of public affairs, who notes aloud that I am in the general's seat. I blush, make a clumsy attempt to relocate, but the two men are already seated around me. We talk preliminaries. They then usher me into Townsend's large corner office. Townsend, standing in OCPs, introduces himself (*Steve Townsend!*) and directs me to a seat on a brown leather sofa. He takes an armchair perpendicular to me. Nestor moves to stand behind me at Townsend's desk and takes out a pen and paper. Indovina take a seat in an armchair next to Townsend and clicks on two digital recorders. I fumble for my digital recorder, turn it on, and then turn on my recording app. No small talk as I fumble, just the loud, direct introduction and firm handshake. Townsend watches and waits.

I hit record, twice. Indovina hits record, twice. And I talk with the president of the army's university for thirty minutes about college writing instruction, Army writing standards, the unique relationship between the Army and higher education, and why he prefers grid paper.[1]

Townsend smiles easily. His tanned, youthful face belies his age. He close-clipped hair is tinged with gray. When he listens, he squints his eyes, raising the corners of his mouth into a tight smile.

Townsend knows why I am sitting in front of him. I pitched my research to Nestor before Townsend gave a talk at the AAC&U annual meeting. Townsend was on a panel with the chancellor of Rutgers

University–Camden talking about civic engagement. Before the talk, I approached Nestor with my business card and asked, "Can I interview the general for my book project?" I think it helped that I teach at Townsend's alma mater and that Townsend gave the commencement address the previous year. Nestor was open to the idea and told me to sit next to him during the general's panel. "After the panel," Nestor said, "I will introduce you." He did. I made my direct ask again to the general, and he loudly said, "Let's do it." Then he walked off. Two weeks before the scheduled interview, I sent a one-page letter of intent to Nestor. The letter read much like a document for human-subject research review—short, direct sentences; clear purpose and background; lacking disciplinary jargon and extensive citations. I included my brief bio statement and an article I coauthored with an Army major about cadets in civilian first-year composition courses (Rifenburg and Forester 2018).

As I prepare to voice my first question for Townsend in TRADOC's headquarters, I see a folder open in front of Indovina; I see my letter of intent, bio statement, and the article I coauthored. Then I talk.

I ask Townsend about his experience as an undergraduate at what was then North Georgia College, now the University of North Georgia (UNG). He starts by telling me about his college writing professor, Professor Guy Lail. Throughout our thirty-minute interview, he will mention Lail by name ten times. A four-star general, reflecting back forty years to his first-year writing professor. When I return to campus, I will head to the library archives, dig up a yearbook from 1980, and find a picture of Lail, one of just a handful of English-faculty members then at UNG. Townsend says,

> He [Guy Lail] taught me how to write an argumentative essay designed to argue a point, convince. There was a sort of fairly simple template with your introduction and thesis and then you gotta discredit the opposition, what the opposition is going to say. Then you get one to three points in support of your argument, and you conclude. And it was so effective that I still remember today what he taught me. That has held me in good stead throughout my Army career.

I keep my eyes on Townsend as he speaks, but I try to steal glances at the space. Typical military decorations on end tables and walls: plaques, pictures, flags. I offer a question about his experience with Army writing, specifically focusing on what he remembers writing as a young cadet and what he finds himself writing now as a general. He entertains my question but doesn't agree with the underlying assumption that cadets and generals are writing different genres for different purposes:

> The whole purpose for writing is to inform or convince, right? You either want to inform someone so that they know what you know. Or you want to convince someone to do something you want them to do. I think, really. That is what is boils down to, why are you writing? . . . In the military, you are trying to inform someone and convince a decision maker to decide something. I see this as a continuum of writing. I see this as a continuum. And you are up and down the continuum all the time.

Townsend returns to his college writing professor:

> For me, the continuum started in college. . . . But Professor Lail, I just got what he was trying, he communicated in such a simple way that I got it. And his point was your writing should be simple and clean, and if you follow a general organization then you will kinda get all the key points across in a style that flows logically and convincingly. That just resonated with me . . . I find that writing to inform and writing to convince . . . that I learned first from Professor Lail in 1979, 80 . . . that writing has stood me in good stead, and I employ those things I learned 36, 37, 38 years ago, I employ them almost every day in this job.

I grab a glance at Nestor behind me. He is behind Townsend's standing desk. I see two monitors and a keyboard. On the desk perpendicular to the standing desk, I see a laptop. A large television hangs in the corner of the office. Later, when posing for a picture with Townsend, we stand behind his desk together. The television is and muted. It's turned to Fox News with coverage of Michael Cohen's testimony regarding his relationship with then-president Donald Trump before the House Oversight Panel.

I have eased my way into the interview and now ask him about the tools he uses when he writes. With a laugh, he reaches for a pocket on his left ankle and pulls out a small black notebook held together with a black string. He tells me he has been carrying this notebook since he was a second lieutenant (the rank one receives upon graduating from college and commissioning). The notepad contains grid paper, which he used extensively earlier in his Army career. Though he no longer needs grid paper, he still prefers the boxes and lines. He then pulls out a writing device: a pen and pencil in one.

"But I am also a modern soldier," he tells me with a grin and reaches for his right ankle pocket in which is a black iPhone, "so, I also have my electronic device. And sometimes I take notes on this and I write. Actually, it is easier to disseminate if I write on here [holds up his iPhone] than if I write on here [holds up his notepad]. But this [holds up his iPhone] has its uses, and I never expect to find myself without it. This [holds up his notepad] also has its uses. But there are times when I prefer this [notepad]. Between these two things, this is how I communicate."

We exchange a few remarks about our sloppy penmanship and why we both prefer blue ink. I notice the four stars arranged vertically on the center of his OCPs. When we conclude, Townsend agrees to a picture, after which I depart. I spend several minutes debriefing with Indovina, the chief of public affairs, who will serve as the point person for any writing I seek to publish based on my interview with Townsend. Indovina then escorts me down the hall, to the elevator, and to the ground floor of Building 950, where I turn in my visitor's badge in exchange for my driver's license. Before I step into my rental car, I take the sign off the orange cone in front of my reserved parking sport. The sign fits nicely in my bag; it reads RESERVED PARKING DR. MICHAEL RIFENBURG 27 FEB 2019.

As I take a left onto Jefferson Avenue, headed toward Washington Avenue and the Newport News airport, my mind returns to the University of North Georgia, where Townsend developed his writing skills, graduated, and commissioned. My mind returns to the seven hundred plus senior cadets at UNG. In my bag, I have two audio files with Townsend's voice describing his writing maturation, his views on the purposes and tools of writing. Townsend's words provide a bird's-eye view of Army writing instruction. But he is far removed from the classroom, far removed from the cadets I work with at UNG.

I have a late flight back to Atlanta. From my view thirty-five thousand feet in the air, I see the sun falling below the horizon. In a few short hours, driving to campus, I'll greet the sun again, this time as it pushes above the Appalachian Mountains and spills across the UNG campus, ushered along by the sounds of reveille. I'll greet the cadets coordinating the raising of the flag and the shooting of the howitzer. I'll greet the one cadet, Logan Blackwell, who, over the course of four years, will walk me through how the ROTC at UNG teaches the Army writing standard and common army genres. To better understand how the army teaches writing to cadets, I need to sit with those being taught.

. . . A HOWITZER . . .

Army Training Circular (TC) 3-21.5, *Drill and Ceremonies* (US Army 2021), provides doctrine for reveille and retreat. This doctrine composes one of the shorter chapters in the roughly three-hundred-page TC, but it still exhibits the exacting specifics one expects from Army writing: proclivity for passive voice and masculine pronouns, crisp sentences stripped of adjectives and adverbs, all caps for verbal directives. Over two hundred words of doctrine dedicated to a daily exercise on all Army posts and any school campus where the Army has a presence. This is a daily choreographed exercise undergirded by the Army writing standard. Section 13-6, "Reveille Sequence of Events," reads,

> The sequence of events for conducting reveille are discussed herein:
>
> *The unit is formed facing the flag 5 minutes (if possible) before the sounding of reveille. Four minutes before the sounding of reveille, the adjutant or other appointed officer (normally the duty officer) takes their position centered on the line of troops, commands the unit to ATTENTION, and commands REPORT.*
>
> *All subunits (companies, batteries, or troops) report in succession from right to left, "Sir or Ma'am, _____ Company, all present or accounted for," or "Sir or Ma'am, _____ Company, ____ Soldiers absent." Salutes are exchanged with each report.*
>
> *The adjutant commands Parade, REST and then assumes Parade Rest themselves. If a band is present, about 30 seconds before reveille, the adjutant commands ATTENTION, directs SOUND REVEILLE, commands Present, ARMS, and then faces about. The adjutant's Salute is the signal for the band to sound reveille and to fire the morning gun. When reveille is sounded by a recording, the call ATTENTION is sounded about 30 seconds before reveille. This ensures that the adjutant has sufficient time to command the units to Present, ARMS before the first note of reveille.*
>
> After the last note of reveille has sounded, the adjutant terminates their Salute, faces about, commands Order, ARMS, and then directs TAKE CHARGE OF YOUR UNITS. The adjutant returns all Salutes with one Salute. This terminates the ceremony.

On UNG's Dahlonega campus, I watch five cadets stand at attention in preparation for reveille. Two cadets stand astride a 75mm Pack Howitzer cannon. The cadets check their watches, adjust their earplugs. Three more cadets wait by the flagpole ready to unfurl a US flag. At 0700 hours, one cadet signals. In response, another cadet yanks a cord attached to the howitzer; the howitzer coughs up a full-throated *bang*. Three cadets raise the flag. Speakers blast reveille. The few civilians on campus stand still. Cars driving through campus stop, as do the shuttle buses, the lawnmowers, the service vehicles. There is a calm in the air with familiar music bouncing around the mountains, campus buildings.

Another day at UNG: a regional multicampus public institution enrolling roughly twenty thousand students and classified as Carnegie Basic Classification of Master's Colleges and Universities (larger programs). UNG is one of six federally designated senior military colleges (SMCs). Norwich, Citadel, Texas A&M, VMI, and Virginia Tech are the other SMCs. This designation comes from the National Defense Act of 1916, signed at the height of the First World War and establishing the Reserve Officers' Training Corps (ROTC) at select colleges and universities through Title 10 2111a(f). Now, over seven hundred schools—SMCs, military junior colleges, civilian colleges—offer ROTC through other sections of the law. US military historians Allan Millett, Peter Maslowski, and William Feis (2012) write that the 1916 NDA "represented the most comprehensive effort to organize a land force structure for future mobilization" (307). This act, along with the Naval Act of 1916 that provided plans and budgets for the construction of additional fleet, "culminated two decades of unsteady but consistent growth and modernization of the American armed forces" (308). The early decades of the twentieth century laid the foundation for the current structure and size of the US military, particularly the Army.

Since the 1916 NDA, ROTC has shifted its role and scope, but the general purpose remains the same: establish a process by which colleges and universities train commissioned officers for the armed forces. In this book, I look at Army ROTC, operating with an FY18 budget of $821 million for the 29,775 senior cadets in 925 total army ROTC programs at US colleges and universities. I look at one of these 30,000 cadets, who attended UNG for four years, received his commission from UNG, and now serves as a first lieutenant in the Chemical Corps.

The *Corps* is the colloquial umbrella term for the Army presence on UNG's campus. During an average academic year, the Corps comprises over seven hundred cadets, about 35 percent of the university's residential student population. Unlike cadets at four of the five federal service academies, cadets at SMCs are not required to commission following graduation.[2] Most UNG cadets do not; 106 UNG cadets commissioned in the 2019–2020 academic year. However, if cadets do commission, they enter the Army as officers at the rank of second lieutenant and are placed into a branch of the Army such as artillery, Chemical Corps, Signal Corps, or military intelligence.

In accordance with the 1916 NDA, cadets take military-science classes each semester. These classes include a physical-fitness lab and leadership-lab components. One key portion of these military-science classes is preparing cadets for the doctrinally defined Army standard of writing and common Army genres that animate the work of an Army officer. The Army writing standard is doctrine found in a variety of Army publications. For example, Army Regulation 25-50, *Preparing and Managing Correspondence* (US Army 2020c), defines this standard: "Effective Army writing is understood by the reader in a single rapid reading and is clear, concise, and well-organized" (1-38). This standard informs Army genres. One common genre cadets learn through the ROTC curriculum are the operations orders (OPORDs), which, are written and orally delivered directives issued down the chain of command in preparation for executing an operation.

As faculty at a SMC, as a teacher who works with cadet writers in required first-year writing courses, and as a researcher invested in how writers develop, I approached the construction of this research project and book with a single research question: *How do cadets leverage the resources offered through the ROTC curriculum to learn the doctrinally defined Army writing standard and key Army genres with which they will engage upon commissioning as an officer in the Army?* This question rolled around my head during the four years I worked with one cadet, Logan Blackwell, and in the two years I spent analyzing my findings and drafting and revising my findings and argument. Logan is the representative case study for my research question. Therefore, I narrowed my research question by focusing on Logan: *How does Logan Blackwell leverage the resources offered through the ROTC curriculum to learn the doctrinally defined Army writing standard and key Army genres with which he will engage upon commissioning as an officer in the Army?*[8]

Pursuing an answer to this question has taken me inside military-science classes, drill fields, and commissioning ceremonies. I spent two days with the First Brigade, 25th Infantry Division at Fort Wainwright in Alaska and participated in morning physical training with officers there in the arctic morning air. I slept in base housing at West Point. I toured and led a workshop for English-writing instructors at General Tadeusz Kosciuszko Military University of Land Forces in Wrocław, Poland. I delivered a lecture at the New Mexico Military Institute and, following the lecture, found myself to be the only civilian in a sea of cadets at the mess hall. I shaved off my beard and cut my hair multiple times in advance of meeting with Army generals, colonels, majors, captains, and even cadets. I pitched my research to busy distrustful colonels in hopes of gaining access to military classrooms. I surveyed over seven hundred cadets and sat down for one-on-one interviews with a handful. Cadets at UNG yelled at me for accidently walking on the grass; cadets at Clemson yelled at me for wearing a hat inside the barracks. One hot summer night, I drank beer with cadets at a private club reserved for fourth-year cadets at West Point. I coauthored a paper on cadet writing with an Army ranger who served as an instructor of political science at West Point. I heard then-Secretary of Defense Donald Rumsfeld deliver a commencement address. I heard General Townsend deliver a commence address and listened to General Mark Milley, then-Army chief of staff and current chairman of the Joints Chief of Staff, reflect on the nature and character of warfare. I talked with cadets and soldiers worried over Obama's decreased defense spending and calmed by Trump's increased defense spending.

As Elizabeth L. Angeli (2019) writes at the beginning of her immersive study of emergency medical services, published scholarship tends to start with a literature review, "but the literature is often not where research projects begin. They begin with people—and these people have stories" (2). Like Angeli, my interest in and entrance into Army writing began with the varied people and places in the paragraph above. Angeli reminds us these people and places carry stories, some of which I account for in these pages and some of which I am still trying to understand. But through these varied people and places, I tried, though a civilian, to enter the Army community over the course of almost two decades. These experiences shaped how I approached my conversations with Logan, how I watched and thought about military-science instruction, and how I approached the Army's never-ending quest to teach critical thinking and literacy—goals I, as a writing teacher/researcher/administrator, share but just with a broader student population.

When relaying my experiences and findings, I'm careful about disclosing too much information about the when and where of Army movements and training. Army Regulation 530-1, *Operations Security* (US Army 2014b), provides guidance on how and when to disclose places and locations related to Army operations. These regulations are directed to soldiers and cadets but also to contractors and consultants. The locations and timings of Army operations are prized information for enemy forces. When I wrote an article on the writing practices of active-duty soldiers within a brigade headquarters (Rifenburg 2019), I had to run a draft through an Army public-affairs office. The public-affairs office asked me to remove specific dates and locations of a training the brigade was preparing to undertake. I complied. With this book, I focus attention not on current soldiers but on cadets. Because of my close reading of *Operations Security*, and my conversations with multiple stakeholders within the Army, I feel legally and ethically and morally comfortable including specifics about cadet training because cadet training is transparent and uniform. What I mean is that all cadets who plan on commissioning attend Advanced Camp at Fort Knox through USACC, which runs an active twitter feed and YouTube channel dedicated to pumping out promotional material showing cadets jumping, climbing, shooting—all the soldiering that might entice a high schooler browsing YouTube to sign up. My writing that Logan attended Advanced Camp does not provide a foothold into Army operations for our enemies. Now that Logan has commissioned, I aim for caution and elide dates and locations. As I draft this paragraph, Logan is three years into his Army career, has already received his first promotion, and is no longer an eighteen-year-old college student taking ROTC classes between trips to Walmart and PlayStation games and general education classes. His movements, in line with the movements of the other roughly half million soldiers in the Army, are designed for readiness and cloaked in security measures.

I engage with *Operations Security* in these two body paragraphs and not in an endnote because the ways we—researchers on writing and literacy and rhetoric—make decisions about how we collect data and analyze data, how we build and maintain relationships with all the stakeholders in our research, affect the work we do. These are choices we all make—or are asked to make—but these choices and the reasoning behind them are often dropped from publications. I believe strongly in foregrounding the ethical and moral and legal and spiritual decisions we make as researchers and in not dropping these decisions from publications or relegating them to ancillary notes. The research I undertook with Logan, and the research Logan and I offer in these pages, is filtered through our interaction with each other and our engagement with Army doctrinal publications and regulations that govern this over two hundred-year-old government-sanctioned force.

As we follow Logan through his college career, I am aware that, as a colleague told me, I have an *n of 1* study. I'm only looking at one person in these pages. I dig into my reasoning and my data collection and methodology later, particularly in my Intersections and conclusion, but my *n*=1 study pushed me to think about what it means to offer findings filtered through the eyes of just one researcher and one participant: What do I lose from *not* interviewing his instructors? His peers? What do I gain? I do balance my findings with the words of General Townsend. I also offer excerpts from cadet Robert "Trent" Morrell's unpublished memoir in which he reflects on FROG week, the orientation week for incoming cadets. But the main voice is Logan's. At its heart, this is a book about Logan's literacy development. I make the bold assertion that a rich, sustained portrait of one learner can carry a book.

To situate my understanding of Logan, I draw from three layers of material. The most immediate layer is the qualitative data I collected on Logan: hours of in-person interviews over the course of four years; Logan's hand-drawn pictures of his writing space; images of Logan's commissioning ceremony and various pins and ribbons on his uniform; Logan's middle-school, high-school, and college-writing outputs (curricular and extracurricular) and class syllabi; my observation notes from his military-science classes and commissioning ceremony.

I pair these data with a second layer: primary and secondary material pertaining to, among other issues, Department of Defense budgetary allocations, Army organizational planning, and the relationship between the Army and civilian educational institutions. Some primary documents I reference in this second layer are Army Regulation 25-50, *Preparing and Managing Correspondence* (US Army 2020c), Army Cadet Command Regulation 145-9, *Cadet Command Reserve Officers' Training Corps Branching, Commissioning, and Accessioning Regulation* (US Army 2016), the *Summary of the 2018 National Defense Strategy* (US Dept. of Defense 2018), and the 1916 National Defense Act. For secondary material, I draw from Michael Neiberg's (2000) *Making Citizen-Soldiers: ROTC and the Ideology of American Military Service* and Donald Downs and Ilia Murtazashvili's (2012) *Arms and the University: Military Presence and the Civic Education of Non-military Students*. I look to these resources because this book engages with questions broader than just Logan's literacy development and with the uniquely US phenomenon of civilians working with soldiers to develop future Army officers.

The final layer of research from which I draw comes from rhetoric and composition/writing studies (RC/WS).[4] This book responds to previous book-length longitudinal studies of writing and writers (Beaufort 2007; Carroll 2002; Chiseri-Strater 1991; Gere 2019; Herrington and Curtis 2000). However, these studies approach writing development linearly, which is understandable when we study writers moving through an undergraduate course sequence: we follow writers as they progress from year 1 to year 4 or 5 and then graduation. Our school curriculum is sequenced, so our studies of writers within these curricula are sequenced accordingly. As Kevin Roozen (2020) writes, when we view writing development along well-structured schooling pathways, "development is depicted as a fairly straightforward process of taking up the already-established genres and identities available within the well-policed borders of an already-made social world" (227). To balance this "straightforward" approach, I follow the lead of Roozen and attend to the dynamic phenomenon of writing development across time and space. As Roozen and Joe Erickson put it in their ebook (2017), writers are constantly "historically developing persons." Writers are always *becoming*—as the subtitle of this book suggests. Writers are fashioning identities along a trajectory of engagement with text across their lifespans and lifeworlds (Bazerman, Applebee, and Berninger 2017, 2018; Dippre and Phillips 2020; Ivanič 1998; Prior 2017; Roozen 2020). I follow Logan beyond his "well-policed" (Roozen 2020, 237) academic pathways and turn to his cocurricular and extracurricular literacy practices. I look at Logan interacting with artifacts, people, spaces, and practices across time and space. I look at his literate becoming—stretching from essays he wrote in sixth grade to emails we exchanged two years after he graduated and commissioned. I look at how his identity as a writer is shaped by his steady engagement with literacy practices inside, alongside, and outside the academic classroom. In the aggregate, these three layers place ROTC in a historical and contemporary context within higher education and provide readers an analysis of how Logan developed as a writer over four years, with particular attention to the various literacy activities in which he engaged that formed his identity as an Army writer.

The research question at the heart of *Drilled to Write* is timely. As I wrote the first draft of this book, the Trump administration was adding more soldiers across all branches of the armed forces. According to an *Army Times* news article (Myers, May 7, 2018), the army alone was looking to add eighty thousand more soldiers in 2018 to support a return to conventional, force-on-force warfare expressed in the 2018 National Defense Strategy. The 2018 National Defense Authorization Act (US Congress, National Defense 2018) signaled the Trump administration's dedication to military might through increased defense spending. ROTC is a prominent source for meeting the new staffing demands placed on our armed forces; therefore, just as US higher education is experiencing a rise in student veterans in the wake of the Post 9/11 GI Bill, we will also experience a rise in cadets. As I make edits to the final draft of this book—roughly two years after finishing the first draft—the United States has moved through another presidential election cycle, and the Army has a new chief of staff. New leadership leads to changes. The Army is experiencing one of its largest transformations in forty years: modernizing major systems and capabilities, developing new doctrine, standing up whole new organizations, and reforming how the Army manages talent (i.e., the Army Talent Alignment Process). In an October 2020 Army press release, with the author noted as simply "US Army," we read that the Army's chief of staff announced a new priority: people first. This priority emphasized leader development, and, more broadly and simply, taking care of people. The article states, "We are prioritizing People as the #1 Army priority" (US Army 2020a). New national-security strategies emerge. New national-defense strategies emerge. New internal challenges arise. But the emphasis remains on people.

Though my focus is not directly on our student veterans, my thinking about cadets crosses into scholarship on student veterans animating RC/WS. Responding to the growing enrollment of student veterans and cognizant of the unique literacy practices student veterans bring with them into a writing class, RC/WS endorsed a position statement on supporting student veteran writers (Conference on College Composition

Figure 0.1. Cadets train on UNG's drill field as two helicopter circle above. Image by UNG's University Relations. Used with permission.

and Communication 2015b), published articles and edited collections, and launched new journals. I take this important scholarship into account in the following pages. I add to this scholarship by inviting readers to consider a writer at the *beginning* of a military career, not at the end, as is the case with scholarship on student veterans. RC/WS has produced little work on cadet writers, which I find surprising considering the field's long history of student-focused pedagogy and advocacy. As Patricia Bizzell (2014) states, "We in this field want to know who our students are" (442). Therefore, instead of asking how writing teachers can create an inclusive writing space for student veteran writers, a question currently discussed, I ask a slightly different question: How does one cadet move through a federally established military-science curriculum and prepare to write as an Army officer?

Back on the Dahlonega campus, the speakers finally fall silent as the flag reaches the top of the mast. Reveille ends. Civilians and cars continue again. Cadets march away. In the words of TC 3-21.5 (US Army 2021), "This terminates the ceremony" (13-3).

Another day begins. First-year cadet Logan Blackwell steps out of the barracks and into the sun.

... AND A CADET

I met Logan during the fall of his first semester as a cadet. He enrolled in an honors section of English 1101 I taught. Our class met in a space with a long wooden table, roller chairs, and a glass wall. An aged brick fireplace, spared during recent renovations and signaling the university's Appalachian heritage, sat opposite the glass wall. Above the fireplace hung an oil painting of a prominent white male from the university's past. Two flat-screen televisions decorated the two other walls.

One-third of the students in the class were in the Corps of Cadets. These cadets, like all the students in the class, were authoring thoughtful analyses of their own writing processes and musing on the definition of writing and the rhetorical power of such a definition—all assignments taken from our class textbook, the second edition of Elizabeth Wardle and Doug Downs's *Writing about Writing* (2014). However, these cadets were also taking their first steps into am Army discourse community. This community is infused with reading and writing practices defined and codified in Army doctrinal publications. These cadets were faced with the dual challenge of honing college-level writing knowledge and skills while also gaining the necessary knowledge and skills to succeed in the textual world of the Army, a world populated with a codified writing standards and common genres. Additionally, as Chris Anson and Shawn Neely (2010) show in their webtext on military writing, these doctrinally defined writing practices stand in contrast to writing practices espoused in traditional first-year composition courses. Challenging literacy development, indeed.

By following Logan over the course of his four years at the University of North Georgia (UNG)—as he moves from a cadet private during his first year to commissioning as an officer in the Army following his graduation—I show how he leveraged resources offered through the ROTC curriculum to learn the doctrinally defined Army writing standard and key Army genres. My many years working with Logan, teaching at UNG, writing with an Army officer, and observing Army officers write from their desks at forts around the country has shown me the centrality of written deliverables for getting Army work done. These written deliverables manifest as a wide variety of text: PowerPoint presentations, synchronization matrices, memos, OPORDs, WARNOs, FRAGOs, 9 Line MEDEVAC reports, counseling forms, recommendation for award forms, and countless other texts grease the wheels of Army readiness, communication, and execution. As I sat in on military-science classes at UNG, the class content of that day often directed itself back to a written deliverable. For example, I observed a class focused on cordon and search techniques: how to secure an area and conduct an efficient and safe search of the area in hopes of securing a high-value target. Cadets brainstormed and then delivered an operations order (OPORD) to the class instructor outlining their course of action. Another class focused on awards soldiers can receive. How does a soldier receive a new ribbon for their rack? Answer: Department of Army Form 638 (US Army 2017). The class ended with an overview of this form. Operations at all levels—from securing high-value targets through cordon and search techniques to recommending a ribbon for a subordinate—hinge on text. The life of an officer is often more clerical than gladiatorial. As Logan told me once with a wry smile, most of the word *officer* is *office*.

Logan is my representative case into ROTC's writing curriculum and cadet literacy development because of his love of literacy. As we formed our research partnership, Logan provided me with a thumb drive of his writing in middle school and high school; he brought with him a deep desire to write, authoring bylaws for student organizations he either joined (a fraternity) or started (ballroom-dance club), spending hours honing a short story for pleasure, submitting essays to our local college magazine and winning an essay contest run by the magazine. I also focus my study on him because he entered UNG with a signed agreement to commission. When I began piecing together this study in my mind, I saw Logan as a student immersed in multiple layers of literacy, a student who entered UNG with a singular goal of commissioning into the Army.

Drilled to Write offers a qualitative, longitudinal case study. I bounded the case study temporally (four years) and spatially (the University of North Georgia). I focused on a single case: *How does Logan Blackwell leverage the resources offered through the ROTC curriculum to learn the doctrinally defined Army writing standard and key Army genres with which he will engage upon commissioning as an officer in the Army?* My data collection included hours of in-person, audio-recorded semistructured interviews with Logan. I conducted all interviews in my campus office, and I transcribed all the interviews. Our ongoing and long conversations allowed Logan and me to have "cyclical dialogue around texts over a period of time," which Theresa Lillis (2008, 362) argues is crucial for understanding how people develop as writers. I triangulated this data by observing Logan's military-science classes and reading over any syllabi and writing (curricular or extracurricular) Logan shared. Through putting in conversation his words on the page, his actions in class, and his comments during our interviews, I paint a rich portrait of Logan as he moves through the ROTC curriculum. I attend to how he develops the Army writing standard and writes common army genres.

In total, I gathered the following textual data written or drawn by Logan. Logan completed all written artifacts during his four-year enrollment as a student at UNG:

- 62 documents from middle and high school. These documents include traditional research-based essays, letters of recommendation for classmates, lecture notes, annotated bibliographies, outlines, and poetry
- 5 pieces of self-sponsored fiction
- 26 curricular essays
- 2 PowerPoint presentations
- 2 memos
- 1 cover letter
- 1 resume

To this textual data, I add

- 16 syllabi from Logan's classes
- 13 interviews with Logan.
- 45 images, 41 of which I took and 4 of which Logan took
- 2 hand-drawn images by Logan: 1 of his writing space and 1 of army echelons

Logan's voice is the prominent voice in my data collection. However, I do invite readers to hear the voices of other key stakeholders in cadet writing development. I climb high up the Army chain of command and offer an interview with General Stephen J. Townsend in the chapter that serves as the prologue for this book. As I write in this chapter, Townsend was a four-star general, who, at the time of our interview, served as commanding general of the US Army Training and Doctrine Command. No one sat higher on the Army chain of command regarding training future and current soldiers.[5] Just one of the many Army components falling under his purview was US Army Cadet Command (USACC) stationed at Fort Knox, and a portion of USACC is ROTC at UNG. I also offer the voice of cadet Robert "Trent" Morrell.[6] I introduce Trent in more detail later, but when word went through the campus that a professor was writing a book about ROTC, I received periodic emails from cadets. One email came with a Word attachment. The email and attachment came from Trent, with a note asking me to look over and provide feedback on a memoir he was writing about his experience in ROTC. We exchanged emails. I asked to use an excerpt in this book. He agreed. The excerpt I provide is self-sponsored writing in which a young adult works through his experiences in honest prose. I am honored to include his voice detailing an experience I—as a civilian—can only begin to understand. Finally, I include my experience at General Tadeusz Kosciuszko Military University of Land Forces (MULF) in Wrocław, Poland, where I led faculty-development opportunities for the instructors who oversee English writing and speaking classes for Polish cadets. UNG and MULF recently signed a memorandum of understanding, thus establishing a relationship for cadet and faculty exchange. This partnership is bearing fruit. As I collected data for this book, two Polish cadets attended UNG for a semester. The intersection of higher education and military preparedness is not a US-only phenomenon. Other countries, too, have developed productive models for training future military officers. By expanding my perspective beyond one student at one US institution, I aim to add much-needed nuance to not only our understanding of how students develop as writers but also how writing curriculum is intertwining with cultural needs.

What I purposefully elide in this book are the direct quotes from Logan's civilian and military instructors. I didn't ask his instructors about his performance or ask instructors to help me better understand their assignments and their feedback on Logan's work. Though I use the verb *triangulate*, Logan is largely the angle in all three points of this data collection: I collected his writing; I collected his voice; I collected his actions in a classroom and on the drill field. I am offering an *n of 1*. I'm aware of the limitations I face with such an approach and the dismissive comments such an approach may solicit. However, a result of the rise of the neoliberal university is greater attention to big data analytics (Scott 2017) to often justify labor casualization and more privatization and outsourcing of student life and academic services (Scott and Welch 2016). We witness more initiatives designed to get students in college and out of college faster. Again, these initiatives, like Complete College America, while admirable for their stated goal of keeping student debt low and streamlining pathways to graduation, lead to our forgetting individual student experiences and privileging big data analytics. We don't see students as single mothers juggling classes and homelife or older adult males coming back to school after years working as mechanics. We see students as DFWI rates, one-semester persistence rates, degree-to-completion rates. Big data and predictive analytics can flatten student experience and misrepresent authentic student learning, as we saw with the reactionary and controversial findings in Richard Arum and Josipa Roksa's *Academically Adrift* (2011). I fall in line with Michele Eodice, Anne Ellen Geller, and Neal Lerner, who, in *The Meaningful Writing Project*, push against findings from large-scale studies on student learning and inject life into staid US higher education narratives about literacy deficient students (2016). They counter these narratives with student voices and student experiences. Instead of reading stats, we hear voices, student voices.

To be fair, I find benefit in big data. I find benefit in Kristine Johnson's (2019) corpus of over 2.3 million words taken from articles published in *Writing Program Administration* between 1979 and 2017. I'm fascinated by Benjamin Miller's (2014) use of heat maps to document thousands of dissertations and David West Brown and Laura Aull's (2017) corpus-based analysis of higher- and lower-scoring Advanced Placement exams. Our field benefits from Dylan Dryer's (2019) analysis of keywords in 13.9 million words of RC/WS published scholarship. I hold in high regard university programs, like the University of Michigan's joint PhD program in English and education, which trains students to aggregate and then make sense of large data corpora. I find benefit in large-scale surveys coming out of the Center for Postsecondary Research at the University of Indiana and the Higher Education Research Institute at UCLA. I am particularly interested in the aspects of these large-scale surveys on student writing when placed alongside what RC/WS scholars see as effective writing practices (Anderson et al. 2015).

But in this book, I go small.

I want, for just a moment, to put aside narratives about retention, and one-semester persistence rates, and conversations with local offices of institutional effectiveness and committees on general education assessment. Just for a moment, I don't want to worry about accreditation guidelines and site visits and quality-enhancement plans. As important as these narratives as for our material livelihood, for putting food on our tables and keeping our kids clothed and our homes heated, and even for pedagogical import, I want to place them on hold. I want to hear, and I ask you to listen to, the voice of one student. This is Logan's story. I want his writing and his voice to tell it. I want to slow down the hectic pace dictated by more accountability, more assessment, more accreditation visits, more system- and university-level initiatives. I want to find a bench in the shade on campus, maybe under the ancient live-oak tree near my office, sit down, breathe, and hear the story of a student, of our students. And I want to sit in this story for a moment as these pages unfurl into the literate life of a learner.

When doing this listening, I'm careful with how I write about student voices and how I document our students' voices when they talk about their educational experiences. Alison Cook-Sather, Cathy Bovill, and Peter Felten (2014), influential voices in the scholarship of teaching and learning discipline, rightly point out the dangers of faculty believing students have a voice to lend to conversations about teaching and learning simply because faculty allow students such a voice (136). I do not want to give the impression that I—a tenured, white faculty member—am allowing Logan the chance to speak, that the only reason Logan has a voice is because I, a privileged faculty member, gave him this opportunity. Abbi Flint and Hannah Goddard (2020) contributed a chapter to an open-access collection on students as partners, an international movement with roots in SoTL that reimagines the role of faculty and student as coresearchers, coinquirers, coconstructors of knowledge. Like Cook-Sather, Bovill, and Felten, Flint and Goddard focus on student voice in higher education research. They distinguish between "acting as a 'voice for' students and presenting the 'voice of' students" (81). They see "voice for" as the "collective role of a representative" and "voice of" as reflecting "the individual voice of that representative student" (81). I'm thankful Logan trusted me with his words, that he allowed me to offer the *voice of* Logan in these pages. Logan and I built a book that captures how we understood his writing development through ROTC at UNG.

I also want this book to speak to issues larger than just how Logan and I understand his literacy development; the unique stories all of us carry are caught up in larger stories. In chapter 1, I establish broad connections between US higher education and the US military. A central premise of my thinking in this book is that US higher education and the US military are inextricably linked, and for English studies, this link is most notably seen in the importance the Army attaches to critical thinking exhibited in literacy, broadly, and writing, specifically. To unpack this premise briefly, I draw from primary and secondary material to detail this broad link between higher education and the military and the role literacy and writing skills play in this link. The implications that come from zooming in on Logan can help readers in English studies, curriculum development, student affairs, and education history understand better the role higher education plays in national defense and the role literacy and genre acquisition play in preparing our citizen-soldiers—our students.

Drilled to Write unfolds in sections, each section devoted to one year of Logan's undergraduate experience. Within each section, I offer chapters divided into three areas: findings, curricular writing experiences, and extracurricular writing experiences. These divisions are artificial. Self-sponsored writing informs academic writing; curricular writing tasks inform the extracurricular. My chapter divisions are not representative of theories of literacy development but are designed for ease of access to the research Logan and I offer. I hope readers interested in extracurricular experiences can find relevant material. Those interested in the first-year composition through the eyes of a cadet can easily find this material.

Each section opens with my research finding for that academic year of Logan's undergraduate experience. These findings collectively answer the overall research question driving this book: *How does Logan leverage the resources offered through the ROTC curriculum to learn the doctrinally defined Army writing standard and key Army genres with which he will engage upon commissioning as an officer in the Army?* To foreground these findings for readers, I offer them in bullet points below, return to them in more depth in each respective chapter, and return again to them in my conclusion:

- During his first year, Logan dipped a toe into the doctrinally defined Army writing standards and genres with which he would soon engage as an Army officer by learning what they are *not*.
- In his second year, Logan, encouraged by the ROTC Order of Merit List, turned to self-sponsored nonschool writing, which, in turn, helped him develop a writerly agency he brought to bear on his curricular writing.
- During his third year, Logan offloaded the cognitive challenge of authoring operation orders onto tools provided by ROTC and tools Logan developed himself.
- As a senior and preparing to graduate, Logan learned the doctrinally defined Army writing standard and key Army genres with which he would engage upon commissioning by gaining knowledge of a specific critical-thinking heuristic (i.e., the military decision-making process [MDMP]) and receiving his branch assignment that would, in a few short months, provide a more nuanced approach to applying the MDMP to his future writing tasks.

Logan's writing development is evidence of cross-domain learning transfer. He integrates and synthesizes and rearranges writing knowledges and practices refined in curricular, cocurricular, and extracurricular spaces. His ultimate goal, and the ultimate goal of the broader UNG ROTC curriculum in regard to writing, is to develop strong Army writing skills for future use as an Army officer. But this goal is a shared endeavor at UNG because writers develop through a confluence of forces—some academic, some not. Logan develops as a writer through general education classes; through his business management major classes; through authoring blog posts about his time in Rome; through writing bylaws for a dance club, letters for his fiancé, and fiction for himself. He develops strong Army writing skills by moving through the nicely sequenced MILS classes. He develops strong Army writing skills by immersing himself in writing inside and outside the classroom. My broad research question addresses how Logan leveraged resources offered by the ROTC curriculum to strengthen his Army writing skills. This book largely focuses on ROTC, but Logan moves into other academic spaces that exist alongside ROTC. At UNG, and at other SMCs, the ROTC curriculum exists alongside the non-ROTC curriculum. Logan's ROTC classes and his non-ROTC classes collectively pushed him to strengthen his Army writing knowledge and practice. As we zero in on my findings for each year of Logan's undergraduate experience, we see the importance of non-ROTC classes during Logan's first year; we see the importance of extracurricular writing during Logan's second year; and we see both self-sponsored literacy production and ROTC-sanctioned literacy production as important to his third year. Finally, during the fourth and final year, we see the importance of the ROTC curriculum foregrounded as Logan nears the end of his undergraduate experiences and prepares for life as an Army officer less than a month after graduation. In sum, the findings I offer here are further testament to what we know about how people develop as writers: that writing development occurs as a result of a confluence of forces across time and space. We can add structure and a tidy throughline to writing development by tracing it against the four-year undergraduate curriculum sequence. To be fair, I do so in this book. But writing development is messy; it does not follow the tidy path our university administrators, local, state, and federal politicians, accrediting bodies, and even faculty members value. As Roozen (2020) writes, when we trace writing development within *just school*, we risk "an overdetermined, incomplete, and ultimately very confusing account of the pathways for disciplinary development" (230). Therefore, I look beyond Logan's academic writing experiences. I trace Logan's development, his *becoming*, across multiple settings. I look at how his essay in seventh grade anticipates his future immersion in ROTC. I look at how his business-writing class figures into how he authored bylaws for a student club he founded. I look at self-sponsored fiction he wrote late at night while listening to jazz, and I conclude with him reflecting on letters he wrote his fiancée while he was deep in the woods for Advanced Camp. These artifacts, written across various times in his writing development, collectively constitute and give rise to Logan's becoming a cadet writer.

In the Intersections, I offer implications about methodology and data collection for longitudinal research on writing and writers. I labor in this broad area of research methods in response to specific exigencies I feel in my own research-teaching-service life as a dad/tenured faculty member at a predominately white institution/husband/faculty fellow of my university's Center for Teaching, Learning, and Leadership/citizen/coeditor of an open-access book series. Instead of opting for the conclusion that speaks to pedagogical implications of this study, I take on the task of understanding how my positionality influences how I collect, analyze, and circulate my findings. I want to foreground the flesh and bones and spirit of who I am and how these things constructed *Drilled to Write* in ways I see, am beginning to see, may never see. For one, it's not lost on me that I gained a foothold into the Army world because I can run four miles. A brief explanation: I received funding to travel to Fort Wainwright in Fairbanks, Alaska, to observe the writing practices of an Army major who invited me to join him for two full days. His days started at 0500 hours with coffee and exercise. So, there I was, lacing up my Brooks running shoes and taking off on a four-mile run with an Army officer. It is not lost on me that my physical ability to run, my financial ability to afford running shoes, and my living situation that afforded me time to exercise helped me gain introduction into this community and led to my first publication on Army writing (Rifenburg 2019). Who we are is what we know.

As important as pedagogical implications are, as necessary as discussion about thesis statements and transitions and rhetorical moves are for supporting the student writers with whom we labor, I want to step back for a moment and think about how the research we undertake—the research that informs our pedagogy—is tied up physically with who we are and what we believe and know and feel. I return to these issues in my conclusion but here state that my positionality and my varied (visible and hidden) identity markers constructed this book.

I draw on the work of Leigh Patel (2019), Amy Stornaiuolo, Gerald Campano, and Ebony Elizabeth Thomas (2019), and Tukufu Zuberi and Eduardo Bonilla-Silva (2008) to bolster my thinking about how our methods and methodologies reflect our own positionality. I draw attention to three parts of the research process, what I call *getting there, staying there, leaving there.* I see these three parts as representative of the research moments we have.

Looking to autoethnography (see Sanchez 2021) and inspired by scholarship that brings the researcher more directly into the narrative, research design, and argument (see Angeli 2019), this book, then, is the journey of a researcher and participant, a teacher and student, learning together about how writing drives the Army.

NOTES

1. Unless otherwise noted, my use of *army* throughout this book refers to the US Army.
2. The five federal service academies are the Air Force Academy, the Coast Guard Academy, the Merchants Marine Academy, the Naval Academy, and the United

3. States Military Academy at West Point. Graduates of the Merchant Marine Academy are the only ones not required to commission upon graduation.
3. The name Logan Blackwell is a pseudonym chosen by the research participant. When Logan signed the human-subject informed-consent paperwork during his first year at UNG, he self-elected for me to use his real name. His real name remained in this manuscript during our four years working together, during my first draft of this book, and in the draft of this manuscript that made its way to reviewers. The anonymous reviewer feedback encouraged me to consider Army Operation Security (see US Army Regulation 530-1, *Operations Security* [2014b]), which forbids the disclosure of timing and locations of Army operations. I emailed Logan, who was them a first lieutenant stationed in the southeast United States, about whether he preferred his real name or a pseudonym. In his email response, Logan selected this pseudonym: Logan Blackwell. Informed consent is fluid, ever changing, not complete once the ink dries on the signed consent form (see Bivens 2018). Logan changed his mind seven years after signing the form.
4. My use of rhetoric and composition/writing studies (RC/WS) as a disciplinary descriptive is taken from the National Center for Education Statistics' "Classification of Instructional Programs" (CIP) (2019). This broad descriptive includes professionals who research, teach, and administer literacy-related fields. CIP 23.13 (rhetoric and composition/writing studies) captures the following: "writing, general; creative writing; professional, technical, business, and scientific writing; rhetoric and composition; rhetoric and composition/writing studies, other." In using this term, I follow the lead of Edward White, Norbert Elliot, and Irvin Peckham (2015) and Derek Mueller (2017).
5. At the time of this writing, Townsend serves as commander of US Africa Command.
6. His real name. Trent provided me permission to use his real name when he first passed along this writing. Two years later, during the revision of this book, I emailed to ask, again, if he preferred his name or a pseudonym. Again, he preferred his real name.

SECTION 1

Becoming a Cadet

A Textworld in Preparation for Year One

We gave up our lives and it's finally over. It's time for us to go where soldiers live in peace and harmony and angels sing amazing grace. . . . Army and Navy, Air Force and Marines it's always the same. Someone will always be there to keep our homeland safe at night.
—Logan Blackwell, written in seventh grade

The President is hereby authorized to establish and maintain in civil education institutions a Reserve Officer's Training Corps. . . .
Section 40, 1916 National Defense Act

All of us, from [Army] Chief [of staff] down, need to improve our skills. Learning to write is a lifelong endeavor.
Former Army Chief of Staff General John A. Wickham Jr., Department of Army

1
ROTC, HIGHER EDUCATION, AND CITIZEN-SOLDIERS

On June 3, 1916, the Sixty-Fourth Congress of the United States of America convened in Washington, DC. Beyond the muggy environs of DC, the Western world was at war, with all waiting to see what President Woodrow Wilson, the stoic former president of Princeton University, would do. He was nearing the end of his first term in office and invested in campaigning for a second. In a few months, he would run against Charles Evans Hughes. Wilson would win.

Roughly two years previously, Gavrilo Princip, through a well-coordinated attack plus a liberal dose of chance, gunned down the Archduke Franz Ferdinand and his wife, Sophie, outside a deli in Sarajevo. In retaliation, Austria-Hungry issued an essentially impossible ultimatum to Serbia. Serbia's boisterous ally Russia mobilized in reaction. Austria-Hungary's equally boisterous ally Germany mobilized. France, Italy, and England jumped in. Germany pushed into Belgium with eyes on Paris. Belgium, then, jumped into the fray. The world was at war and few knew why. As Christopher Clark (2012) argues in *The Sleepwalkers: How Europe Went to War in 1914*, civilians and military alike didn't know why: "But who *was* the enemy?" Clark writes in his final chapter, "Nobody knew . . . Rumors abounded" (554). Nevertheless, the armies of Europe mobilized.

The United States watched anxiously from the sidelines. When Congress met, Germany and France had already clashed along the western front; trenches were dug; armies dug in. No-man's land was established with barbed wire, machine guns, flamethrowers, and gas. The first and second Battle of Ypres had already been fought. Both sides registered over one hundred thousand casualties in the first battle; the Germans decided to use poisonous gas in the second.

The Battle of Verdun—the longest battle of the war—was in its fourth month. The Battle of the Somme was to begin in one month. Over one million soldiers would die when Britain and France clashed with Germany in southeast France. Closer to home, Pancho Villa was staging bold raids on the newly US-acquired land of New Mexico. Rumors swirled that Germany was providing support to Villa and his entourage in hopes of destabilizing or, at the very least, distracting the United States. From the Oval Office, Wilson kept his eye on Villa to the south and the massive slaughter of soldiers to the east, forgoing direct intervention much to the frustration of some members of his cabinet. Earlier in the year, Secretary of State William Jennings Bryant resigned over how Wilson handled the sinking of the RMS Lusitania, a British passenger ship torpedoed by Germany. Over one hundred Americans died. The United States flexed her muscles, but the brawny gesture was just a show. Wilson did not ask Congress for a war declaration.

With conflict all around, Congress met on June 3, 1916.

They adopted and Wilson signed the National Defense Act of 1916, which established, among other key military provisions, a Reserve Officers' Training Corps at "civil educational institutions."

ROTC was birthed during conflict.

With the stroke of a pen, Congress linked war, armies, and higher education in an intricate—and oftentimes uneasy—relationship. This relationship is still in place.

Section 40 of the NDA focused on ROTC programs:

> The President is hereby authorized to establish and maintain in civil education institutions a Reserve Officers' Training Corps, which shall consist of a senior division organized at universities and colleges requiring four years of collegiate study for a degree, including State universities and those State institutions that are required to provide instruction in military tactics under the provisions of the Act of Congress of July second, eighteen hundred and sixty-two, donating lands for the establishment of colleges where the leading object shall be practical instruction in agriculture and the mechanic arts, including military tactics, and a junior division organized at all other public or private educational institutions, except that units of the senior division may be organized at those essentially military schools which do not confer an academic degree but which, as a result of the annual inspection of such institutions by the War Department,[1] are specially designated by the Secretary of War as qualified for units of the senior division, and each division shall consist of units of the several arms or corps in such number and of such strength as the President may prescribe.

In this exhaustive sentence, three points are worth mentioning. For one, the president oversees ROTC programs ("establish and maintain"). As the commander in chief, the president is de facto head of US armed forces. Walk inside the military-science building at the University of North Georgia, and you see a picture of the current US president at the top of a chain of command. Second, this act establishes the process through which one moves from a cadet to an Army officer. Upon graduating from a four-year school and completing the ROTC requirements at a four-year school, one can commission as an officer at the rank of second lieutenant. This commissioning process, according to the language of the act, reaffirms existing policy in a similar 1862 Act of Congress. That date, like the date of 1916, is noteworthy. In 1862, the US Civil War was in its infancy, and Congress passed similar legislation providing parameters for using higher education as a mechanism for moving people from civilians to officers. Third, this 1916 act points to the importance of A&M colleges and universities and the federal government's role in establishing these colleges. Like the federal government's work with the Morrill Act (also of 1862), which established land-grant colleges across the United States, the federal government and state governments entered a complex relationship through which state governments used federal land to establish college programs in agriculture, mechanics, mining, and military instruction. Historian of education John R. Thelin (2004) argues that though the military focus has not been of much interest to historians, it was this specific focus that was "one of the most successful provisions of the Morrill Act" (78). Through the Morrill Act, land-grant institutions were required to establish and maintain military training units, but individual schools were granted autonomy in deciding whether this training would be compulsory for their students or not. By 1914, just two years before Congress passed the NDA, roughly thirty thousand college students were taking part in this training. According to historians of education John S. Brubacher and Willis Rudy (1968), "Land-grant institutions had furnished three times more officers to the Army than West Point" (226). The Morrill Act, in effect, paved the way for the citizen-soldier of ROTC programs in the early twentieth century. Indeed, Justin Morrill, the representative from Vermont who sponsored the legislation, was good friends with Alden Partridge, who, in 1819, founded the American Literary, Scientific, and Military Academy. This academy is now known as Norwich University, the oldest senior military college (SMC). Inspired by the mix of civilian and military students at this college in Vermont, Morrill molded an act that would encourage other schools to take up Norwich's example—and many schools and colleges did. The Department of Defense recognizes Norwich as the birthplace of ROTC. The road the Morrill Act paved led to the NDA.

Section 42 of the National Defense Act of 1916 details the need for "physically fit male students" to enter into this program and for schools with an ROTC program to hire a "professor of military science and tactics" and "at least one hundred physically fit male students." Section

43 establishes the secretary of war as the determiner of curriculum (i.e., "to prescribe standard courses of theoretical and practical military training") and determines that institutions provide at least three hours per week per academic year of training. Section 44 ensures that these physically fit male students are US citizens and at least fourteen years old. The act continues fleshing out the details for the newly established ROTC before moving into training camps and the National Guard.

But the fourteen sections of this act, then and now, bond US higher education and military preparedness.

Returning to Logan, US Army Cadet Command Regulation 145-9 (US Army 2016) stipulates that once he "completes all ROTC requirements, including Advanced Camp [a thirty-one-day training event at Fort Knox], and possesses a baccalaureate degree from an accredited college or university, [he is commissioned into the Army according to] Army Regulation 145-1." Additionally, Logan, and all cadets seeking a commission, must be US citizens, pass medical and physical tests, meet the height and weight standard in Army Regulation 600-9 (2019d), and pass a drug test. With all these boxes checked, Logan, with final approval from the secretary of defense, will enter the Army and move through accessions, the process by which he is given a duty component (e.g., active duty, National Guard, or National Reserve) and branch (i.e., job description). Most UNG cadets receive active duty.

Logan will enter as an officer at the rank of second lieutenant. The Army has three broad types of personnel: enlisted, noncommissioned officers (NCOs), and officers. Active-duty enlisted personnel make up the bulk of total Army strength. According to the Army Demographics, FY 20 Army Profile report (US Army 2020b), the total Army strength was 1,010,217 soldiers as of September 2020. This number includes members of the National Guard, Army Reserve, Active Duty, and cadets at West Point. Active-duty soldiers numbered 485,383, nearly half the total strength. Breaking down the active-duty soldiers into officers and enlisted shows us that only 16 percent of active duty are officers, with 81 percent enlisted.[2]

Officers are formed through a tight relationship between school and state, as most officers have a college degree. The officer rank comes with more prestige and responsibility. NCOs, technically, start as enlisted personnel at the rank of private (E-1); officers start at second lieutenant (O-1). The pay gap between the two is prominent: according to 2019 pay-table data available on the Army's website, a second lieutenant with less than two years of experience receives a base salary of $38,260.80 (in addition to a living allowance or other bonus pay); privates with less than two years of experience receive $20,170.80 (US Army 2019a). An asterisk on the pay table signifies pay will be lower for the first four months of service for privates. Officers start as second lieutenants and then are promoted up the ranks: first lieutenant, captain, major, lieutenant colonel, colonel, and then the general ranks, one star to four stars, the rank of full general.

The Army develops officers in three ways: West Point, Officer Candidate School, or ROTC. West Point reports a 10 percent acceptance rate, charges taxpayers around $250,000 per cadet for tuition, and graduates roughly one thousand cadets yearly. That's a small drop in the bucket out of the nearly eighty thousand total officers currently serving. The twelve-week Officer Candidate School produces a few thousand officers, but again, just a small fraction of the nearly eighty thousand total officers. ROTC supplies the bulk of the officers, the bulk of the leaders needed to guide the enlisted.

Just prior to graduation, Logan will move through accessions to receive a duty slot (active, guard, or reserve) and branch, or job description. The Army breaks these branches into four broad categories: combat arms branches, combat support branches, combat service support branches, and special branches. A cadet receives a duty component and branch according to their performance on the Order of Merit List (OML) and talent management process. The OML ranks all cadets at a university or school who have completed Advanced Camp (usually juniors). UNG posts their OML on a board inside the Military Leadership Center, the building that serves as the physical hub of ROTC at UNG. The rank is dependent on a host of factors, including academics, extracurricular activities, and fitness tests. These factors are assigned weighted values that change each year. The talent management process is like a test one would take with a high-school guidance counselor that helps cadets identify their talents and interests. Based on these data points, cadets are branched.

Returning to World War I history: Wilson went to war in 1918, buoying the flagging spirits of England and France with a US troop surge.[3] The war ended a little over a year later. Wilson took a prominent place at the peace-negotiating table in Paris.

FROM ISOLATIONIST TO INTERVENTIONALIST (AND BACK AGAIN?)

Foreign-policy decisions are determined, it seems, miles away from the here and now of everyday life. But they impact us and our students.

The United States struggled to find her way on the world stage as an independent country following the Revolutionary War. As England and France continued their near century-long skirmishes, George

Washington issued a Proclamation of Neutrality in 1793 that stated just that: the United States would remain neutral in yet another conflict between France and England. When John Adams assumed the presidency following Washington's retirement after two terms, Thomas Jefferson, as vice president, pushed his old friend Adams to lend support to France. Adams, like Washington, didn't want to get pulled into a war, partially because of his frustration with the haughty French and Jefferson's infatuation with their sophisticated airs and partially because of the projected cost of waging a war across the Atlantic Ocean. Adams won out; the United States remained neutral. And when Jefferson succeeded Adams as president, Jefferson, too, kept to this policy of neutrality. In 1821, under the presidency of James Monroe, Secretary of State John Quincy Adams, whose father several decades earlier boldly fought to keep the US out of a foreign conflict, delivered a speech on July 4, 1821, to the US House of Representatives that offered a succinct view of US foreign policy, a view that, though delivered by a secretary of state, set the stage for how the US viewed foreign conflict for almost a century. Dressed in his Harvard gown, Adams (2013) declared, "[The United States] goes not abroad in search of monsters to destroy. She is the well-wisher to the freedom and independence of all. She is the champion and vindicator of only her own." He concluded his speech by pointing to a common personification of the US: a female with a shield and spear, and upon the shield is inscribed Freedom, Independence, Peace. Adams said, "This has been her Declaration: this has been, as far as her necessary intercourse with the rest of mankind would permit, her practice." During the uncertain early years of this republican experiment, no matter that an Army general or a polymath farmer from Virginia held the presidency, the US sought no "entangled alliances," no "monsters to slay."

Until, largely, Wilson went to war almost a century later.

World War I. World War II. Vietnam. Korea. Bosnia. Somalia. Iraq. Afghanistan. The US goes in search of monsters now. And sometimes the monsters come for us. We have looked for monsters in Mogadishu, Kosovo, and Baghdad. Seeking out these monsters, we have journeyed to Fallujah, the Ho Chi Min Trail, and Kabul. Interventionist foreign policy guided the United States in the twentieth century. When Logan entered UNG in 2014, Barack Obama had just won reelection. He inherited a foreign-policy mess from George W. Bush. The US, in reaction to the horrendous attacks of September 11, had gone in search of monsters to slay and stumbled her way into a war in Iraq and a commitment to toppling Saddam Hussein. The US quickly found itself embroiled in conflict in almost too many countries to name, with no clear course of action. The US shifted from conventional force-on force warfare—with a clear enemy lined up against a clear opposing force—to asymmetrical warfare, walking the dusty, winding streets of Fallujah in search of . . . a target? Weapons of mass destruction? But try as Obama might, he could not fully wrest US troops from our varied military engagements. Despite winning the Nobel Peace Prize, despite scaling back troop levels, despite opting for drone warfare over boots on the ground, our troops largely remained abroad in search of those elusive monsters. Our total Army strength registered roughly five hundred sixty-two thousand active-duty troops in FY10 (US Army 2010). Army profile reports offer total army strength each year over the past decade and 2010 is at the top of the bell curve, so Obama oversaw the peak of the troop surge. In chapter 12, I cover in more detail shifts in foreign policy from Obama to Trump, particularly highlighting how Obama responded to Syria's government's gassing its own people in 2013 and how Obama scaled back out troops across all services, including active duty army. But here I simply point to how foreign policy has largely shifted from isolationist to interventionist. Cadets, really *all* of us, feel the result of uncertain and challenging foreign policy.

CIVILIAN CONTROL OF CITIZEN-SOLDIERS

US higher education may be the proverbial ivory tower standing high above the hoi polloi, but it is higher education administrators, and not uniformed officers, who were and are the driving force behind the inextricable link between higher education and the military we see starting with the Morrill Act of 1862 and culminating in the National Defense Act of 1916. Military historian Michael Neiberg (2000) writes,

> Civilian colleges and universities, not the armed services, led the way in creating on-campus military training programs. From the early nineteenth century to the present, the administrators of American higher education have believed firmly that the national defense requires skilled young officers, but that these young men should not be prepared exclusively by the military itself. (2)

This belief, Neiberg reminds us, is part and parcel with how people in the United States approach government and the military. Neiberg writes that people living in the United States firmly believe "that the military must be subservient to civilian interests for it to truly represent and defend the interests of the society it serves" (13). David Axe (2007), in his study of ROTC at the University of South Carolina, writes that the US military represents the "volunteer spirit" (8) of the people living in the United States and that "American soldiers are just American citizens in different clothes" (8). Civilians have final authority over the military. The president, no matter their military background, enters the office as a civilian. So does the vice president. So does the sectary of defense, even if they have a military background. So do members of Congress, who alone have the power to declare war. The secretary of the Army is the highest-ranking civilian in the Department of Defense, and even though the chairman of the Joints Chief of Staff is a four-star general (or the equivalent of), by law that person does not have operational command authority over any aspect of the military once they assume office. Nor does the chief of staff of the Army. Historical events shaped our desire for civilian input in the development of future soldiers (think colonialists' frustration with quartering British soldiers, a frustration that led to the Third Amendment).

We also stress local autonomy and an all-volunteer force. Each campus with ROTC decides on its own whether ROTC is compulsory for students who matriculate. VMI only enrolls cadets, for example; UNG is a mix of civilian and military, with cadets only on one of its five campuses. And all cadets at senior military colleges have the option of commissioning or not. Americans are historically squeamish about federally mandated military service; jettisoning conscription was a political inevitability in the wake of Vietnam. Only cadets at four of the five federal service academics are required to serve. As political scientist Donald Alexander Downs and public policy professor Ilia Murtazashvili (2012) write, "At root, the citizen-soldier ideal [articulated in ROTC] is a product of distrust of a standing military, coexisting with a belief in the obligation of citizens . . . to defend themselves, their communities, and the nation with arms." (80). Higher education, as representative of the people it serves, seeks an active role in the development of future soldiers, even as the "military has often resisted diverting resources toward programs that it has perceived as citizenship programs, not essentially military programs" (Neiberg 2000, 4). ROTC is woven into the fabric of the United States: it represents a balance between the military and civilians; it represents choice and local autonomy. ROTC is also woven into civilian institutes of higher education. For example, at UNG, a professor of military science (PMS) heads up ROTC. The PMS is a colonel and holds the position for three years. While the PMS is a Title 10 federal employee and draws a paycheck from the federal government, not the state government as I do, the academic curriculum he oversees falls under the jurisdiction of the College of Arts & Letters, the same college I, in the English department, fall under.

Because schools and the military are coupled, stakeholders of higher education feel the impact of military decisions. During my lifetime, the United States has known little international peace. I remember a soldier in camouflage visiting my second-grade classroom. Operation Desert Storm was in full force, and an active-duty soldier was standing in my classroom. It was the first time I saw such a sight. Beyond remembering the name of my second-grade teacher, it's the only memory I have of that school year. Fast forward to the US intervention in Kosovo under the Clinton administration when I was in high school, and then that September 2001 morning. I was a first-year college student getting ready to head to my first-year composition course, watching sports highlights on ESPN that were interrupted by chaos and terror. Since the Towers fell that day, the US has sent thousands and thousands of military and civilian personnel into war. Six men stood next to me in my wedding: my father, my brother-in-law, and four high-school friends. My father had been in the Corps of Cadets at UNG but did not commission. Three of my high-school friends deployed, one as active duty, one as reserve, one as a lawyer with the Air Force. My active-duty friend deployed three times, a total of thirty-one months during his first sixty months of marriage. I went through undergrad, grad school, and my years as a professor in this post-9/11 era. My children have only known this era. Many of our students only know this era.

Because the United States has known little international peace in the last thirty years, college educators are faced with an increased student population that has known combat, students who have completed basic training, sworn an oath to serve, been deployed. Through interdisciplinary research, educators are developing attunement to this population and pedagogical best practices for working with and supporting them. The University of Utah hosts a national research center and international conference focused on veteran studies. The National Endowment for the Humanities (2014) invited projects that "encourage humanities programs that focus on the history, experience, or meaning of war and military service." Virginia Tech, an SMC like UNG, hosts the *Journal of Veteran Studies* and also hosted an NEH summer institute on veteran studies. Many schools offer Green Zone training to help faculty and staff understand and support student veterans on our campuses. I completed my Green Zone training through our student affairs office as I finished revisions to this book.

RC/WS scholars and scholarship, too, have contributed to more acute understandings of the unique challenges and affordances student veterans bring to US college campuses. Christian Weisser, Michelle

Ballif, Alexis Hart, and Roger Thompson (2013) coedited a special issue of *Composition Forum* devoted to student veteran writers. *Kairos: A Journal of Rhetoric, Technology* published a special issue on military writing edited by Mike Edwards and D. Alexis Hart (2010). *Pedagogy: Critical Approaches to Teaching Literature, Language, Composition, and Culture* hosted a round table titled "Veterans' Voices" that became as special issue edited by Hart and Thompson (2016a). Hart and Thompson, with the support of a Conference on College Composition and Communication (CCCC) research initiative grant, visited over seventy US college campuses to learn about support systems in place for student veterans and then published an award-winning essay (2016b) on their work and a follow-up book, *Writing Programs, Veteran Studies, and the Post 9/11 University: A Field Guide* (2020). As I was completing the final draft of this book, Mark Blaauw-Hara (2021) published *From Military to Academy: The Writing and Learning Transitions of Student-Veterans*, which, like Hart and Thompson's 2020 book, is poised to serve all US higher education stakeholders who work with student veterans.

To this collection of scholarship in the paragraph above, we can add position statements by professional organizations. In 2011, the CCCC appointed a Task Force on Student Veterans that led to the 2015 document "Student Veterans in the College Composition Classroom: Realizing Their Strengths and Assessing Their Needs." The document opens with a two-paragraph introduction and offers assets student veterans bring to campuses. These assets are practical considerations, easily implemented in a college writing classroom:

> Student veterans have served as part of a team and have often served in leadership roles for which problem-solving and thinking on one's feet were daily requirements. This experience should be valued, honored, and recognized. For example, instructors might invite student veterans to take leadership roles in the classroom, as small group facilitators, or as mentors to other students.

The position statement then provides special considerations regarding student veterans and ends with FAQs and a list of references broken into four sections: "Composition/Writing Studies," "Disability Studies," "General," and "Student Services/Student Affairs."

However, student veterans are not the object of this book. Logan has not commissioned, navigated basic training, been deployed, seen combat. He even cringes at the idea that he is like veterans and tells me when people around town thank him for his service, he is quick to point out he hasn't served. But I offer this all-too-quick overview of how student veterans are considered in RC/WS because, instead of tracing how immersion into the military influences academic performance, I want to start at the beginning and trace how *anticipated* immersion into the military influences academic performance, particularly in regard to literacy development.

The CCCC position paper (2011) details another asset of the student veteran: "Student veterans are experienced writers and communicators who are familiar with military genres of writing and questions of authorship sometimes different from but related to those encountered in higher education. That expertise and familiarity should be acknowledged, explored, and built upon." As I show throughout this book, the military does indeed have unique communication genres. I find myself nodding along with the point that "questions of authorship [are] sometimes different from but related to those encountered in higher education." According to Chris Anson and Shawn Neely (2010), texts such as field manuals, standard operating procedures, and policies are "recycled, repurposed, and appropriated without the need for individual authorial attribution" because "getting jobs done effectively and efficiently" (1) takes prominence over accurate authorial attribution. The CCCC position paper gives readers recommendations for working with student veterans who bring these genres and questions into the classroom. I want to explore how a student starts on the path to being a veteran, how a cadet learns military genres and questions of authorship. In short, to use a literary metaphor, instead of looking at a protagonist at the close of the narrative, I want to flip backwards to the start and see the protagonist at the beginning of the narrative.

As the United States finds itself embroiled in never-ending conflicts, as our colleagues in psychology, sociology, and health sciences develop more acute tests for diagnosing PTSD and TBI, as our federal government creates and implements more initiatives for helping veterans return to college, I anticipate the pedagogical interest in student veterans will only grow. I believe we can learn a great deal about our student veterans by looking at a student on the path to being a veteran. In the next chapter, I introduce my study and align it with other longitudinal studies on student writer development.

NOTES

1. Through several bureaucratic iterations, the War Department became the Department of Defense in 1949.
2. The other 3 percent are warrant officers, a gray area between officers and enlisted.
3. The historical trajectory of WWI and the rise of ROTC is more nuanced than the few quick paragraphs I offer. To add more details: ROTC failed to raise the troop

numbers as quickly as Wilson demanded (Levine 1988). To raise troop levels, Congress pushed to implement a universal draft; Wilson opposed a draft. Through a variety of committees and political negotiating, Congress established the Student Army Training Corps (SATC), which turned participating colleges into full-time Army training locations. SATC was disbanded after only three months (with the conclusion of WWI), but SATC laid the foundation on which ROTC would eventually stand. Additionally, historian of education David O. Levine (1988) points to SATC, specifically, and WWI more generally, as instrumental in shaping positive public opinion about universities in the early twentieth century. Levine argues that "by showing higher education's potential for service to young people and the diverse sectors of society and by creating economic and social incentives for college attendance, the war effort accelerated the expansion of the structure, size, and functions of American higher education" (24).

2
THIS STUDY, LONGITUDINAL RESEARCH, AND RHETORICAL GENRE STUDIES

When I stepped into the honors English 1101 classroom for the first time, I knew I would be working with cadets. Into this class, I brought knowledge about student veterans my colleagues in RC/WS had developed and implemented. However, I found myself in a different research/teaching space than my RC/WS colleagues described. To put it simply, cadets are not veterans. I was not working with soldiers returning from deployment and reintegrating into the civilian world. Cadets have one boot in the academy and one boot in the drill field. One boot at the threshold of the academy and one boot at the threshold of the army. They have not been deployed and have no prior military experience. They are in a liminal position, blank slates upon which the rhetorical demands of writing for the academy and writing for the Army are to be written. They are in a period of three transitions, as the commandant for the Corps of Cadets tells incoming UNG faculty: transitioning from civilian life to military life; transitioning from a sedentary life to an active life; transitioning from a high-school student to a college student. Any of those transitions alone would be challenging, but these cadets are marching into all three at once.

Then there is writing; the leap from high-school to college writing. Howard Tinberg and Patrick Sullivan's (2006) edited collection *What Is "College-Level" Writing?* includes three student-authored chapters that provide writing teachers with a rich account of how students articulate the many challenges that come with moving from high-school to college-level writing. For example, former undergraduate student Amanda Winalski (2006) states that "writing at this [college] level is perhaps an ongoing process that necessitates a persistent willingness to try, fail, and try" (307–308). The cadets in honors English 1101 were transitioning into this space of trying and failing and trying again Winalski describes. In *Drilled to Write*, I invite us to read the words and work of Logan as he tries and fails and tries again.

https://doi.org/10.7330/9781646422784.c002

Midway through the semester, I approached Logan about a long-term project. He expressed interest, and we sat down in my office for several interviews that semester. Through the initial interviews, I gathered snatches of Logan's literate past: a thumb drive containing his curricular and extracurricular writing projects since seventh grade; syllabi from his college classes; PowerPoint lectures he sat through in his military-science classes; a tour of his barracks; and the textual miscellany that directs everyday Army life. After that semester, I made a bold request of Logan: *Let me follow you and talk with you until you graduate.*

Logan agreed.

I received amended IRB approval.

This project began.

LONGITUDINAL STUDIES IN RC/WS

Book-length studies by Elizabeth Chiseri-Strater (1991), Marilyn Sternglass (1997), Lee Ann Carroll (2002), and Anne Beaufort (2007) informed how I began formulating this project. These authors argue for sustained, fine-grained studies of a person.

In *Academic Literacies: The Public and Private Discourse of University Students,* Chiseri-Strater (1991) writes, "Academic literacies . . . cannot be untied from a student's overall literacy" (xvi). This statement serves two purposes for writing researchers. One, it directly knots curricular and extracurricular literacies so writing research can focus not only on classroom writing experience when charting a learner's writing development. Two, by making *literacy* plural, Chiseri-Strater gestures toward many different forms of literacy, some in conflict with each other, some in harmony. These literacies animate one's private and public life (to borrow terms from her title). Using ethnography, she paints a rich portrait of Anna and Nick, two students at the University of New Hampshire. Chiser-Strater's work is one of the earlier ethnographic studies of student writers. Subsequent scholars operate in her tradition.

Six years after Chiseri-Strater introduced readers to Anna and Nick, Sternglass (1997) published *Time to Know Them: A Longitudinal Study of Writing and Learning at the College Level.* Lee Ann Carroll, who later wrote her own longitudinal study, describes Sternglass's work as "one of the few truly longitudinal studies that captures both the academic environments in which students write and, most importantly, their perception of this environment" (8). Sternglass collected data on nine students over the course of six years at the City College of New York. The student population at City College skews toward multicultural urban, a much different student population than Chiseri-Strater studied at New Hampshire. Sternglass articulates the roles writing and writing instruction play in fostering critical-thinking skills, specifically, and learning, generally. Sternglass's framework considers socioeconomic constraints impacting students' access to education and students' ability to devote time and resources to schoolwork. Ultimately, Sternglass argues "students with poor academic preparation have the potential to develop the critical reasoning processes that they must bring to bear in academic writing if they are given the time" (296). Through highlighting the role of writing in learning and by looking at a multicultural urban population, Sternglass asks readers to consider large questions about the role of prior knowledge and socioeconomic standing in the path of learning.

Carroll's (2002) *Rehearsing New Roles: How College Students Develop as Writers* follows twenty students over the course of four years at Pepperdine University. A developmental perspective informed by psychology helps Carroll focus on how students adjusted to moments of transition in their academic writing lives: from class to class, professor to professor, year to year. Carroll draws on student portfolios of academic writing and asks students to complete self-assessments and participate in focus groups and individual interviews. With these data, Carroll argues students develop as writers through taking on "new and difficult roles that challenge their abilities as writers" (9), and, most critically, students did not learn to write better over the course of four years; instead, students learned to write "'differently'—to produce new, more complicated texts, addressing challenging topics with greater depth and complexity" (xii).

For *College Writing and Beyond: A New Framework for University Writing Instruction*, Beaufort (2007) designed a qualitative case study focused on the literacy development of one person: Tim, a history and engineering major at a private university in the southern United States. Beaufort studied Tim for six years. She followed him from his first semester classes to two years after his graduation when he was working for a mechanical design company. Through her exploration of how college students develop as writers, mapping how writers develop expertise in a given discourse community, she hopes for a "re-conceptualization of writing instruction at the post-secondary level" (5). Beaufort's study stands as an early articulation and examination of theories of writing transfer that now dominate the theory and practice of writing instruction. As scholars now look back on Beaufort's book, Tim, as the centerpiece, recedes to the background, while Beaufort's conceptual model of the five knowledge domains jumps to the fore. In this model, Beaufort captures the five domains upon which learners draw when developing expertise in a given community: writing-process knowledge, subject-matter knowledge, rhetorical knowledge, genre knowledge, and, the domain that encompasses the other four, discourse-community knowledge. This conceptual framework undergirds her study and establishes "recommendations for restructuring university-level writing instruction in ways that will increase the likelihood of positive transfer of learning" (21). Beaufort's hopeful stance still drives curricular writing developments, like the teaching-for-transfer curriculum popularized in Kathleen Blake Yancey, Liane Robertson, and Kara Taczak's (2014) award-winning *Writing across Contexts*. Collectively then, *College Writing and Beyond*, is less about Tim's experience as he moves through college and more about college writing instruction, a savvy rhetorical move on Beaufort's part that helps assuage concerns that qualitative case studies offer limited generalizable findings. Though Beaufort fails to consider any literacy practices that may populate Tim's nonacademic life (she quickly acknowledges then forgets Tim "wrote song lyrics in his spare time" [92]), Beaufort delivers a rich picture of one student's academic writing over six years at one university.

These four studies of writing development most directly shaped how I approached, implemented, and wrote about my study of Logan. Chiseri-Strater tells readers literacy practices and histories extend beyond the classroom, and Sternglass tells readers writing and critical-thinking skills are caught up in a vast web of socioeconomic and sociohistoric forces. Carroll tells readers that writers learn to write differently—not necessarily better or worse—and Beaufort offers a conceptual model of writing development that writing-related transfer theorists and practitioners now use as a springboard to developing curricula that facilitate transfer.[1]

Longitudinal studies like these have recently shifted to bring the focus more clearly on how students describe their writing experiences in undergraduate programs. I appreciate this pivot toward student agency and listening to students tell stories of their writing experiences. Eodice, Geller, and Lerner's *The Meaningful Writing Project* reports findings on how over seven hundred students describe their most meaningful writing experiences. Jonathan Alexander, Karen Lunsford, and Carl Whithaus (2020) are steadily working on an expansive study on how undergraduates from their undergraduate programs describe their writing experiences. They offer the framework of wayfinding as a "metaphor for conceptualizing, examining, and studying writing experiences" (125).

In sum, these studies keep the focus largely on US undergraduate programs and map students' pathways through varied collegiate writing experiences. However, with the financial support of organizations like the Spencer Foundation, and the institutional support of universities like Elon University, writing researchers are tracing trajectories of writing development that journey beyond school. We are developing more robust understandings of literate becoming by interrogating and sharpening our theoretical and methodological models. We are attending to lifespan writing research in rhetoric and composition/writing studies.

LIFESPAN-WRITING RESEARCH IN RC/WS: PERILS AND POSSIBILITIES

As I was finishing this book, Elon's Center for Engaged Learning, an innovative hub in the world of teaching and learning under the guidance of Peter Felten and Jessie Moore, was concluding a three-year research seminar titled Writing beyond the University. This research seminar gathered over forty scholars, including me, from across multiple countries to form three-year multi-institutional research projects that examine writing beyond the university. Through this seminar, I had the chance to labor and learn with colleagues around the world; findings are still pending as I write, but the resources the team at Elon has poured into this initiative signal scholars' growing commitment to tracing the trajectories of writers' literate becoming.

Additionally, in 2012, the Lifespan Writing Development Group (LWDG), comprised of Charles Bazerman, the late Arthur Applebee, Virginia Berninger, Deborah Brandt, Steve Graham, Paul Kei Matsuda, Sandra Murphy, Deborah Wells Rowe, and Mary Schleppegrell came on the scene. With financial support from the Spencer Foundation, the group gathered multiple times in Santa Barbara, California, and arrived at principles on writing development.[2] The people composing the LWDG brought with them a range of methodological and theoretical approaches to studying writing, and they offered their consolidated eight principles around writing and writing development in a brief essay (2017) and book-length study (2018). A snippet of their argument serves as an epigraph for this book, namely that writing development occurs across all the spheres in which a person engages with and enacts literacy practices (Bazerman et al. 2017). They conclude their essay by arguing that these principles should inform future research into lifespan-writing research and guide how we teach writing, how we test writing, how we design and enact government policy on writing and writing instruction.[3]

The work of the LWDG is not without detractors. In his pointed response to the LWDG's 2017 essay, Paul Prior (2017) states that "if we want to produce rich accounts of writing development over the lifespan . . . we need to constantly interrogate and refine our theoretical and methodological frameworks . . . the *just-writing, just-in-school* agenda will not capture the rich complexity of writing development across the lifespan" (217). Prior focuses attention on what should be our unit of analysis when seeking to better understand how people develop as writers. "Indeed," he writes, "it is long past time for us to accept that embodied, mediated, dialogic, semiotic practice is the matrix of all so called 'modes' and to recognize that semiotic (including literacy) development is a ubiquitous cultural process, not the special provenance of school" (217). Placing literacy development within the broader category of semiotic development, Prior urges us to attend to how people's semiotic development occurs across all communicative spheres and through coordination with other people, objects, and tools.

I read tones of lament and frustration in Prior's response. If Prior intended these tones, I can understand that because he has been steadily pushing RC/WS scholars to consider and attend to these issues for over three decades. Prior's voice is an important one that has long called for writing research to move beyond *just writing* and *just in school.* The scholarship Prior advocates for can operate *alongside* the work the LWDG offers and advocates for. Collectively, Prior's position and the position of the LWDG hold great promise for pushing us to innovate and reinvigorate our research methods and methodologies, for asking us to draw on cross-disciplinary theories of languaging, and for pedagogical import and local, state, and federal policy import. In the remainder of this section, I outline scholarship that looks beyond just writing and just-in-school writing and suggest how, in this book, I work alongside these two traditions: sometimes I focus my attention on just Logan's alphabetic prose churned out in the confines of the four walls of a first-year composition class; sometimes I turn an eye to his doodles in a sandbox tucked in the corner of the Military Leadership Center at the University of North Georgia.

Scholarship pushing against just writing and just in school attends to a broader range of meaning-making modes such as inscriptions (Latour 1990; Roozen 2020) or embodiment (Halley 2021; Syverson 1999) and attends to how people take up and refine and learn these meaning-making outputs in varied communicative spheres, not just in school. This scholarship doesn't narrowly consider writing development; instead, in Prior's words (2017), it considers "semiotic becoming." Prior's word choice is key: semiotics can include writing but is larger than just that. *Becoming* suggests an always coming into existence; *development* suggests an end point, for at some moment all organic objects have developed and are no longer developing. Semiotic becoming maps trajectories of how people engage with meaning-making modes across their lifetime and how, and now I am borrowing from the title of Prior's (2018) webtext, these moments add up to lives. By way of example, consider his webtext, which first appeared as a talk at the Thomas R. Watson Conference hosted by the University of Louisville. Prior introduces us to his daughter, Nora, now an adult biologist. Prior describes how Nora became a biologist. He provides images of Nora's fourth-grade school project; he describes an imaginative game he played with Nora when she was a child; he talks about her field work in Uganda when she was an undergraduate student and shows presentation slides from her talk at an academic conference about her work in Uganda. By moving across time and space, by looking beyond just writing and just in school, he traces a lifetime of becoming a biologist. Prior concludes: "From a *trajectories-of-semiotic-becoming* perspective, learning happens not *in* domains but across the trajectories of a life. It may turn out that music is important to becoming a biologist, that home is the primary site of academic work, that laboratories are teeming with social relationships, that rational stories of the progressive acquisition of knowledge need not apply." Research like this articulates rich, fine-grained studies of literate becoming by making use of theoretical models of writing development that map "trajectories people chart across their lifeworlds" (Roozen 2020, 230) and methodological frameworks that help capture such expansive becoming.

If we do this work of moving beyond just writing and just in school, we need new models and frameworks. The employed writing-research methods and methodologies that have served us since we started publishing a steady stream of journals in the mid-twentieth century no longer hold when we attend to more than writing and more than writing in school.

Zooming out from this scholarship and thinking more broadly, I see two approaches to understanding better how people develop as literate persons, and these approaches turn on the just-writing, just-in-school position. One approach focuses attention most squarely on traditional understanding of writing as alphabetic script composed by a person within the social demands of schooling. We follow students—for the research participants are often students—through a sequenced curriculum at an accredited university most often in the United States. We find ourselves reading about how this student encounters the dizzying array of disciplinary approaches to writing driven by a dizzying array of disciplinary epistemologies. We find ourselves reading that the writing produced in classrooms and writing produced in workplaces is "worlds apart"—to borrow from the title of *Worlds Apart: Acting and Writing in Academic and Workplace Contexts* (Dias et al. 2013). We conclude by reading about implications for the classroom or curriculum. The locale of writing development is, in Prior's (2017) words, the "special provenance of school" (217). I then see an approach to writing development that moves beyond writing and moves beyond school so that these studies attend to Prior's admonition that the just-writing, just-in-school agenda will not capture the rich complexity of writing development across a life. These studies look at how people develop semiotic resources in response to varied communicative demands they encounter. These studies challenge traditional pillars of RC/WS: that writing is alphabetic script and that writing development occurs in school.

In this book, I work amid these two broad approaches. I don't pit one against the other but seek harmony between the two as a way forward with writing research. I stay with the word *writing* in the phrase *writing research* because it is more readily understood by audiences and publics outside RC/WS. I also use *writing* because that is the word the community I am focused on uses. The Army has a definition of writing. The Army does not have a definition of semiotics, semiotic development, or the like. Since I believe my findings should be answerable to the Army community, I use their language. But I use *writing* with an invisible asterisk because, like Prior, I want to broaden our understanding of writing to include, for example, Logan manipulating toy soldiers in a sandbox and Logan coordinating his physical movement during a tactical operation in response to a written and then orally delivered operations order. I want to look at people acting with inscriptions. I want to note the importance of inscriptions for becoming a solider. Bruno Latour (1990) writes that inscriptions are "so practical, so modest, so pervasive . . . that they escape attention" (21). Cadet life is filled with such inscriptions. I want to broaden my view of writing so I do not look only at authored OPORDs but also at the sandbox inscriptions that help Logan produce an OPORD. I also trace Logan's writing development linearly against the backdrop of a four-year ROTC curriculum. I spend time reflecting on Logan's writing practices in middle- and high school. And I spend time reflecting on his nonschool, non-RTOC writing and the emails the two of us exchange now that he has graduated. But the bulk of this book is Logan in school: year 1, year 2, year 3, year 4. Again, I follow this tidy path—even as I advocate fiercely for the tangled and divergent and recursive and messy path of literacy development—because this is the sequence in which he is operating. I want to learn how ROTC helped Logan develop as a writer. Therefore, I need to study the sequenced four-year undergraduate ROTC curriculum designed and implemented at UNG. I need to play within the lines to offer feedback about the lines. So, returning to just writing and just in school: at times, in this book, it is just writing; at times it is not. At times we are just in school; at times we are not. As RC/WS develops research questions and findings derived from specific communities of study and answerable to different communities, we need to consider how the just-writing and just-in-school perspectives serve those with whom we research. My work with the Army and ROTC has led me to believe that offering findings on a cadet's semiotic development outside school does not best serve that community—though it may serve our RC/WS community. But I believe a study that at times attends to just writing and at times attends to just in school can serve both the Army and ROTC community and RC/WS. I seek harmony between our discipline and the communities we seek to serve with our work.

TAKING UP GENRES OF A COMMUNITY

For a foothold into Logan's becoming a cadet writer, I take up research on writing-related transfer, specifically how writers transfer genre and style across domains. Like the compulsory general education writing courses that populate US higher education, Army writing is predicated on the notion of successful transfer: cadets, through writing activities within the ROTC curriculum, learn the Army writing standard and bring this standard to bear on the writing tasks they eventually take up as Army officers. More specifically, ROTC curriculum is predicated on the notion that cadets will transfer the common Army genres and styles into their writing lives as Army officers. As Mikhail Bakhtin (1986) taught us, style and genre are linked, and we particularly see this linkage at play in Army writing. The Army has a coherent definition of the Army writing style, and the Army has detailed examples and templates and uses for common Army genres.

RC/WS knows a great deal about transfer. For example, we know about the role prior knowledge plays in transfer (Anson 2016). We know how to construct effective curricula to support transfer (Yancey, Robertson, and Taczak 2014) and how learners transfer knowledge across media (DePalma 2015). We can point to documents like the Elon Statement on Writing Transfer (Elon University 2014) that crystallize and communicate our findings to broad audiences. Additionally, through connecting with our colleagues working in the scholarship of teaching and learning, we continue to explore what transfer might mean for our teaching practices (Moore and Bass 2017). Indeed, Yancey (2017), in her contribution to Jessie L. Moore and Randall Bass's collection, argues that a key difference between high-school and college writing is the "elaborated writing processes that students develop in [FYC] . . . that they repurpose for writing tasks in their other classes" (42). Bass (2017) takes this point one step further and argues that intentionally designing curricula to foster transfer is a hallmark of higher education. With the emphasis in the original text, Bass writes, "Designing for writing transfer entails acts of intentionality and integration that speak precisely to what we mean by *higher* education" (146). In this book, I extend Bass's point to a cocurricular activity like ROTC and argue that the intentional design of classes to facilitate writing transfer is an element of the ROTC curricular sequence at an SMC like UNG. Given that argument, then, how does Logan experience his movement through this curricular sequence? How does Logan experience the intentional design of ROTC classes and the intentional building of skills in preparation for the writing life of an Army officer? Additionally, given that the Army offers a definition of the Army writing standard, which we can understand as a *style* of writing, how does Logan bring this standard to bear on common Army genres?

Before hearing from Logan and entering classroom spaces with him, in the remainder of this chapter I lay a foundation for engaging with how Logan experiences genre and style in his ROTC classes. I start with genre by offering two broad arguments about the role genre plays in writing development and then turn to specific genres Logan will write as a cadet.

To begin, two broad arguments about genre: genre is a tool that does and a key factor in the transfer of writing knowledge and processes and, thus, an organizing principle in writing pedagogy.

I offer these broad arguments as a blueprint for how I construct my argument on Logan's literacy development. Genre holds a prominent place in writing pedagogy because we understand genre as an action and define it as a central feature of writing development.

Genre: A Tool That Does

Pick up a publication within RC/WS on genre and genre studies, and you will see Carolyn Miller's (1984) work is either directly referenced or indirectly reflected. Miller shifts the current focus in genre studies away from textual features of a genre to what the genres help accomplish (thus the *social action* dimension in her title, "Genre as Social Action"). Her emphasis on *action* in her title draws attention to the concept that genres *do*. Genres are not just offering textual features; instead, rhetors adopt or do not adopt genres based on the opportunity of a chosen genre accomplishing something another genre cannot. I like to think Miller is offering us a verb concept of genre instead of just a noun concept.

Charles Bazerman (2004) follows this notion of genre as verb and projects genre through activity theory. Activity theory comes to us largely from Soviet-era psychological theory concerned with how people interact with each other and with tools to accomplish something. The unit of analysis is the activity system. Within an activity system, people share a common goal and use common tools to accomplish this goal over time. A concrete example is the Army. Through training and doctrine and accumulated historical processes and lore, the over one million Army soldiers coalesce around a communal goal and organize their action toward this goal around (textual) tools such as OPORDs, WARNOs, FRAGOs, memos, PowerPoint presentations, synchronization matrices, planning horizons, 9 Line MEDEVAC reports, and handwritten miscellany and other (textual) tools leveraged and coordinated to accomplish a collective goal. Activity theory organizes collectively agreed upon action around the coordination of people and tools, with the two holding equal agency in pursuit of this goal. Following Bazerman, genres are tools, critical cogs in the machine of community building and doing. Bazerman even offers us a conception of a genre system in line with an activity system: a fluid and dynamic organizing action spurred and supported by genres. Disruption or continuation of community goals hinges on genres. He writes, "Understanding the form and flow of texts in genre and activity systems can even help you understand how to disrupt or change the systems by the deletion, addition, or modification of a document type" (311). Taking Miller and Bazerman together, RC/WS offers genres as tools that do. Such a perspective ushered in what is now referred to as *rhetorical genre studies* (RGS). RGS, with its perspective of genres as typified social action grounded in recurrent situations, holds great promise for articulating for us and for our students the roles genre knowledge and genre acquisition play in writing development.

Genre: A Key Factor in the Transfer of Writing Knowledge and Processes, Thus an Organizing Principle in Writing Pedagogy

Beaufort (2007) offers a visual of how writers develop expertise. This visual contains five overlapping domains: writing-process knowledge, subject-matter knowledge, rhetorical knowledge, genre knowledge, and discourse-community knowledge. Beaufort nests the first four knowledge domains within the last: discourse-community knowledge. In line with RGS, Beaufort offers a traditional understanding of genres as "tools for writers" (20) formed through and in discourse communities. Genre is a tool writers handle as they seek to transfer writing knowledge and processes from one context to another.

Working in Beaufort's wake, Mary Jo Reiff and Anis Bawarshi (2011) illustrate that more successful student-writers recognize the prevalence and helpfulness of prior genre knowledge, whereas the less successful students do not. They introduce readers to the concept of "not" talk, a phrase taken from their student transcripts. Reiff and Bawarshi found that when students struggle to verbalize a writing assignment, they often describe what the assignment was *not*—not a literary analysis, not a research paper. According to Reiff and Bawarshi, "Our analysis suggests that the recognition of 'not' genres allows students to abstract and repurpose strategies from prior genres into less familiar ones" (328). I argue students' "not" talk highlights genres as tools that do. Novice writers approach an unfamiliar task by describing how the task functions differently from what they already know. Through this negation, novice writers understand what a thing is not, what that tool does not do.

Gwen Gorzelsky, Carol Hayes, Ed Jones, and Dana Lynn Driscoll (2017) provide findings from their Writing Transfer Project, a two-year project of student writing across four institutions using mixed-methods data collection. They write, "Students who viewed genre as a means for inquiry and analysis, rather than as formulaic conventions, made the greatest mean scores on the year 1 pre- to end-of-semester writing samples" (116). They point to this "statistically significant" finding to emphasize the importance of "genre awareness in writing growth." (116). Both multi-institutional studies—Gorzelsky and colleagues and Reiff and Bawarshi—approach genres as "tools of cognition" (Bazerman 2009, 283) in that both studies see genres as tools for accomplishing specific tasks within specific activity systems. The successful student writers from the Writing Transfer Project study viewed genre as something that does, as a "means for inquiry and analysis." The successful student-writers at Tennessee and Washington gained traction in unfamiliar writing tasks by understanding what the genre was not.

We now have empirical data within RC/WS on the role genre knowledge plays in transfer and writing development broadly. This data informs our pedagogical practices. For example, the third version of the Council of Writing Program Administrators' "WPA Outcomes Statement for First-Year Composition" (2014) places genre as key in what students should develop proficiency in: "Write in several genres," "Understand how genres shape reading and writing." In my role of writing program administrator, I receive scores of writing textbooks that now populate the shelves in my office. The fourth edition of Mike Palmquist and Barbara Wallraff's (2020) *Joining the Conversation* incorporates a textual feature they call "Genre Talk," which highlights design and genre conventions for a given assignment, such as informative writing, analytical writing, and evaluative writing. They also include a table representing how their textbook aligns with the CWPA outcomes statement (OS). The third edition of Amy Braziller and Elizabeth Kleinfeld's (2020) *The Bedford Book of Genres* also makes use of a chart to show how it aligns with the OS. Braziller and Kleinfeld take genre as the focus of the book because, as they write in the note to the instructor, "Working in a variety of genres and modes gets students to invest in what they do in first-year writing" (vii). The first edition of Robert Yagelski's (2015) *Writing Ten Core Concepts* provides ten concepts that are organizing principles for the book and are taken from the OS. Yagelski grounds six of the ten concepts in what the OS calls "rhetorical knowledge," which includes knowledge of genre. All three textbooks operate from the foundation that genres are not just containers through which we organize and classify text; instead, genres are things in action that organize and are organized by social interaction and that—returning to Bazerman and activity theory—genres are tools that accomplish the goal(s) of a community. Textbooks are accumulations of knowledge reflecting disciplinary shifts in thinking and doing. Textbooks are physical representations of the scholarship populating journals and conferences and books, and textbooks respond to what Paul Lynch (2013) terms the "Monday Morning question" (xi). Textbooks represent genres as tools that do and as a guiding principle in writing pedagogy. In this book, I look at genre through these two principles.

ARMY GENRES

The Army writing standard informs Army genres. For UNG cadets, three genres guide most of their writing: operations orders, 9 Line MEDEVAC reports, and counseling forms.

Operations Orders

As a first-year cadet, Logan anticipated operations orders (OPORDs) would be the "biggest military writing." Army Doctrine Publication 5-0, *The Operations Process* (US Army 2019c), provides a clarifying definition of the term *operations*: "Military operations are human endeavors conducted in dynamic and uncertain operational environments to achieve a political

Figure 2.1. OPORD form from Logan's self-assembled notebook. Photo by author.

purpose" (v). Key to this definition is the emphasis on *human, dynamic,* and *uncertain.* These variables require precise writing and precise delivery of writing. In other words, these variables require a detailed OPORD to facilitate success. OPORDs (see figure 2.1) are directives issued down the chain of command in preparation for the coordinated execution of an operation. The Department of Defense mandates the five-paragraph version, which includes situation, mission, execution, sustainment, and command and control. Coupled with OPORDs, warning orders (WARNOs) prepare soldiers for the execution of an OPORD, and fragmentary orders (FRAGOs) modify small portions of OPORDs. OPORDs are, in Logan's words, "like five-paragraphs briefing troops on 'this is the problem, this is what we are going to do, this is how we are going to do it, this is what we have available, this is the time frame.' And it is a big, long, extremely technical document that gets every single possible detail of an operation." According to Army Doctrine Publication 5-0, *The Operations Process* (US Army 2019c), OPORDs require critical and creative thinking:

> Commanders and staffs apply critical and creative thinking throughout the operations process to assist them with understanding situations, making decisions, directing actions, and assessing operations.

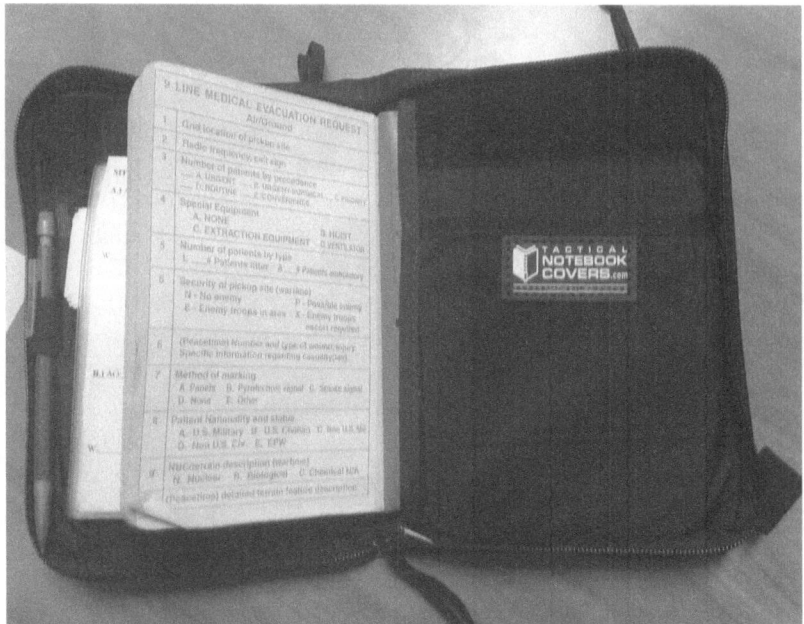

Figure 2.2. 9 Line MEDVAC report form from Logan's self-assembled notebook. Photo by author.

Critical thinking is purposeful and reflective thought about what to believe or what to do in response to observations, experiences, verbal or written expressions, or arguments . . . Critical thinking helps commanders and staffs identify causes of problems, arrive at justifiable conclusions, and make good judgments . . . Creative thinking examines problems from a fresh perspective to develop innovative solutions. Creative thinking creates new and useful ideas, and reevaluates or combines old ideas to solve problems. (1-65, 1-67, 1-68)

9 Line MEDEVAC

Unfortunately, 9 Line MEDEVAC reports (see fig. 2.2) may follow an OPORD. 9 Lines assist in the event of casualties. When engaging with hostile forces, casualties (which, for the military, include deaths and soldiers who are captured, injured, or missing) often occur. OPORDs invite critical and creative thinking because the genre gives writers time to consider options. Soldiers rapidly write and then radio in 9 Lines; a soldier's life may be at risk if the 9 Line is not relayed quickly and clearly.

Counseling Forms

The most common genre Logan will write during his four years at UNG are developmental counseling forms. As Logan rises through the ranks of the Corps, he will be asked to perform one-on-one counseling with his subordinates and complete DA Form 4856 (US Army 2014a), which will require his signature and the signature of the individual counseled. If OPORDs are on one end of the critical and creative thinking continuum and 9 Lines are on the other, I see the developmental counseling form in the middle. Logan will fill in specific boxes on the form—it is a government form, after all—but he does have the opportunity to offer narrative responses to sections such as "Purpose of Counseling," "Key Points of Discussion," and "Assessment of the Plan of Action."

These are the genres in which Logan will engage, the metaphorical molds into which he will pour his prose. But what of style? To continue the metaphor, what kind of prose is Logan pouring into these molds?

ARMY WRITING, PLAIN WRITING, AND THE IMPORTANCE OF LITERACY

The Army conveys its writing style largely through one document: Army Regulation (AR) 25-50: *Preparing and Managing Correspondence* (US Army 2020c). AR 25-50 is a one hundred plus-page document outlining three forms of correspondence authorized for Army use: letter, memorandum, and message. Within the eight chapters of this regulation, the Army constructs a clear "how-to" manual. For example, chapter 1 provides guidance on ink color and how to express times and dates; chapter 6 covers signatures and signature blocks. In section 1.11, the AR provides a clear description under the section heading "Writing Quality":

> In accordance with the Plain Writing Act of 2010 . . . DA [Department of the Army] writing will be clear, concise, and well-organized. Army correspondence must aid in effective communication and decision making. The reader must be able to understand the writer's ideas in a single reading, and the correspondence must be free of errors in grammar, mechanics, and usage. Use electronic spell check when available, but always proofread; spell check is only a tool and is not infalliable.

Indeed, the Army writing standard predates the Plain Language Act of 2010. DA-PAM 600-67, which is no longer an active document on the Army Publisihing Directorate's website, is a briefer document, only seventeen pages. The pamphlet opens with a foreword by former Army Chief of Staff General John A. Wickham Jr. With the underlined text present in the original, Wickham Jr. writes,

We must be able to articulate our intentions so that soldiers and civilians two echelons removed will know the end we seek. One way to assure such clear and concise communication is by improving the quality of our writing. This pamphlet, Effective Writing for Army Leaders, can help if used correctly. It introduces a new, simplified writing style which establishes writing standards and guidelines, and outlines editing tools to help reinforce the standards for ourselves and our subordinates.

Wickham adds one more paragraph before signing his name to the document. But he adds curious handwritten marginalia, a final call for clear writing: "All of us, from Chief down, need to improve our skills. Learning to write well is a lifelong endeavor." A powerful, accurate summation.

DA-PAM 600-67 (US Army 1986) defines the Army writing standard in this first chapter: "The standard for Army writing is writing you can understand in a single rapid reading, and is generally free of errors in grammar, mechanics, and usage." The pamphlet continues: "Good Army writing is clear, concise, organized, and right to the point." Using active voice, clearly separating each section, and opening with a "short, clear purpose statement" achieves this concision and organization. Such a descriptor does not seem unique to Army writing. Aside from the spoken-word poetry of the Dadaists or the playful poetry of Lewis Carroll, one would be hard pressed to find a person or organization that espouses opaque and disorganized prose to communicate.

The 2010 Plain Writing Act also strengthened the Army's understanding of the importance of clear writing. In 2010, Barack Obama signed into effect the Plain Writing Act with the directed purpose to "improve the effectiveness and accountability of Federal agencies to the public by promoting clear Government communication that the public can understand and use" (US Congress, Plain Writing Act 2010). Section 3 of the act provides a definition of plain writing: "The term 'plain writing' means writing that is clear, concise, well-organized, and follows other best practices appropriate to the subject or field and intended audience." Like the definition of Army writing in DA-PAM 600-67, plain writing is clear, concise, and organized. This act finds its genesis in a 2009 memorandum titled "Transparency and Open Government" in which Obama (2009b) wrote, "My Administration will take appropriate action, consistent with law and policy, to disclose information rapidly in forms that the public can readily find and use."

The Department of Defense (DoD), under which we find the Army, falls under the purview of "Federal agencies" described in the act. To this end, the DoD developed and maintains a "Plain Language" page on the Washington Headquarters Services (n.d.) website. This webpage includes training videos, writing-style guides, before and after examples of plain-language prose, and a pdf of an Army *Action Officer: Staff Writing Guide*. Additionally, users of this webpage can read annual Plain Language Act compliance reports. In the April 2020 Plain Language Compliance Report, we learn there were no plain-language amendments requests in 2019 and steps the DoD took during 2019 to implement plain-language requirements such as the direct but vague statement, "The DoD Plain Language Committee met to share ideas and information" (Washington Headquarters, *DoD Plain* 2020). Users of this webpage can also suggest a DoD document for plain-language review.

The act charges federal agencies with overseeing their own implementation and continued use of plain language. Nonpartisan watchdogs advocate for plain-language bills at the state and federal level and review current federal-agency websites and documents for plain writing. The Center for Plain Language (2018) is a 501(c)(3) nonprofit organization that helped lobby for the passage of the act in 2010. Founded in 2003, the center provides an annual Federal Plain Language Report Card in which they give a grade on a scale of A to F for the "organizational compliance" and "writing quality" of twenty-three federal agencies. According to the 2018 report card, "organizational compliance" entails "staffing, communication and training required by the Plain Writing Act." The DoD received an A+ for organizational compliance and a B for writing quality. Department of Commerce, Department of Housing and Urban Development, Department of Transportation, and the Department of Treasury all received an F in one category.

As evidenced by the Plain Language Act and the enforcement of the act, the executive and legislative branches of the federal government place an emphasis on the clarity and organization of writing, with the expressed purpose of building better bridges of communication between the federal government and its constituents. The Army, too, emphasizes clarity and organization but not because it has a goal of communicating more clearly with civilians. The Army does not have constituents. Clarity and organization lead to the rapid transmission of information. Speed is a priority. Additionally, to achieve speed in the transmission of information, the Army does not emphasize source attribution. In a word, plagiarism is of little concern for the most common internal Army genres.

In their webtext for the special issue of *Kairos* on military writing, Chris Anson and Shawn Neely (2010) write, "Disseminating what would ordinarily be considered intellectual property is often encouraged—and attribution beyond the local command level rarely happens" (3). What

Anson and Neely found is that policy letters, for example, are written and rewritten on an as-needed basis:

> Although an incoming commander will review the previous policy letter and perhaps change a few sentences to reflect his or her personal command philosophy, the majority of the original text often remains the same. The new commander's signature block replaces the old commander's, the date is changed, and a "new" policy letter is born. By common definitions . . . this is plagiarism. (4)

But for the sake of efficiency and the common good, the Army does not cite all the hands that crafted the document. Army writing does not adhere to the rigid standards of attribution governing writing within Western education.

The above paragraphs signal the importance federal government agencies place on plain writing and how the Army, in particular, privileges the rapid transmission of information over source attribution and appropriation. Through their various publications, the Army conceptualizes writing as a tool—a tool used for the specific unique tasks that constitute soldiering. Writing also carries cultural cachet within the Army. Writing is not just a tool soldiers use to pass memos up and down the chain of command. Writing and broader literacy initiatives are key for building Army community. For example, the Army Morale, Welfare, and Recreation (MWR) Program is designed to support and build community for DoD civilians, Army soldiers, and their families through hosting recreational and leisure activities but also overseeing the Army's own library system. With seventy libraries across seven countries, the Army MWR library traces its roots back to 1903 when Congress instructed the Army to develop and maintain recreational services for their soldiers and families. In 1920, the Army founded the Motion Picture Service, and in 1923, the Library Service. Soldiers serving in remote locations can request a monthly paperback-book kit containing twenty-five paperback books and an mp3 player loaded with twenty-four audio books—all matched to the interest of the soldier. The DoD, too, has a library system, the DoD MWR. Like my local library, the Army MWR library hosts summer reading camp for kids. From ensuring readiness for a tactical exercise to building the cognitive skills of preschoolers living on an Army base, literacy has a central role in the work of the Army.

During his four years at UNG, these genres will constitute the text world of the Corps for Logan. This book asks and answers questions such as, How does Logan move from Googling OPORDs on his iPhone during his free time to leading the writing and reading of one of his subordinates? How will he learn the genre of DA Form 4856, the urgency and clarity needed for the 9 Line? I turn to Logan's four years as an undergraduate student at the University of North Georgia to answer these questions and my larger research question. But the seeds that grow into Logan's postsecondary literacy experiences were planted earlier—through his curricular and extracurricular experiences with reading and writing. Anne Ruggles Gere (2019) reminds us most studies of writing development focus on the "undergraduate years without much attention to what came before or after" (325). To be fair, I have this myopic perspective because, in this book, I largely look at Logan's undergraduate years. But Logan entered into this research process with me equipped with a thumb drive full of various writing projects stretching back to his time in seventh grade. These one-page reports, PowerPoint presentations, annotated bibliographies, and narratives collectively constitute the text world of Logan Blackwell, the artifacts buried within years of official schooling that tell a tale of literacy. Like an inquisitive archeologist, I turn in the next chapter to introducing in more detail the research participant of this study and examining and considering the artifacts he created. The Elon Statement on Transfer (2014) calls for more "longitudinal studies [that] will enrich disciplinary understandings of transfer, particularly as scholars examine learners' development as writers" (9). *Drilled to Write* aims to respond to this call by examining Logan's development as a writer, how he moved knowledge across domains within, alongside, and outside school.

NOTES

1. These four books are not the totality of book-length RC/WS longitudinal studies on writing development. Anne Ruggles Gere's (2019) edited collection *Developing Writers in Higher Education: A Longitudinal Study* is a recent open-access offering, in addition to Albert Kitzhaber's (1963) work and publications by Richard Haswell (1991), Chris Thaiss and Terry Myers Zawacki (2006), and Anne J. Herrington and Marcia Curtis (2000). I also encourage readers interested in an additional overview of recent longitudinal studies on writing development to browse Paul Rogers's (2010) synthesis of this work. I found the table he constructed about how various authors have attended to extracurricular and curricular factors related to writing development to be particularly informative.
2. Thank you to Chuck Bazerman for talking with me one Sunday afternoon so I could better understand the history of the LWDG.
3. During the fiftieth anniversary of the Dartmouth Institute and Conference, Bazerman (2021) delivered an address in which he highlighted the work of the LWDG and called for continued lifespan writing research. The Writing through the Lifespan Collaboration is an output of his call. The collaboration held its inaugural conference in 2018 and has since published the collection *Approaches to Lifespan Writing Research: Generating an Actionable Coherence* (Dippre and Phillips 2020).

3
THE ARMY'S VERSION OF THE FIRST-YEAR EXPERIENCE
FROGs, Hills, and Haircuts

Logan Blackwell grew up in a large suburban city in east Georgia. His father works as a plant manager at a rock quarry, and his mom is a part-time nurse. Logan comes from a civilian family except for his grandfather, who was an E-4 (a low-level enlisted rank) until he was medically discharged. Logan attends UNG on an Army ROTC scholarship and has already signed paperwork and is contracted with the Army to commission following graduation. Few cadets enter UNG with such a contract. He entered UNG with a plan to branch military intelligence, infantry, or aviation. If he sticks with his plan, he will be the first military officer in his family. He admits that is part of the attraction to such a career. When he talks with you, Logan maintains strong eye contact and speaks with an air of confidence that belies his age. In class, he is focused: sitting straight, his fingers near his keyboard, ready to write. When we sat in my office for interviews, I followed his lead, dropping small talk in favor of getting down to business. I can respect a disinterest in obligatory small talk, but with Logan, such a disinterest speaks to what he is interested in and not what he isn't: since seventh grade, Logan has known he wants to pursue a commission in the military. With such a focus, I can understand why he doesn't have an interest in entertaining my barracks joke or my inquiries into how his day is going.

He does open up and ease into conversation when talk turns to books and writing. He has an effusive love of language with strong memories of books in his home and his parents reading to him at night. He remembers books on the bookshelf: Nicholas Sparks's novels, the *Left Behind* series, the popular relationship book *Men Are from Mars, Women Are from Venus*, and a biography on Dale Earnhardt, the late race-car driver. As a child, he read the *Magic Treehouse* series, Hardy boys, *Harry Potter*. He ambitiously attempted Jules Verne's *20,000 Leagues Under the Sea* in third grade but gave up.

https://doi.org/10.7330/9781646422784.c003

When I asked about early memories of school-supported literacy, he began with sixth grade. His sixth-grade English curriculum was divided between literature and writing; he had a separate teacher for each. His writing class was taught by a teacher with a PhD. In this class, according to Logan, "It was all writing with no extra literature stuff attached to it." The teacher was "very particular grammatically" and took extra time responding to student writers. Logan remembers working on a research paper and locating his own sources and then participating in a peer-review session in which students used different colors to respond to a classmate's writing. Logan produced a paper on ethical hunting, which he still has on a thumb drive and which he shared with me. Logan wrote the document in 18-point single-spaced Georgia font and lined the border of his document with trees. It is almost three pages long. He starts his paper with a bold statistic and two equally bold, succinct statements. I quote directly from the document without altering the language or usage: "About 1.5 million deer related car accidents occur each year causing 1 billion dollars in damage and one hundred fifty-seven human deaths. Hunters can change this. Hunting is an ethical practice."

That same year, Logan authored an expository paper on wilderness survival. He opens, as he did with his persuasive paper, with a hook: "Are you scared of getting lost in the woods?" Written in the same 18-point single-spaced Georgia font, but without a decorative border, the three-and-a-half-page paper is broken into five sections: "Rules of the Wilderness," "Shelter and Warmth," "Finding Food," "Medical Treatment," and "Equipment." As with his ethics of hunting paper, Logan addresses the reader as "you" and concludes with a nod of encouragement to his reader: "If you get lost, stay calm and think . . . you'll know what to do." Throughout, Logan weaves in phrases that hint at his tough-guy persona, a persona that may be connected to his burgeoning military interest. He writes, "Pain is usually not noticed in a survival situation" and suggests to his readers that they use the stomach of an animal for a water pouch; but Logan recommends that, first, the reader should "wash out the stomach."

When Logan reflects on his interest in the military and his literacy history, he begins at the same place: sixth grade. Logan does not have copies of papers prior to sixth grade and did not offer substantial narratives or memories of events prior to sixth grade. He did, however, write of his experience in third grade. In the honors English 1101 class, I assigned a group analysis of literacy history taken from chapter 1 of the second edition of Elizabeth Wardle and Doug Downs's (2014) *Writing about Writing*. After students read literacy narratives and full-length academic articles that chart writers' literacy development, I invited them to collaborate on what I call a *literacy task*. I borrow this term from Lee Ann Carroll (2002) to refer to writing assignments that call for "high-level reading, research, and critical analysis" (xiv). Logan worked with two civilian students. The three authored a text that explored their individual literacy histories and then offered a collective argument that united their narratives. They argued that they all experienced some "barrier" in their literacy history and, as a result, their love of literacy was squashed before they entered high school. Logan's narrative section in this paper did not focus on sixth or seventh grade, as I expected when I sat down to read and assess the literacy task. Instead, Logan brings the reader into his third-grade classroom and writes that "teachers were always concerned with themes in reading and writing." Logan's frustration with needing to find "some deeper meaning or cultural study in the books" and a "highly specific format to writing with a very specific purpose" erected "creative barriers." He wrote that his writing felt "robotic." Through these experiences in third grade, Logan moved away from the humanities. I do find it a bit odd for Logan to suggest that seeking deeper meanings in a text resulted in creative barriers, and I also find it odd that Logan, who wants to make a career out of the Army, expresses frustration with "highly specific writing" with a "specific purpose." But these potential contradictions sketch a picture of complex literacy development. The experiences that form literacy development do not dovetail, do not point to a singular meaning. Literacy development is messy, recursive, an amalgamation of school-sponsored and self-sponsored writing. Literacy development is not charted in a pie chart, graphed on a coordinate plane, or quantified on an Excel spreadsheet, as much as administrators, legislatures, our colleagues, and the public may want. As Carroll found in her study of college writers at Pepperdine, students learn to write differently as they move through varied curricular and extracurricular literacy encounters; their writing development cannot be charted as better or worse. So, too, in this study. Throughout *Drilled to Write*, contradictions arise; data gleaned from interviews may not align with data gleaned from textual analysis, gleaned from observation. At the fore, I want to be clear I don't paint—the data don't allow it—a linear and tidy picture of Logan developing as a literate cadet; instead, I offer a thick description of this process in all its rich messiness that comes from qualitative research.

What Logan learned about writing in sixth grade was toppled in seventh. Logan admits that because of the positive feedback he received from his sixth-grade writing teacher, he was "a little arrogant." He didn't receive the same high level of praise from his seventh-grade teacher as he did from his sixth-grade teacher. In Logan's words, "My seventh-grade teacher absolutely hated how I wrote." He adjusted his writing to fit with what his teacher was looking for, and then he "switched back to the way [he] wanted to in eighth grade."

In seventh grade, he took steps toward an eventual career in the military. He also wrote "A Soldier's Will," which I quoted from in the epigraph to this section and which I quote again here (see fig. 3.1): "We gave up our lives and it's finally over. It's time for us to go where soldiers live in peace and harmony and angels sing amazing grace. . . . Army and Navy, Air Force and Marines it's always the same. Someone will always be there to keep our homeland safe at night." He penned these bathos-heavy lines as a seventh grader at Greenbrier Middle School for his teacher, Ms. Pond. In a swirling font complete with an image of a headstone and US flag, his work offers a glimpse into how his literate identity is informed by the amalgamation of worlds he inhabits: religion, military, family. The worlds Logan inhabited in seventh grade are worlds he will inhabit throughout his four years as a cadet. He will populate these worlds with texts, and he will populate texts with these worlds.

About the text, Logan told me,

> In seventh grade, I got into the military. I just had this revelation one day. I thought all these normal civilian jobs . . . I couldn't really find a place. I felt like I could do any of them. It was just I didn't know what I liked. I knew things I really, really liked were speaking in front of people and being able to change situations and make policy and being the acting catalyst for something. I grew up quite a bit.

Logan offers many ideas in this excerpt. He speaks with confidence, almost arrogance, which he hinted at as a cause for some of the friction with his seventh-grade teacher: "I felt like I could do any of ['these normal civilian jobs']." He also offers the first glimpse into the importance he places on oral delivery, linking oral delivery with writing. This theme runs through many of the discussions Logan and I had about writing and what constitutes good writing for the Army and for his academic classes. He often returns to the idea that good writing should sound pleasing to the ear. Such a belief about writing links Logan with fifth- and fourth-century BCE Greek understanding of rhetoric and writing, a period in which Western rhetoric flourished through the work of Aspasia, Plato, and Sappho and the rise of the democracy. During this period, writing was largely, but not exclusively, an oral art form. Language took on a largely civic and public dimensions. Many of the great thinkers from this period, such as Isocrates, made a living as logographers. Public debate in

Greenbrier Middle School
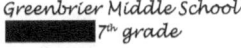 7th grade

A Soldier's Will
By:

As I lie here in this valley I think of my homeland. Surrounded by the dead bodies of my brothers, I wonder where I would be in the land of the free. I am hopeless to find where I belong. I answered the call to duty and now my time is finally up. I gave my life to this land of sin and lost souls. Our guns are down and our boots are hung. It looks like the job is done. We gave our lives and it's finally over. It's time for us to go where soldiers live in peace and harmony and angels sing amazing grace. Between war and peace, love and hate, America is together once again. Army and Navy, Air force and Marines it's always the same. Someone will always be there to keep our homeland safe at night. The children will once again play without fear of their joyous laughter being heard. Let them sleep in peace and their voices be lifted up to the heavens. We're up here with God watching you live out your lives in peace. May God preserve the land of the free and everything it holds dearly. It's what our fathers fought bravely and died for, a place of peace, our safe haven we call America. Let freedom forever reign in the place I call home.

Figure 3.1. An excerpt of Logan's middle-school paper "A Soldier's Will."

the polis formed the foundation of democracy. In a sense, the Western rhetorical tradition was born from practical civic roots. Logan maintains such a view of writing and often spends time considering how the text he authored would sound if spoken aloud. Though orality has largely waned in US higher education, the Army places importance on the rapid and effective oral delivery of key information. In seventh grade, while

Logan struggled to adapt his writing to a new audience, he discovered an interest in the military and in his ability to speak successfully in front of his classmates. As he said,

> The speech thing didn't really start until seventh or eighth grade. That came along with the military stuff. I just loved the idea of a guy in uniform standing in front of people. I noticed the power that delivery has on speech. And that is kinda the unique facet of writing. I could read you something on paper, and it would mean nothing. But my delivery can change the entire thing. So, that was what got me into speeches . . . the oral delivery making a difference.

He decided to pursue a life in the military in seventh grade and began working toward that goal in eighth. Logan told me his goal in eighth grade was to get "unfat."

Logan entered high school with a checklist he believed would help him get into a federal service academy: "That was my baseline for everything: Will this help me get into an academy? Will this help me get scholarships?" He accumulated extracurricular activities: Beta Club, the national honor society, the Spanish honor society, a foreign-language society. He had at least one AP course each year and placed in gifted math for three years. His high-school writing portfolio contains common high-school topics. He wrote a four-page paper on *Antigone* in which he argues that Creon, the antagonist of this Greek drama, "exhibits all the defining characteristics of the tragic hero as defined by Aristotle." Inspired by *Animal Farm*, he wrote an allegory about the Annapolis Zoo. He wrote a three-paragraph argument titled "A Modest Proposal: Setting a New World Order" in which he offers an alternative model to the crooked world of college athletics. He penned a paper for his junior American literature class titled "*A Lesson Before Dying*: Ernest Gaines's Lessons of Manhood." In the same class, Logan wrote a three-page fictional account of his experience at the Navy Junior Reserve Officers Training Corps (NJROTC). During his senior year, he completed the seemingly obligatory *Beowulf* essay in which he describes themes in the ancient poem and how these themes reflect the Anglo-Saxon culture.

Logan wrote in other classes. Most of this writing incorporated his growing interest in the Navy, just as his allegory based at the Annapolis Zoo did. For NJROTC, Logan produced "The United States Navy's Role in the National Strategy." The following year, he wrote an APA-format seven-page research paper titled "The Battle of Tripoli: A New Look for the American Navy," in which he provides the reader with background on the 1801 US conflict with Tripoli and then considers new strategies executed by the Navy during the conflict. Logan's "What I Learned About

Selecting a Career" does indicate his overall interest in the military; he writes about choosing to pursue a career as an officer in the Marines.

The thumb drive Logan shared with me also contains writing not directly connected to the classroom. Midway through his junior year, Logan wrote a one-page single-spaced reference letter for his friend and fellow NJROTC cadet. His friend was seeking to advance to Eagle Scout, the highest scout rank. Logan writes glowingly of his friend and signs "C/CPO Logan Blackwell" at the bottom of the reference, C/CPO standing for his rank, cadet chief petty officer, in the Navy junior ROTC program. For his NJROTC academic competition, Logan wrote a three-page essay on lessons he learned in NJROTC. Written one day after Christmas, while he was on winter break during his senior year in high school, Logan's essay explores the idea of a "spiritual commitment" about NJROTC. He writes, "I am different in this respect because this spiritual commitment is the basis of everything I have ever done." For Logan, spiritual commitment does not carry religious connotations, but it speaks to cadets seeking "something bigger than themselves." He tries to identify this deeper sense of personal sacrifice that characterizes military life. He knows there is something there, and he attempts to give voice to this something through describing a spiritual commitment. He talks of his legacy and the importance of leading the 142 "cadets of mine." Near the end of his essay, he writes of his "dream of becoming a commissioned military officer."

In our interviews, Logan didn't talk as much about high school as he did middle school. But these slices of text constitute Logan's literate life. As with any inexperienced writer, Logan is given to sweeping generalizations in his arguments and even dips into periods of bravado that can come off as arrogance. But I read this potential arrogance as a writer reaching. Logan is not a commissioned officer, has not been deployed. Yet through his dedicated interest in the military, he has gained an awareness of the personality characteristics constituting an effective military career. Logan tries to assume these characteristics in his prose, his mannerisms, and his overall worldview. His writes of his legacy, the 142 cadets under him, and his spiritual commitment. Logan doesn't have the ethos to talk legacy yet, but his research into the military over the course of the five plus years following seventh grade has taught him of the ethos desired and espoused by the military. Logan attempts to mimic this ethos.

When it came time to apply to schools, Logan focused on senior military colleges (SMCs) and federal service academies. He applied to Virginia Tech, UNG, VMI, Navy, West Point, and the Citadel. Logan hoped for West Point, which admits roughly 10 percent of applicants. He believed his grades were strong, and he received the all-important congressional nomination. He scored in the 79 percentile in the mathematics component of the SAT, the 92 percentile for verbal/critical reading, and the 95 percentile for writing. His combined English/writing ACT score was 28, and his reading score was 33. He already had AP credit for four classes (World History 1, US History 1, American Government, and Calculus 1). He was active outside the classroom.

He did not get in.

He believes he failed because he didn't throw a basketball far enough. West Point, like all federal service academies and SMCs, requires a fitness test in their admissions process. Applicants undergo a Candidate Fitness Assessment administered by a PE teacher or someone officially connected with the military. According to West Point's admissions page, potential cadets' physical abilities are tested in six areas: a basketball throw from a kneeling position; cadence pull-ups or flexed-arm hang (for woman); forty-yard shuttle run; modified sit-ups; push-ups; and one-mile run. Though West Point does not advertise desired times and number of reps, Logan believes he was denied entry into West Point because his basketball throw was four feet short. UNG offered Logan the best financial package, so, in Logan's words, "the money decided on Army."

He entered UNG on an Army ROTC scholarship, an academic scholarship, and contracted with the Army to commission as a second lieutenant following graduation, just like the Army cadets who labor and learn along the banks of the Hudson River.

Before classes started for the fall semester of Logan's freshmen year, he arrived on campus one week early for Freshman Recruit Orientation Group (FROG) week. During six physically challenging days, Logan and his fellow cadets experienced a rapid transition from a civilian to military life.

His first year as a cadet, a time he began planning for in middle school by starting a checklist and getting unfat, was about to begin with FROG week.

FROG WEEK

On a relatively mild day in August, Logan and scores of incoming cadets stepped foot on the mountainous Dahlonega campus of the University of North Georgia. For the next six days, Logan would be run through the storied process of transitioning from a civilian to a cadet. On day 0, new cadets undergo what the Army calls "in-processing." Cadets ensure their paperwork is in order; they receive a haircut at Woody's Barbershop, a

Figure 3.2. First-year cadets move through in-processing during FROG week. Image by UNG's University Relations. Used with permission.

tiny store barber shop on the Dahlonega public square. They receive their uniform, room, and company assignment (see fig. 3.2). They line up in formation with their company for the first time, eat dinner, and hear brief talks by the president of the university, the commandant, and the professor of military science. The physical tests begin the next day. Cadets are timed in a two-mile run, sit-ups, and push-ups. Cadres (i.e., groups of junior and senior cadets) provide a series of military-oriented classes before cadets head to bed and prep for the next day, when cadets are introduced to military traditions, such as lowering and folding the flag, and traditions of UNG. Cadets also begin learning drill and ceremony. The last three days are the most strenuous. Cadets work through the grenade-assault course and receive survival-skill training from an elite specialty unit: the Mountain Order of Colombo. The next day, cadets travel to Camp Frank D. Merrill, home to the 5th Ranger Training Battalion and the Mountain Phase of the Army Ranger School. They repel from a tower and rock face and head home to prepare for a three-mile uphill run on the final day of FROG week. The Corps holds graduation for those who complete the six days of training. Academic classes begin the next day. The campus transitions into a dizzying array of coordinated movements. Civilian students and family unloading cars and moving into dorms. Cadets carrying armloads of gear to the military leadership center. The rush of activity that brings a sleepy summer college campus to full tilt, ready for another semester. The August heat breaks when the sun hides behind the Appalachian Mountains. The movements slow as cadets and civilians settle in for the night. Then the darkness of campus and the calm. Reveille to come in seven hours. Cadets and civilians alike are off to the first day of classes.

A Memoir

I include portions of an unpublished memoir cadet Robert "Trent" Morrell provided me. Trent allowed me permission to include his firsthand experience. I include excerpts from Trent's memoir below and honor his original language, spelling, style, usage, and mechanics. I place his writing in italics to visually separate his exact words from mine. He emailed me close to three thousand words. I include ellipses to signify when I have elided portions of his writing:

Ch3 FROG Week

My time at UNG began with FROG week, and during FROG week cadets are indoctrinated in the rules and regulations of the Corps of Cadets. FROG stands for Freshman Recruit Orientation Group. On the first day, I Day, [I as in "initiation"] everyone shows up in a plain white tee-shirt and khaki shorts. Fear is in the face of every future cadet, and each stands close by their family while they look on with dread and anticipation to begin the day. I remember standing next to my father, anxiously awaiting orders to move out of the parking lot. Next to me was another young boy named Dan. Dan was from the Miami area, and we chatted about Florida to kill time before orders were barked at us to move our cars to the offloading area. This started the first day of a new life for me.

I was assigned Alpha Company. This was a pleasant surprise as it meant not only would I live on the top floor of Liberty Hall, but I would also be in the first company in the chow line. Alpha company has a tradition of upholding the standard and makes sure every new FROG is taught just how to do this.

The first day is packed with events. The first thing we were given was our knowledge sheet. It was a single double-sided piece of paper in a Ziplock bag, and both sides were packed full of information in tiny font. The knowledge sheet had to be read while you stood at parade rest and had to be held straight in front of your face. At no time could it be looked down on. The knowledge sheet contained important information like the rank structure of the Army, every cadet from company commander and above, and a very detailed description of every cannon on campus.

We got handed what seemed like uniform after uniform and, most important, got a room assignment. My father waited around to attend the parents' briefings, and later in the evening I said my goodbyes to him. This marked a turning point in FROG week. The cadre (a sergeant in charge of us) who had previously been nice and helped me move in switched to an intense, disciplined machine. We were "smoked" for making mistakes on how we addressed them or for not standing at attention or parade rest. Smoking is the nice term used for an excessive amount of physical activity, whether this was push-ups, flutter kicks, or front-back-goes, it didn't matter.

That night we also conducted the reporting-in ceremony. This entailed all of us standing in a stairwell as one by one we were sent running down the hallway to memorize a white board and report to the first sergeant of the company. The board read:

> "FROG Robert Trenton Morell
> Reporting in to Alpha company 1st Battalion Boars Head Brigade
> On this the lord's day 12 August 2014
> With the highest honor to be selected as a cadet for Alpha company
> Commanded by Cadet Captain Sara S. and Cadet First Sargent James J.
> I submit myself to further review in the hopes of becoming a member of Alpha company."

We were given not more than twenty to thirty seconds to memorize this entire board. The task itself was set up for failure, and failure meant being sent back to the stairwell. By the end of the night no one had completed the report-in, and we were all smoked for it.

When we were released to our rooms, I finally met my roommate, Haddon R. from Michigan. An instant friendship was formed. The last thing we did before bed was surrender all our electronics and watches for the rest of the week.

...

The third morning came even earlier, and we all rushed to shave and get dressed in a clean PT uniform. We were all ordered to go out to the drill field where we took a PT test. The test is three events: two minutes of push-ups, two minutes of sit-ups, and a two mile run. I had spent the summer training for this, however, there is a huge difference between the flat land of Florida and the mountains of northern Georgia. This became very apparent to me on the 2-mile run as I struggled with the hills. I didn't pass the run, but I learned where I needed to improve. The rest of the day we attended classes about title IX and school traditions and the history of the Corps.

The school has multiple land marks of historic importance. The first we looked at was Purcell plaza named after COL. Ben Purcell an alumnus and Vietnam vet who was held in the infamous Hanoi Hilton. Purcell plaza sits between the three-cadet barracks, and every cadet walks by it multiple times a day. The second is the memorial wall next to the flag pole. This wall has every name of North Georgia alumni that have been killed in the line of duty while serving the country in combat. A smaller wall sits adjacent with the name of every student who has died while at school. The third is down by the military leadership center and has the names of all the alumni who died while serving not in combat. The forth is the memorial arch way on campus. This was a gift from the class of 1952 to the class of 1951, who went to Korea where the majority of them perished in the war.

I remember learning about each of these and going to sleep that night thinking about each name on that wall. I wondered what kind of people they were, and what it must have been like for them to be a cadet here at UNG. I asked myself if I was following in their path honorably or just tarnishing the footsteps they left.

...

That evening began the longest smoking yet, we were all formed up in the main dayroom and told that a can of dip had been found in someone's room. Immediately we began doing push-up after push-up while being yelled at. About half way *through they said if someone claimed it we would all be set free. Derrick immediately stepped forward and claimed it. Little did we know that he actually had left a can of dip out. However, this was not his can. He was willing to take the big one for the team and claim it as his own. They told him to shut up and began smoking us more. Finally, when the majority of were no longer able to do any more physical activity they took us for a run. The run was a full sprint and became a challenge to keep up the pace. The run ended coming around the back side of the barracks.*

As we rounded the back side, we saw the entirety of our cadre holding flags, tiki torches, and a large log. Each item they held was explained to us and handed down to one of the FROGS. The shield was given to the one who looked out for others and was given to Gabriella B. The stick nasty which is a large walking stick adorn with antlers and different Army patches this was given to my roommate Nick R. The log was given to the two who put the team on their backs and helped carry others, and it was given to me and Charlie A. Finally, the guide on was given to the cadet who best embodied what it meant to be a member of Alfa company. This was given to my roommate.

That night we all went to our rooms and prepared for graduation the next day. We made our beds again for a final time and talked about how excited we were to see our families again. We also talked about the last obstacle—the Crown Mountain Run. We both agreed that night to make sure the other would finish the run.

The Crown Mountain Run began the next morning after chow. Some of us more daring individuals took the Alfa challenge, which is drinking a glass of milk and a red Poweraide. This was so that anyone who threw up would puke Alfa red. We all formed up on the drill field carrying the icons we had been given the night before.

The run is done at an "airborne shuffle," or a light jog, faster than a walk but way slower than a run. Charlie and I had to carry the log for the whole run. This wasn't a problem until the last 100 yards uphill. The incline increases heavily and carrying the log didn't make it any easier. Despite this we made it to the top and back down together. As we circled the drill field for the last part of the run we raised the log above our heads, so everyone knew we were Alpha company.

The run ends with the new cadets being formally welcomed to the Corps and all of our parents pinning the Corps of Cadets recruit pin. My whole family came and were so proud to see me graduate. We took pictures of me in uniform, and I proudly showed them my perfectly made bed. It was one of the proudest moments of my life. My family took me to lunch and Walmart. It was a bitter sweet goodbye as they left that afternoon, and I not only began my life as a cadet but also as a Freshman in college.

Trent is now a commissioned officer stationed in Europe. He continues to work on his memoir.

Intersection 1
GETTING THERE
Stepping into Longitudinal Research

A commitment to self-reflexivity in the research process . . . requires considering the researchers' stance and relationships to others in the study, the conceptual and epistemological foundations of their work, and recognition of what is at stake and for whom.
—Amy Stornaiuolo, Gerald Campano, and Ebony Elizabeth Thomas

The very basis of Writing Studies as a knowledge-producing discipline rests upon the idea of students as knowledge-makers, not merely knowledge consumers.
—Rita Malenczyk, Neal Lerner, and Elizabeth H. Boquet

I find solace in definitions. Maybe that is why I began this project. One day, thinking about the four cadets in my honors English 1101 classroom, I wondered about what writing they might be expected to do for their MILS classes, what type of writing they might be expected to do when they commissioned into the Army. From that inquiry point, I browsed Army doctrinal publication pdfs, and from that browsing, I found a definition of writing: "Effective Army writing is understood by the reader in a single rapid reading and is clear, concise, and well-organized" (US Army 2020c). I link this definition of Army writing with three definitions of the field of rhetoric and composition/writing studies (RC/WS), for just as I find solace in researching an organization with a unifying vision of writing, I find solace in laboring in a field of inquiry that seeks (even if it ultimately fails to find) a communal understandings of what we do.

Susan Miller (2002) locates RC/WS in our public work by writing that "it is knowledge of how texts 'got this way' that justifiably defines our recognized expertise. . . . We find identity there, in taking up what, who, to what ends, and, especially how people have written and write. . . . That is the greatest benefit of writing studies to all: the provision of well-formed, vividly engaging information about how and to what far-reaching ends people write and have written" (51–52). Bazerman (2011) emphasizes our work with writers in RC/WS when he submits that "as a field its motive comes from helping people use written language more effectively, for both production and reception" (15). Both Miller and Bazerman place our labor with and for *people*. For many of us, those people with whom we labor are students. I often return to Bizzell's (2014) statement that the heart of RC/WS is "want[ing] to know who our students are" (442). If RC/WS car had a bumper sticker, for me, Bizzell's quote would be it. Through this committed desire, many within RC/WS view students as coproducers of the knowledge driving our field. Rita Malenczyk, Neal Lerner, and Elizabeth H. Boquet (2018) argue that "the very basis of Writing Studies as a knowledge-producing discipline rests upon the idea of students as knowledge-makers, not merely knowledge consumers" (70). They write that the knowledge students produce "continues to guide how we structure our classrooms and programs" (81). This argument shows how students actively contribute to the building of RC/WS. Broadly, then, RC/WS illustrates a historical commitment to writers and writing and building knowledge *with* writers. The historical commitment exhibited in these definitions of what RC/WS does influences how we conduct research. I engage with these influences in the Intersections of this book, which invite readers to think about how we study writers and how we move forward with what we learn from studying writers.

I organize Intersections 1, 2, and 3 into three subsections: getting there, staying there, leaving there. I intentionally placed these Intersections throughout the book—not just in the introduction or just at the ending. The *there* unites these three subsections. The *there* is not just spatial; the *there* is not just temporal. The *there* is the coming together of researchers and participants to wrestle with the phenomenon of writing during a research moment. Sometimes *there* is spatial and temporal—such as my two-day observation of an Army major writing inside a brigade headquarters in Alaska (Rifenburg 2019). But so often our research projects aren't bound by time and place. We follow writers and writing and research questions and curiosities across times and spaces. Such is the case with this four-year study of Logan, which began in one space (UNG) during one specific time period (four consecutive years). But our conversations have extended. He keeps writing for his job as an Army officer. I keep arriving at questions as I draft this book, and we talk through email. When does the study end? Does it?

I cover these three sections linearly—entering, staying, leaving—even though such an order is misleading. Regardless of how and when and where we bound studies of writers, researchers enter a research moment with participants, stay with their participants in this research moment, and leave this research moment to circulate findings locally, globally, and, hopefully, publicly. I start with getting there: how we arrive at and gain access to a research moment. The challenges that come with getting there.

Qualitative research design helps us elucidate "what, who, to what ends, and, especially how people have written and write" (Miller 2002, 51–52). But qualitative research design comes fraught with issues of coercion and misrepresentation. To safeguard against illegal and/or unethical conduct, we have disciplinary ethics statements like the "CCCC Guidelines for the Ethical Conduct of Research in Composition Studies" (Conference on College Composition and Communication 2015a), the American Educational Research Association's Code of Ethics (2011), and the Modern Language Association Statement of Professional Ethics (2004). We also receive guidance from the Department of Health and Human Services, Indigenous governing bodies like the Navajo Human Research Review Board (Navajo Division 2018), and local human-research-subject boards. But polished research statements, detailed federal oversight, and the lockstep process of conducting human-subject research offered by handbooks and research guides cast a misleading shadow of ease onto the challenging process of qualitative research. Gnarled questions of ethics arise when we conduct research with people. And we wonder, Can we? Should we? Or, as the poet Elizabeth Bishop (1979) muses, "Is it right to be watching strangers in a play / in this strangest of theatres?" (93).

The last literature course I took was during my first semester as an MA student at Auburn. I started graduate school with a love of eighteenth-century British literature and a hope to talk Walpole, Smollet, Fielding, and Burney with undergraduates, maybe publish on faith and virtue and the rambunctious frivolity pulsing through this dynamic century when monarchs kept losing their heads, the Western novel rushed onto the literary scene, and erudite poets took jabs at each other in scathing verse. But I never made it far enough in my studies to take a graduate class on this period; I struggled mightily in my first literature class, a modern American poetry class, at the same time as I found great joy and questions in my work with first-year student writers. I switched my focus, my career path. Though modern American poetry and I never connected, I kept many of the books, and when I found myself stuck as I was writing this book, I flipped through Bishop's work. Sometimes the flow of poetry helps disentangle my knotted thoughts. Bishop's verses did just that, even with my sophomoric marginal notes from this class distracting me at times. I found myself reading her poem "Questions of Travel," which she wrote while living in Brazil. In the poem, she wonders in writing about her positionality, about sitting and watching and living in a foreign country. She muses, "Is it right to be watching strangers in a play / in this strangest of theatres?" (93). Bishop drops the question almost one quarter of the way into the sixty-seven-line poem, almost as if this question serves as the thesis for the argument she unfolds in flowing verse.

I don't think she fully answers it. That doesn't matter though. The question matters, and it's a question I bring to my thinking. Bishop brings ethics to our discussion through choosing the word *right*, which, in turn, implies a *wrong*. This word also begs the follow-up question *for whom?*—a question implying audience and purpose. Bishop brings people and place into the discussion by speaking of *strangers* and *theatres*. Bishop brings multiple people and places into the discussion by dropping making both nouns plural. Bishop's words were with me in Poland as I walked the streets of Wrocław and sat in the classrooms of the military university. Bishop's words came back to me as I reflected on my observational logs from a MILS class.

For my study of Logan, for my work with Polish cadets and Polish writing instructors, I found myself wondering if it was *right* for me to be present: to sit in Logan's class, roam the barracks with him, walk around Army bases, and provide advice on writing assignments to Polish instructors. Who am I to ask? To watch? To even wonder or declare? At the surface level, I mitigated these nagging concerns by shaving my beard, tidying my hair, and tucking in my shirt when I entered a military space. Even then, with my smooth face and generic white-collar dress, who am I to think I can enter this space? Who am I to watch these strangers in a play? Bishop's question, broadly put, also drives discussions of ethical human-subject research in literacy studies. In their editor's introduction to *Research in the Teaching of English*, Amy Stornaiuolo, Gerald Campano, and Ebony Elizabeth Thomas (2019) push readers to assume a position of self-reflexivity in literacy research. They write that

> such a commitment to self-reflexivity in the research process involves more than being transparent about the mechanics of a research study (e.g., reporting the number and kinds of interviewed conducted or including details about the schools and individuals who participated); rather, it requires considering the researchers' stance and relationships to others in the study, the conceptual and epistemological foundations of their work, and recognition of *what is at stake and for whom.* (194)

I am particularly taken by the last phrase. In italics, Stornaiuolo, Campano, and Thomas write "*what is at stake and for whom.*" This recognition is all the more important when working with writers for extended periods and tracing how they develop as writers. Who is served by my data collection, my findings, and how I circulate my findings? While I do not have definitive answers—although I completed this study—I have questions. In the spirit of coproduction of knowledge and in the spirit of our field's commitment to studying what people write and have written, in this first Intersection, I offer access and data collection concerns inherent in longitudinal studies of writers. I offer the challenges with getting there.

GETTING THERE

When I began formulating this long-term research project, I knew I was preparing to enter a ROTC space that was a part of my campus. I also knew I was entering a cocurricular space. On my campus, ROTC is headed by the professor of military science (PMS), an active-duty officer holding the rank of colonel. The MILS classes that constitute the ROTC curriculum fold under the College of Arts & Letters; however, when I chatted with the PMS, he was clear he did not report to the dean of this college as I do. Instead, the PMS is a federal employee whose salary, unlike mine, is paid by the Army, not the state of Georgia. Cadets take classes within the MILS curriculum mainly taught by active-duty soldiers. Cadets also take civilian classes and receive one of five bachelor's degrees granted by UNG.[1] Part of their day falls under the purview of civilian instructors; part of their day falls under the purview of ROTC, inside barracks and on drills fields hidden away from the eyes of civilians.

As a researcher, I had ready access to cadets. As faculty in the College of Arts & Letters, I emailed my dean, who could email the PMS and provide approval and support of my research project. The dean and PMS served as gatekeepers (Jones, Torres, and Arminio 2014) to my research project.[2] Entering a research moment hinges on locating and working with gatekeepers (Rifenburg 2020). According to Irving Seidman (2013), gatekeepers "control access to people [and] can range from the absolutely legitimate (to be respected) to the self-declared (to be avoided)" (47). Gatekeepers allow initial access. Once researchers gain access, the gatekeepers fade out of the study. My dean served in this capacity by emailing the PMS on my behalf. The PMS served in this capacity by approving the dean's request to allow me access to

MILS classes and forwarding my email down the chain of command to whoever was scheduled to teach the class I opted to observe. Before I could gain access to spaces Logan circulated through, I needed nods of approval from gatekeepers.

From my experience, I draw implications regarding self-reflexivity and positionality that could guide current and future longitudinal studies of writers. Recall the argument forwarded by Stornaiuolo, Campano, and Thomas (2019): self-reflexivity "requires considering the researchers' stance and relationships to others in the study, the conceptual and epistemological foundations of their work, and recognition of *what is at stake and for whom*" (194). They make this point after stating self-reflexivity is more than writing a clear and clean methods and methodological section, what they term the "mechanics of research." Instead, throughout the research process, we must attend to "what is at stake and for whom." In this spirit and in the spirit of not just offering my method and methodology—which appears early in the book—I offer what is at stake and for whom and place it alongside my desire for self-reflexivity, for acknowledging how my positionality allows me into spaces and helps me see and causes me not to see phenomena surrounding Logan's writing development.

In *White Logic, White Methods: Racism and Methodology*, sociologists Tukufu Zuberi and Eduardo Bonilla-Silva (2008) draw from their experiences researching, teaching, and publishing within their predominately white discipline of sociology (Zuberi and Bonilla-Silva 2008). Zuberi reflects on his book, *Thicker Than Blood: How Racial Statistics Lie* (2001), in which he sketches a powerful argument that connects the rise of statistical research to the "racially bent eugenic mind" of Francis Galton in the mid- to late nineteenth century (8). Zuberi argues statistics came about through a desire to quantitatively represent the superiority of whites and denigrate the position of people of color. In his personal narrative in the introduction to *White Logic, White Methods*, Zuberi reports on reactions he received from fellow sociologists when he gave talks about his book, when he bluntly called out the inherent racism in the discipline. Zuberi then writes, "Data do not tell us a story. We use data to craft a story that comports with our understanding of the world" (9).

I'm drawn to the broad argument that research methods and research methodologies can be racist, that researchers, even with the best intentions, may promulgate racism through employing these methods, and that a field itself may enable racism or simply be racist. I'm drawn to these broad arguments because I'm seeing them play out in my field. Asao Inoue (2015, 2019) has called out the racism and white supremacy and white ideology he sees permeating the teaching practices, research methods and methodologies, and even service initiatives animating the field. During a full-day workshop, I watched Inoue, in a small group of English-department faculty at a predominately white institution, work through audience Q&A with people who pause and take umbrage at the idea that a field and the people in it, a field ostensibly dedicated to inclusivity and the democratization of education, may be racist. Inoue is right. Specific writing practices and teaching practices promulgate white supremacy.

I'm also drawn to these broad arguments, and specifically Zuberi's words, because I'm white and because I'm working within a field that is fractured and grappling with issues of representation and inclusivity and diversity. I'm drawn to Zuberi's thinking because I'm trying to do the work of foregrounding—not forgetting—my positionality and understand the best I can the ways all my identity markers influence how I collect data, analyze data, represent data, circulate data. Pulling from Zuberi's language, I try to foreground how the data I collect and think and write about are a "story that comports with [my] understanding of the world" as a tenured, white, middle-class, heterosexual, Christian, cisgender dad, husband, brother, teacher, researcher. As a person. My research is coming from me, the flesh and bones and spirit that comprise Michael Rifenburg.

These varied identity markers granted me relatively easy access to the Corps of Cadets at UNG and the broader US and Polish Armies. My tenure status and publication record granted me gravitas when I approached my dean, the PMS, even a four-star general, about this book project and helped me receive internal funding to support my travel to Poland. Being able-bodied, I could participate in Army physical training in Alaska. During our four-mile run, I gained insight into how the Army officers I was running with understand the Army; running along the Chena River at 0600 hours allowed conversation to flow a littler freer than it might if we were to sit in an office at 0900 hours with a tape recorder whirling in the background. I ran because my body allowed it. Because I could afford $95 running shoes to train. Because I had family support in place to watch my three kids when I went on hour-long runs in the cool of the evening. Because I lived in an area where being outside is safe. I identified as heterosexual and cisgender, two identity markers helpful for entering the Army, with its mercurial and sometimes damaging policy on transgender troops and homosexuality. I was also white—like 71 percent of Army officers (US Army 2020b). I was also married—like 66 percent of male Army officers (US Army 2020b). I use past tense in this paragraph to describe my positionality and identity markers in Alaska. But nothing has changed. I still hold these points of privilege.

As I think about my positionality and reflect on my position in relation to my research participants, I believe how we gain access to a research moment leads to what we find in our research moment and what we then circulate from our research moment. How we gain access leads to what we find and what we publish. For one, to gain approval from my dean and the PMS, I needed to articulate a research plan in line with what they might support, what the institutional mission and accreditation reports might support. I needed to write up my research plan in an email that rhetorically worked for buttressing the work of my gatekeepers. I needed to define my course of action. As I would if writing an application for human-subject research, I had to be clear with what I was researching, why, how long it would take, and what I was asking permission to do (take pictures? interview? observe? photocopy material?), and I needed to be clear that my presence would not place an undue burden on the Corps (as has been the case with previous external and internal researchers). How I gained access based on navigating these rhetorical constraints led to what I found.

Additionally, gatekeepers, as important as they are, can lead to issues of coercion. Once I received permission from my dean, from the PMS, and from the Army major who taught Logan's MILS class, how free was Logan to say no to additional interviews with me, to opt out of the project, to stop sending along his class syllabi and extracurricular writing? Though the dean and PMS faded away after granting me access, their presence loomed over my study and, in ways I may never see, shaped the data I collected and how I collected it; they may have placed an undue burden on Logan to continue in the study. I don't know. But when writing researchers take the necessary steps to form relationships with gatekeepers to enter a space, the possibility of coercion looms large.

As I continue growing as a writing researcher, and as current and future writing researchers engage with additional much-needed longitudinal studies of writers, I/we would do well to think through how our positionality gains us access to spaces and times we want to enter. Additionally, we must work with editors and publishers and reviewers to get these narratives into our publications because knowing how a researcher gained access carries rhetorical weight similar to knowing how many participants a researcher interviewed. Let's report on how we gained access just as we report on research mechanics.

To do this important work, we can follow the lead of Indigenous education research scholars like Julie Kaomea (2001) and Eve Tuck and K. Wayne Yang (2012, 2014). We can look to the collaborative work of Heather J. Shotton, Amanda R. Tachine, Christine A. Nelson, Robin Zape-tah-hol-ah Minthorn, and Stephanie J. Waterman (2017) to read how relationships and positionality help us live our research; we can look to the research-methods books by Leigh Patel (2015) and Linda Tuhiwai Smith (2012) to understand how to build relationships and answerability into our education research and reflect on the baggage that comes with the word *research* itself.

Entering these research moments is just a step. Once we are there, we must stay there. We must still hold an understanding of our positionality as we collect data and analyze data. In Intersection 2, I argue that to do so, we must adopt what Amy Stornaiuolo, Anna Smith, and Nathan Phillips (2016) call an "inquiry stance."[3] This stance allows us to story our research in meaningful ways. More on that, several chapters from now, in Intersection 2.

NOTES

1. By comparison, all West Point graduates receive a bachelor of science.
2. Thank you to Todd Ruecker and Vanessa Svihla (2020), whose work on the messiness of educational research and subsequent editorial guidance helped me generate some of my early thinking on the importance of gatekeepers (see Rifenburg 2020).
3. Thank you to Kevin Roozen for introducing me to this article over coffee in Louisville, Kentucky.

SECTION 2

Year One, Cadet Private

I wanted to get contracted. I wanted to start getting paid. I wanted to do well in the Corps and make sure people know I am not normal. I want to get somewhere. And really stay on top of things and not fail college and be a statistic.
—Logan Blackwell reflecting on his first year of college

4

FINDING 1
What Writing Is Not

Data collected from year 1 led me to argue my first finding in response to the research question driving this book: *How does Logan Blackwell leverage the resources offered through the ROTC curriculum to learn the doctrinally defined Army writing standard and key Army genres with which he will engage upon commissioning as an officer in the US Army?* I found that Logan dipped a toe into the doctrinally defined Army writing standards and genres with which he would soon engage as an Army officer by learning what they are *not*.

Logan saw Army writing standards as one of many skills to master as a cadet—just like rappelling, folding his bed sheets, marching in formation, reading map coordinates. With his checklist mentality, writing was just one of many different skills (some academic, some athletic, some Army) he needed to display either mastery of or proficiency in to advance as a cadet and receive high marks for the National Order of Merit list. The Army uses this list to place commissioned officers into branches. High marks on the OML lead to a greater chance a cadet receives their desired branch. To matriculate at the premier US military college, the United States Military Academy at West Point, Logan needed to display athletic prowess in given categories, categories with quantifiable outputs like X number of pushups in Y amount of time, a two-mile run in Z time. To prepare for these athletic achievements, he created a checklist in seventh grade. This checklist guided his athletic preparation for almost five years. Though he did not get into West Point (like 90 percent of applicants), such a checklist mentality brought him to UNG and was reinforced through additional quantifiable rankings and metrics, like the OML. When the time came for Logan to take a seat in an honors English 1101 class, he approached writing as a skill he needed to display proficiency in so he could amass high marks on the academic aspect of the OML. Writing, in a sense, was no different than a timed two-mile run; an event for him to display proficiency in and mastery of for a higher ranking. For Logan, writing became a codified and specific skill so that he saw just one form of writing. Writing was not a cognitive phenomenon for which a person drew from various literacy practices honed across a lifetime of literate engagement. It was a narrowly defined skill with specific classroom-based utility. Like a syllabus, writing was an artifact unique to schooling. Logan brought this understanding of writing to bear on how he began to conceptualize Army writing. He learned about the Army writing standard from self-sponsored explorations of Army OPORDs on his iPhone, his brief immersion into Army writing from his Military Science (MILS) class taken during his first year at UNG, and his work with the JROTC in high school. He struggled when it came time for him to see how writing adapts according to ever-fluid rhetorical situations, such as the writing within an American literature course. For him, writing was not responsive to ever-changing needs and audiences and moments. There was one form of writing, and when this form of writing collided with audience expectations or did not connect with the needs of the moment, the audience should adapt, the needs should adapt, not the writing. Just as the students in Linda Bergmann and Janet Zepernick's (2007) study struggle to connect general education writing instruction with discipline-specific writing instruction, Logan struggled to see the need for English writing; he saw it as distinct from the writing that served his checklist mentality, his commitment to the Corps. Instead, Logan demonstrated what Reiff and Bawarshi (2011) call "not talk"; the students in Reiff and Bawarshi's study "describe[d] their written work (and writing process) by explaining what genres it is not" (325). I saw an example of this "not talk" when Logan and I spoke about his experience in American literature:

> [The instructor] really enjoys, really, really in-depth analysis of, I guess, symbolic meaning. It's not enough to say the room was blue. You gotta say the room was blue because. No, he didn't write the room was blue because he wanted it to be blue but he because of some imagery of him being sad or some really abstract meaning. And that's always been a struggle for me because I have always been a numbers guy and take it for what it is.

He continued his response: "With [the American-literature instructor] and all those implicit meanings, I really don't think it's applicable to the military."

In these interview excerpts, and the excerpts forthcoming in the next chapter, Logan demonstrates burgeoning understanding of what Army writing is not. Logan's response is similar to an argument articulated by Neal Lerner and Mya Poe (2014) following their three-year study of science undergraduate students. Using coded data interviews and textual analysis of student writing, Lerner and Poe mapped the shifting identities of their research participants onto the research participants' developing scientific knowledge. Lerner and Poe make arguments about the need to listen to students' stories of learning and becoming, an argument all the more prescient as US higher education moves deeper into quantifying student learning through a dizzying array of spreadsheets, metrics, and datasets. But Lerner and Poe also make the argument that we must listen more closely to moments in which our students experience "failed initiation into discourse communities" (58), as these moments may forecast turning points in students' developing identities as writers. To be fair, Logan did not enter UNG with hopes of receiving a degree in English with a concentration in literature. He took American Literature I to check a box off on his plan of study. But regardless of his exigence for taking the course, he, as the data indicate, failed initiation into the American literature discourse community. This failure, not marked by the letter grade of D, F, W, or I but marked by frustration and dismissal, shaped Logan's understanding of the writing practices and broader literate activities of his chosen focus: the Army.

At the time, I wondered whether his frustration and dismissal might hinder him as he processed into his next year. As scholars and professional organizations have argued, successful college writers develop helpful dispositions or habits of mind that help them navigate the ever-changing nature of college-level writing. Dana Lynn Driscoll and Jennifer Wells (2012) draw from psychological theories of motivation to argue that individual dispositions need greater focus in writing-transfer research. Early in their work, the coauthors directly call upon the eight habits of mind in the *Framework for Success in Postsecondary Writing* (Council of Writing Program Administrators et al. 2012) and see their work on dispositions as an extension of these habits: curiosity, openness, flexibility, creativity, engagement, metacognition, persistence, and responsibility. Sure, even as the *Framework* is the "'go-to' source for WPAs who wish to do advocacy work within governmental, legislative, and institutional contexts" (Perryman-Clark and Craig 2019, 104), RC/WS scholars have scrutinized the document. Katie Kalish, Holly Hassel, Cassandra Phillips, Jennifer Heinert, and Joanne Baird Giordano (2019) find that imposed austerity through neoliberal policy causes instructors and students alike to "practice resilience, often in ways that contradict disciplinary standards like the habits of mind" (261); therefore, they signal a note of caution and ask readers to "think more carefully about how and why we invoke the *Framework* as guidance for our programs and classrooms" (269). Inoue (2019) points out that all the authors of the *Framework* are white, pushing his audience to wonder about implicit racial bias in the *Framework*'s construction.[1] However, I see great value in Reiff and Bawarshi's (2011) conceptualization of "not talk," and I see this conceptualization as linked to Driscoll and Well's (2012) argument that we must understand better students' individual dispositions when undertaking the cognitive challenge of authoring. I believe an initial step in Logan's writing development is developing a *not* disposition.

I offer this finding with a positive spin. I believe the rigid view of writing Logan carried during his first year was how he leveraged the resources offered through the ROTC curriculum to learn the Army writing standards and common Army genres. By learning what they were not, he better learned what they were. In other words, he found the prose he rolled out for a MILS assignment and the prose he rolled out for the Anne Bradstreet explications in American Literature I were the same prose, but he graded the prose differently: praise for the MILS prose, slight censure for the Bradstreet prose. Here, he learned the limitations, or, better put, the rhetorical flexibility of what he perceived and understood to be attributes of Army writing. Logan, at this point, has yet to adjust his prose accordingly based on this feedback. Instead, he reacts by shaking his head in frustration at literature classes. But the seeds are planted. He is not learning how to write for the Army but learning when not to write for the Army. He is learning by struggling. Maybe the most effective thing for Logan's literacy development broadly and growth in writing according to the Army standard is a wide range of writing assignments, with a wide range of instruction and course materials and exigencies, just what he and thousands upon thousands of other first-year students receive during their first year of college: disciplinary growth dependent on course work across the disciplinary spectrum.

In the next chapter, I back up these findings with evidence from Logan's first year as a cadet at the University of North Georgia.

NOTE

1. The *Framework* has met with detractors and admirers alike. To see how writing instructors and programs have taken up the *Framework*, see The Framework for Success in Postsecondary Writing: *Scholarship and Applications* (Behm, Rankins-Robertson, and Roen 2017). For additional critiques of the *Framework*, see the special issue of *College English* that offers an overview of how the *Framework* came together (O'Neill et al. 2012) and critical responses by Bruce McComiskey (2012), Kristine Hansen (2012), Judith Summerfield and Philip M. Anderson (2012), Carol Severino (2012), and Patrick Sullivan (2012). Anne Ruggles Gere, Anne Curzan, J. W. Hammond, Sarah Hughes, Ruth Li, Andrew Moos, Kendon Smith, Kathryn Van Zanen, Keely L. Wheeler, and Crystal J. Zanders (2021) drew from critical language awareness and communal justicing to recommend specific revisions to the *Framework*'s section titled "developing knowledge of conventions."

5
BANNED BOOKS, ANNE BRADSTREET, AND FIRST-YEAR COMPOSITION

Large-scale quantitative data point to the importance of a student's first year of undergraduate education. We can look at Excel spreadsheets provided by local offices of institutional effectiveness, identify which students received a D, F, W, or I, and predict, with statistical precision, how many of these students will graduate within four years.

We can chart which students are most likely to return to campus for their second semester of their first year based on their performance in general education classes like FYC. At UNG, for example, during the 2018–2019 academic year, 60.8 percent of students who received a D, F, W, or I in English 1101 during fall 2018 returned to campus in spring 2019.

These data linking student's academic performance in first-year courses with their retention, one-semester persistence, and degree-to-completion pacing have pushed US higher education to cull decades-old research on undergraduate education like the Boyer report (1998), to redesign their general education course offerings in hopes of (to spin this positively) providing more equitable and accessible and meaningful pathways of learning for students or (to spin this more cynically) ensure efficiency to appease federal-government oversight and local legislatures who decide on annual budgets. Either way, US higher education and many external not-for-profit and for-profit organizations offer a wealth of services designed to help schools redesign their first-year courses and first-year student experience. The American Association of Colleges and Universities (AAC&U), for example, offers an annual conference on general education and, in tandem with George D. Kuh (2008), articulates eleven-high impact practices, one of which is first-year seminars and experiences, that support student learning and engagement. The Lumina Foundation and the National Institute for Learning Outcomes Assessment (NILOA) authored the Degrees Qualifications Profile. This statement articulates competencies the Lumina Foundation and NILOA espouse for college graduates, which, in turn, shapes how our colleges and universities construct their general education curricula

https://doi.org/10.7330/9781646422784.c005

(Adelman et al. 2014). The John N. Gardner Institute of Excellence in Undergraduate Education, which I have worked closely with and describe more in the conclusion, provides a service it titles Gateways to Completion. The University System of Georgia, under which falls UNG, partnered with the Gardner Institute for three years and asked that all system schools redesign gateway (i.e., first-year) courses with a specific eye to raising DFWI rates for underrepresented student groups. The first year of a student's undergraduate experience has become a space to which varied stakeholders in US higher education have laid claim: politicians wanting to see students enter their first year with more credits that can lead to faster graduation and less student debt; advocates of equity and inclusion demanding these courses to do more than shuttle students more speedily through the academic assembly line; potential future employers hoping students gain marketable skills that lead to social and economic mobility. All in one academic year. And to better learn about the students who are coming to higher education for their first year of college, we have the Beginning College Survey of Student Engagement (BCSSE) that provides robust quantitative data of students in the United States and Canada.

Indeed, the first year of an undergraduate's education has yielded an entire discipline of study. Kennesaw State University, the third largest public university in Georgia, offers a master of science in first-year studies, a fully online graduate program and, according the Kennesaw State (2020) website, the only degree program "dedicated to the discipline of first-year studies." Indeed, first-year studies has all the markers of a nascent and growing discipline: annual conferences, steadily published journals, graduate degrees, and research centers affiliated with US universities. For example, the University of South Carolina houses the National Resource Center (NRC) for the First-Year Experience and Students in Transition. John Gardner, who cofounded the Gardner Institute, once worked with the NRC. The NRC advertises an annual national conference, a consistently published journal (*Journal of the First-Year Experience and Students in Transition*) and other publications, an active listserv, and resources for leveraging ideas forwarded by the conference and publications into the classroom—all characteristics of a fully fledged discipline.

As a writing teacher, researcher, and administrator, I am most interested in data (qualitative or quantitative) about the writing habits and processes and knowledge our students bring into their first-year composition classroom. These data paint various pictures of incoming students as writers. In *Academically Adrift*, Arum and Roksa (2011) chart longitudinal data of 2,322 students enrolled in US higher education. By looking at student transcripts, survey responses, and data from the Collegiate Learning Assessment, a standardized test given to students in their first semester and then in their second year, Arum and Roksa report 45 percent of the students in the study displayed "no statistically significant gains in critical thinking, complex reasoning, and writing skills" (36).[1] Additional reports and surveys focused specifically on writing development paint a similarly bleak picture. The National Commission on Writing in America's Schools and Colleges (Nation Writing Project 2003) reported that writing instruction in the United States is "increasingly shortchanged throughout the school and college years" (3). The National Assessment of Educational Progress (National Center for Education Statistics 2012), in its most recent report on middle- and high-school student writing, maps the writing skills of eighth graders and twelfth graders across three proficiency levels: basic, proficient, and advanced. They found that 3 percent of twelfth graders, students who may be preparing to enter US higher education, performed at the advanced level. Disappointing results are not a surprise to educational researchers familiar with periodic US literacy crises—two being the tumult over poor writing skills of incoming wealthy male Harvard students following the US Civil War, which led to Harvard's implementing one of the first required college writing courses, and the well-known feature article "Johnny Can't Write," published in *Newsweek* in 1975.

Yet self-reporting data paint a much different picture of student writing, particularly incoming first-year college student writing. Acting as a counter to *Academically Adrift*, which privileged the often-critiqued Collegiate Learning Assessment data, Eodice, Geller, and Lerner's *The Meaningful Writing Project* operates from two premises: (1) students display sophisticated rhetorical awareness of writing—in school and out of school writing; and (2) students are engaging in writing projects they would describe as *meaningful*. To bolster their premises, Eodice, Geller, and Lerner (2016) designed a multi-institutional mixed-methods study that included survey data from over seven hundred seniors at three different schools, twenty-seven one-on-one interviews with seniors, and sixty one-on-one interviews with faculty. Of the 707 students who completed the survey, only twenty-eight reported that nothing they authored during their college careers was meaningful. Instead, most students pointed to meaningful writing that was unique and future oriented and that provided them with space to claim agency.

Our students are writing and have stories to tell and knowledge to share about writing—if we design instruments that capture these stories and this knowledge. In this book, I share stories written by Trent, who, as a graduating senior at UNG, sat down on his own to pen his memories of cadet life and generously allowed me to offer his writing in chapter 3. And then there is Logan, who, like Trent, makes time to write for himself, not in response to the exigence of a deadline, a professor, and assignment sheet, a grade—just in response to the innate need to make meaning with words despite the frenzied life of a cadet, a college student. So, he pens short stories, writes blogs, drafts constitutional bylaws for new student clubs.

I cannot help but wonder at the discrepancies among national assessment findings, self-reported data on student writing, and the stories of student writers Eodice, Geller, and Lerner share and that I share. RC/WS has long touted the correlation among student writing and student engagement and meaningful learning experiences, and organizations dedicated to improving undergraduate education have more recently turned attention to writing classes. Kuh (2008), in partnership with the AAC&U, describes high-impact educational practices. Two of these eleven practices fall squarely into the first-year composition class: writing-intensive classes and first-year seminars and experiences.

No matter the data-collection instrument or the organization collecting the data, we know of the critical importance of writing classes, the critical importance of the first year of undergraduate education. We also know that to learn more about the learners in our classrooms, we need to hear directly from them.

I listened to Logan talk and write his way through his first semester as an undergraduate cadet at UNG. I listened to him learn what writing is and what writing is *not* for the various spaces in which he would move during his first year: what writing looks like within an FYC classroom, a literature classroom, a military-science classroom. He would leave this year with a profound understanding of what Army writing is not, the overarching finding that frames this look at Logan's first year.

He matriculated as a management major and tested out of required Spanish 1101 and 1102 through the College Level Exam Program, a group of standardized tests offered by the College Board. Logan started in the honors program and was placed in honors English 1101: English Composition I. This course is the first step in the compulsory two-step composition sequence at UNG. The two courses are collectively labeled first-year composition (FYC). He registered for sixteen hours, a lot for a first-semester student adapting to college life and to cadet life:

- BIOL 1260: Environmental Science (3 hours)
- BIOL 1260L: Environmental Science Lab (1 credit hour)

- CSCI 1250: Informational Technologies (3 credit hours)
- ENGL 1101H: (Honors) English Composition I (3 credit hours)
- MILS 1000: Leadership and Personal Development (2 credit hours)
- MILS 1005: Physical Readiness Leadership and Exercise (1 credit hour)
- PSYC 1101: Introduction to Psychology (3 credit hours)

ENGLISH 1101H: (HONORS) ENGLISH COMPOSITION I

Courses like English 1101 grab the attention of media outlets, politicians, and colleagues around higher education who wish to promulgate a literacy-crisis narrative; this is the course that grabs the attention of state representatives who periodically turn a critical eye to higher education and ask for more data-driven accountability for liberal arts general education courses like English 1101; this is the course that leads higher education organizations like the AAC&U to craft rubrics for assessing student learning in this course; this is the course often tied to ever-important persistence and retention rates; this is course that reflects seismic shifts in US higher education.

This is the course in which I met Logan.

I taught this class. That declarative sentence asks for a moment of unpacking. I'm aware of the potential drawbacks that come with researching one's students. According to Title 45 of the Code of Federal Regulations published under the Department of Health and Human Services (HHS) (2016), researchers should "minimize the possibility of coercion" (§46.116). It is hard to minimize coercion when engaging with power dynamics that come with a teacher researching their own student. Additionally, the Conference on College Composition and Communication's "CCCC Guidelines for the Ethical Conduct of Research in Composition Studies" (2015a), which I helped revise, provides a section on recruiting research participants. This section carries a note of caution:

> To avoid situations in which students feel that their decision to participate (or not) in a study might affect their instructor's treatment of them, we recruit participants from other classes or other sources. If the topic of the research or other special circumstances require that the study involve our own students, then we use measures to avoid coercion or perceived coercion, such as confirming students' voluntary participation after grades are submitted or asking colleagues to conduct the actual data collection.

Aware of this caution and HHS guidelines, I attempted to minimize coercion two ways. For one, I sent my IRB-approved recruitment email to all cadets in the class inviting them to participate in this study. The email stressed that their decision to participate or not would not impact their grade. Second, before they received this email, we had already read several publications in class that offered research similar to what I was proposing: long-term studies of writers' development. Therefore, the cadets had a clearer understanding of what was being asked of them and what a final publication might look like. I do want to emphasize that these methods to avoid coercion might not have been enough. Qualitative researchers cannot erase coercion; we seek to minimize it, as I did. And we minimize coercion not only during recruitment but also through all steps of the research process. I return to these broader issues of coercion and research throughout my Intersections.

All the cadets in the class took me up on my research offer, and I coauthored and published a study that offered qualitative data about the cadets in this class paired with quantitative data on over three hundred cadets at UNG (Rifenburg and Forester 2018). Logan was the only cadet who stayed with me for four years. I wanted to stay with Logan because he was already contracted to commission into the Army following graduation and because he immersed himself in variety of writing projects—curricular and extracurricular.

For the first paper, taken from our class textbook *Writing about Writing* (*WAW*) (Wardle and Downs 2014), second edition, students collaborated on a group literacy narrative in which they collectively detailed their earlier experiences with literacy, charted points of similarities and disconnects among their narratives, and offered a broader argument about the role literacy plays in their lives. Logan and his two coauthors wrote a strong paper that wove their separate literacy histories into a coherent argument. Instead of focusing on his experience in seventh grade—a year he told me was instrumental in his literacy development thus far—he focused on third grade and on his current literacy practices. In the extended passage below, I quote from the entirety of Logan's section of the paper. This section illustrates Logan's literacy history and current literacy practices. But more important, this section is Logan's written reflection on his literacy, a rare form of data in studies for which researchers chart the literacy practices—historical and contemporary—of their participants. He wrote in the third person. I retain his text as he composed it:

> When asked about his literary experiences as a child, Logan most clearly recalls the point at which he developed his distaste for assigned reading and writing. He tells us that as a third grader, his teachers were always concerned with themes in reading and writing. He could never read a book just because he enjoyed it or write a piece to entertain his audience. There

always had to be some deeper meaning or cultural study in the books and a highly specific format to a writing with a very specific purpose. He says his writing felt "robotic." He wrote and analyzed solely for a grade. This pattern of creative barriers would continue throughout his schooling, and by the time he entered high school, Logan informed us that he rarely read for entertainment. But, contrary to expectations, he still maintained creativity in writing. We found he maintained his creativity out of necessity. As a commander in NJROTC [Navy Junior Reserve Officers Training Corps], Logan was frequently called upon to speak in front of large audiences and oral writing is a skill he believes was necessary to maintain a strong command presence in front of his cadets. He often wrote motivational speeches to present before the cadets, and each time a different element of leadership needed to be reflected in his language, thus requiring creativity. This skill was extremely important not only for addressing his cadets, but also for briefing his superiors. One can deduce that if it had not been for Logan's need to do creative writing outside of his academic coursework, he would most likely hold the same writing patterns as reading. So, what is it that gives Logan such a distaste for just the assigned tasks in literature? On the reading elements, Logan says he doesn't always mind the books, but the teacher "ruins" them by trying to pull out some arbitrary literary theme or deeper meaning and making him write about it. He must prove using textual evidence what something represents or why it was written. He strongly believes most of the time, authors of these "academic pieces of literature" originally wrote to entertain and just like him, they would never enjoy writing about vague symbols and underlying messages. With regards to assigned writing, one can tell he has passion, but only because of his previous successes in extracurricular writing. He tells us he hates assigned writing because he never feels his work is good enough. If there's no creative liberties to make the piece in his style, he doesn't think it's quality work. It's this very issue that is turning students off of writing and as seen in our next case, the problem gets even bigger as our research subject tells us why she turned her back on extracurricular writing completely.

In this excerpt, I see seeds that will sprout into more substantial concepts central to Logan's literacy development: a distaste for reading and analyzing literature; a drive toward extracurricular over curricular writing; and a conception of the importance of orality when writing.

In his narrative, Logan describes the importance of extracurricular writing and how the creative element of his nonschool writing informed the literacy practices he undertook in the Navy Junior ROTC program. He argues that he still writes for fun because he inserted creativity into his nonschool writing. He writes, "With regards to assigned writing, one can tell he has passion, but only because of his previous successes in extracurricular writing."

With the phrase "extracurricular writing," Logan pulled from a body of research that links school and nonschool writing in a person's literacy development. In class, we read some of this research found in chapter one of *WAW*. Many stakeholders in student writing development—instructors, parents, administrators, state legislatures, students themselves—perceive curricular writing as the indicator and facilitator of writing development. This perception can become so dominant that students and stakeholders alike see writing as only school based and serving classroom assessment purposes. A myopic perspective like this is damaging to how we understand writing development. Kevin Roozen, in his articles (2008, 2010) and his book with Joe Erickson (2017), undertakes work that locates nonschool writing as foundational for literacy development. Instead of offering an either/or proposition—school-based or nonschool writing—Roozen offers a synergistic understanding: writers drawing on both school and nonschool writing in their writing development. We read Roozen's work in Logan's class, and the teacher part of me hoped Logan was thinking about this reading when he wrote his portion of the paper. Weeks after coauthoring this first paper, Logan demonstrated his commitment to nonschool writing by winning an essay contest hosted by the campus literary magazine.

He also began connecting orality and writing in this excerpt from his coauthored literacy narrative. This theme became stronger throughout my time working with Logan and this piece was the first place I saw it emerge in Logan's writing. I talk later about the importance Logan places on orality in more detail when looking at the third and final paper he wrote for English 1101. Here, however, it is worth noting Logan sees "oral writing" as central to how he presents himself in front of his cadets and his superiors. With the phrase "oral writing," Logan is drawing on an understanding that writing and orality are, or at least can be, conflated. Such an understanding, I believe, comes from Logan's interest in the military, an interest that began in seventh grade. Throughout this book, my chief interest is in how Logan's immersion into the military and his anticipation of commissioning as second lieutenant following graduation shape his literacy development. Here is one clear example.

The second paper Logan and the class authored was an autoethnography assignment taken from chapter four of *WAW*. Using this assignment prompt and modeling a data-collection method based on Sondra Perl's (1979) study found in chapter four of *WAW*, students undertook a think-aloud protocol. This protocol asks research participants to externalize their thoughts through talking aloud while writing in response to a given prompt. I asked students to borrow a digital recorder from our university's library or to download a free audio-recording app on their phones and then record themselves as they talked aloud while completing a writing assignment for another class. The goal was to then have students transcribe their recordings, code their responses using as a model Perl's method of coding her interview data, and then craft a research paper with a clear argument driven by their transcript data. But I made a misstep as a teacher. Few of the students had any writing to complete for other classes and couldn't record themselves writing. Logan was one of these students. But instead of offering an account of my teaching misstep, this tale ends on a positive and unexpected note. Because of my lack of foresight, Logan wrote an award-winning essay.

Logan was one of the honors students who did not have other writing assignments he could record himself writing. I suggested he author something for two contests offered by our campus literary magazine, the *Chestatee Review*. The magazine hosts a variety of campus activities, such as open-mic night, a banned-book essay contest, and PoeDown, a joint celebration of Edgar Alan Poe and Halloween that includes flash-fiction (i.e., five hundred words or less) readings. At the time, the *Chestatee Review* was hosting both a banned-book contest (in honor of Banned Book Week sponsored by the American Library Association) and a flash-fiction contest (in celebration of Halloween). I suggested he author something for the banned-book contest or PoeDown. He did both. His flash fiction was inspired by true events that took place on Parris Island, home of the Marines' training facility, in 1956. He titled his piece "Mors Certa, Hors Incerta: The Heat of the Night." The Latin translates as "death is certain, hour unknown." The story unfolds in one paragraph and ends with a fun, macabre line: "Some say they can still see the ghosts of the recruits near that pike, but no one will ever know what really happened the night the dead rose to punish the living." He did not receive any accolades for his macabre tale, but he did for his essay on censorship.

Logan's essay for the banned-book contest won him $50 and the publication of his essay in the *Chestatee Review* (see fig. 5.1). Titled "In Preservation of Dignity: Censorship Before Catastrophe," Logan defends censorship: "It serves as an attempt to preserve Americans' confidence in their nation's leaders; it provides a means for preserving national security, and it allows the government to process all data before it gets manipulated by the mass media and the general public." His paper unfolded along these three points and settled into a uniform five-paragraph essay structure—though he did add a sixth paragraph. All the reasons Logan provided are grounded in the assumption that the government and people working in and for the government operate in the best interests of their constituents. As such, governments have the right to curtail individual expression for the sake of collective safety.

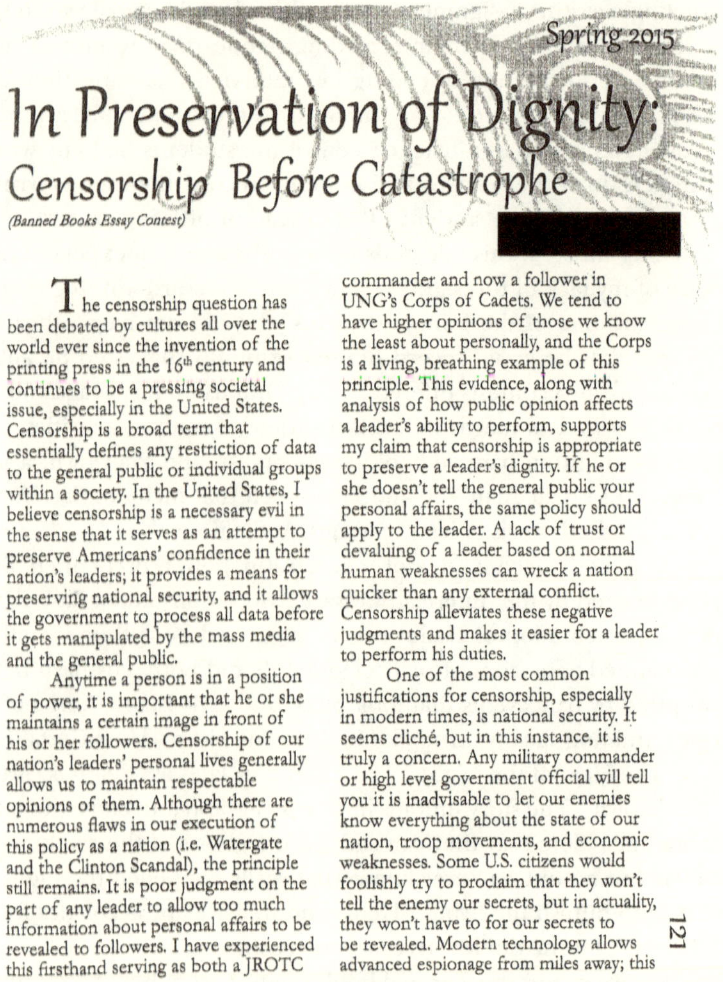

> # In Preservation of Dignity:
> ## Censorship Before Catastrophe
> (Banned Books Essay Contest)
>
> The censorship question has been debated by cultures all over the world ever since the invention of the printing press in the 16th century and continues to be a pressing societal issue, especially in the United States. Censorship is a broad term that essentially defines any restriction of data to the general public or individual groups within a society. In the United States, I believe censorship is a necessary evil in the sense that it serves as an attempt to preserve Americans' confidence in their nation's leaders; it provides a means for preserving national security, and it allows the government to process all data before it gets manipulated by the mass media and the general public.
>
> Anytime a person is in a position of power, it is important that he or she maintains a certain image in front of his or her followers. Censorship of our nation's leaders' personal lives generally allows us to maintain respectable opinions of them. Although there are numerous flaws in our execution of this policy as a nation (i.e. Watergate and the Clinton Scandal), the principle still remains. It is poor judgment on the part of any leader to allow too much information about personal affairs to be revealed to followers. I have experienced this firsthand serving as both a JROTC commander and now a follower in UNG's Corps of Cadets. We tend to have higher opinions of those we know the least about personally, and the Corps is a living, breathing example of this principle. This evidence, along with analysis of how public opinion affects a leader's ability to perform, supports my claim that censorship is appropriate to preserve a leader's dignity. If he or she doesn't tell the general public your personal affairs, the same policy should apply to the leader. A lack of trust or devaluing of a leader based on normal human weaknesses can wreck a nation quicker than any external conflict. Censorship alleviates these negative judgments and makes it easier for a leader to perform his duties.
>
> One of the most common justifications for censorship, especially in modern times, is national security. It seems cliché, but in this instance, it is truly a concern. Any military commander or high level government official will tell you it is inadvisable to let our enemies know everything about the state of our nation, troop movements, and economic weaknesses. Some U.S. citizens would foolishly try to proclaim that they won't tell the enemy our secrets, but in actuality, they won't have to for our secrets to be revealed. Modern technology allows advanced espionage from miles away; this

Figure 5.1. The first page of Logan's award-winning essay published in the Chestatee Review.

Reading again through Logan's essay, I am reminded of the United States' long struggle with balancing liberty and security, in which security, represented by a strengthening of the executive branch and military, often wins out and proves true Cicero's maxim *silent enim leges inter arma* (roughly translated as "when the cannons roar, the laws fall silent"). In 1798 President John Adams signed the controversial Alien and Sedition Acts. A young United States was struggling to gain its footing as a sovereign nation. In Europe, the French Revolution was underway. Vice President Thomas Jefferson, sympathetic to the French cause and seeing parallels to the US Revolution of just two decades earlier, implored Adams to intervene. A cash-strapped and fledgling United States could not afford to enter a costly European war. Adams was bound to stay out of the conflict. After a series of unfortunate diplomatic events between the US and France, and fearing the high number of French émigrés in the US might sow seeds of French sympathy and rally their cause in the US, Adams reluctantly signed four bills collectively known as the Alien and Sedition Acts. The Alien Act included a Naturalization Act, which adjusted how people applied for citizenship. The Sedition Act was, in the words of Adams's biography David McCullough (2001), of "greater consequence" (505). The act allowed the leveling of fines and imprisonment for what the act calls "false, scandalous, and malicious" writings against the government. These acts gained the approval of George Washington, from his retirement in Mount Vernon, and Noah Webster, the prolific writer and lover of language. Jefferson offered his disapproval but—in typical Jeffersonian fashion—fled from the tumultuous center of government in Philadelphia to his idyllic home in Virginia. Adams signed these bills in the context of "tumult and fear" (McCullough 2001, 504), which probably led to his losing his reelection bid to Jefferson in 1803. These bills made a radical statement about the executive Branch's ability to limit individual liberties at the cost of national security.

Logan's essay connected to arguments that animated a young United States. His argument also connected to arguments animating the United States in a post-9/11 world. When he wrote that censorship is a "necessary evil" because "it provides a means for preserving national security," Logan conjured up notions of the Alien and Sedition Acts and, more recently, the controversial 2001 USA PATRIOT Act signed by George W. Bush. I don't want to offer a reading on the proper balance of individual liberties and national security or a treatise on the limits of executive power; instead, I offer this foray to illustrate where Logan's thinking was at this moment in his college career: he believed in a strong federal government and falling in line with the governance of the executive branch. This example also shows Logan's strong interest in extracurricular writing. Though these two writing assignments—the flash fiction and the essay—were completed as an alternative class assignment, during his second year at UNG Logan found himself writing often out of class and for his own growth and enjoyment. He started writing for a popular college-student media platform and authored constitutional bylaws for a ballroom dance club he founded. I saw the seeds of this personal writing planted during his first semester.

Logan's future boss will be the commander in chief—the president of the United States. Once he takes the Oath of Commissioned Officers, his political and ideological beliefs (if the two can even be disentangled) will take a back seat to the dictates of whoever sits in the Oval Office. The Oath of Commissioned Officers reads as follows:

> I, _____, having been appointed an officer in the Army of the United States, as indicated above in the grade of do solemnly swear (or affirm) that I will support and defend the Constitution of the United States against all enemies, foreign and domestic, that I will bear true faith and allegiance to the same; that I take this obligation freely, without any mental reservations or purpose of evasion; and that I will well and faithfully discharge the duties of the office upon which I am about to enter; So help me God. (US Army, *Oath* 1999)

When Logan takes this oath, he will not pledge fealty to a person but to a document: the US Constitution. Even though he is still four years from raising his hand and repeating this oath, his strong adherence to the government and his belief that protecting the government is of utmost importance is represented in his award-winning essay. According to Logan, it's manipulation on the part of the mass media and the general public that needs to be addressed, not the manipulation of the government. Even Logan's title is tinged with patriotic jingoism: "Censorship Before Catastrophe." The Corps of Cadets at UNG is divided into companies, one company being Alpha Company. Their motto? Death Before Dishonor. The ultimatum embedded in Logan's title comes across as aggressive and even hyperbolic but matches with a military ethos, at least as Logan understands a military ethos at this point in his student and ROTC career.

The final assignment Logan completed came from the fifth chapter of *WAW*. This chapter asks students to explore how screen-based writing has shifted understandings of what writing is and how its accomplished. Students undertook readings from this chapter, which wrestles with how technology changes the composing process and changes what we consider writing. To this end, Logan wrote a definitional essay on writing, with particular attention to who has a stake in defining this gerund and why. In other words, Why would, say, college administrators be interested in defining writing? Why would college presidents or state legislatures? Why would the College Board, the owner and operator of the SAT?

Logan's six-page paper, titled "Composing Art without Defining It: The Writing Definition," gets off to a rough start by posing several clunky rhetorical questions in the opening paragraph and adopting a verbose and lofty tone. He does, however, offer his definition of writing in the opening paragraph: "Writing is in essence, a message. It doesn't matter how it's transmitted, so long as it's understood by the intended audience. It may have an underlying meaning, but only if the author intended it to be that way." I was not sure of the purpose behind "in essence," but I appreciated how Logan offered a rhetorical understanding of writing. Writing necessitates an audience; even more, writing needs an intended audience. Logan's definition is rhetor centric in that meaning exists with authorial intent, a supposition formalists and other camps of literary theory would certainly squabble with. But readers of this essay have something to hang onto. Logan gives himself a claim he can follow through his essay.

The odd tone started in the first paragraph continues when Logan introduces a "young undergraduate" on page 3 and then offers a nineteen-line free-verse poem written by "a senior in high school." This "young undergraduate" and "senior in high school" appear to be the same person—which, of course is Logan—but this distancing is balanced by Logan offering several sentences after the poem: "So, my counter argument to this essay . . ." Logan reveals himself to be this young scholar and high-school senior on page 6 and concludes with an awareness that he somewhat stumbled his way through this paper, maybe intentionally so: "Is there one perfect definition of writing? Probably not, but that's where the writer's lesson takes effect. If you're looking for a perfect definition you probably won't find it, but as far as finding an imperfect definition, you just read it."

At this point in my research on and with Logan, and my work on this book, I have read many pages of his writing stretching back to his middle school days. I have read his fiction, poetry, emails, reports, academic essays, and letters of recommendation. But even now when I sit down and reread this essay and begin to write about how this essay marks a certain stage in Logan's literacy development, I don't see Logan in this paper. It's puzzling, so much so that I went back to my grade book and looked up his grade. I gave him an A. I don't disagree with myself because this essay overcomes the clunky hesitant prose in the opening paragraph and does say something, does do something. This paper works, but it doesn't reflect Logan as I have come to know him.

Maybe part of my struggle to see Logan in this paper is because of when I assigned this paper and when Logan wrote this paper: late November, students bracing for the impact of final exams, Thanksgiving Day less than a week away, other assignments pressing in and jostling for attention. I would do Logan a disservice if I did not consider the larger context in which he wrote this paper. But maybe I am struggling to see Logan in this paper because Logan is beginning to withdraw himself from his writing. However, such an argument doesn't seem to resonate with this paper because Logan is in this paper. He uses first person and even quotes himself. But he constructs himself as a distant "young undergraduate," as a "senior in high school." It is as if he wants to insert additional voices into this paper, but instead of quoting from the class readings or findings additional outsides sources, he constructs himself as a source and as an object of inquiry.

As I understand Army writing, I can see why Logan might begin removing himself from his writing so it takes on a distant, impersonal tone. Logan knows that when he begins writing and delivering the common Army genre of operations orders (OPORDs), for example, this genre will not invite him to insert his personal voice and style into the finished text; this genre does not ask how *Logan* wants to run the operation. Certainly, OPORDs and other forms of military writing have a style that influences the composition, but this style seems derived from the genre and not the author. If Logan is distancing himself in anticipation of future genres that require such distancing, then Logan's writing-definition paper takes on additional interesting components. This paper may be a conceptual gateway for Logan into Army writing. For example, the paper takes on a masculine dimension by preferring masculine pronouns, and not just because Logan is writing about himself at times. In his first sentence, Logan writes of the "average human being," which turns into the "average human," and then, eventually, Logan writes of the "average man." I understand Logan as using these three descriptors to cover the same area. He uses "man" or "human" twelve times. To this masculine tone, Logan added a pedantic one largely by posing rhetorical questions: "It's a beautiful concept, isn't it?" "But why?" "So, what is writing?" Instead of offering these questions as statements that drive the main argument, Logan flips them into clunky questions that lend a didactic tone to the paper but also illustrate how Logan believes orality is central to good writing. On page 4, Logan writes in his distance voice: "He said the best pieces he ever wrote were ones he did outside of school or ones that he delivered orally." I appreciate Logan's awareness of the importance of extracurricular writing for his literacy development. This awareness also shined forth in the lengthy excerpt I took from his first paper.

Returning to orality, the questions Logan offered would work if he were to deliver his paper aloud—just as OPORDs are delivered aloud. Asking questions of the audience and offering verbal signposts help listeners negotiate a complex oral argument. In his paper, however, the questions strike me as ineffective and, unfortunately, a bit condescending and pedantic. At the same time, these questions are formed because

Logan believes orality—the ability to deliver text aloud—is critical to good writing. Moreover, orality is critical to Army writing.

In a separate research project, I partnered with a colleague, who, at the time, taught political science at West Point (Rifenburg and Forester 2018). We studied conceptions of writing first-year cadets bring to their FYC classes at UNG. Using a mixed-methods research design, we surveyed over seven hundred UNG cadets and conducted semistructured in-person interviews with four first-year UNG cadets. We found cadets stress orality, credibility, and clarity when writing for their general education writing classes. Orality is a key to Army writing. Three common Army genres (medivac reports, after-action reviews, and OPORDs) are designed to be read aloud. Logan was one of our four research participants we interviewed. In his interview, Logan stressed the need for orality in writing:

> People can get behind a person; it is hard to get behind a piece of writing . . . you can't really stress words and do the repetition and do all the nice little speech things that go in the movies just from a piece of paper. They can't really envision how you want it to be spoken. It just doesn't have the same feel, I think. It can move somebody, but it is better if someone is speaking it. (Rifenburg and Forester 2018, 57)

Logan wasn't in alone in his assessment. A first-year cadet offered the following take on orality and writing: "Whether I am explaining it to somebody or whether I stumble and have to go back, to have good writing it needs to be able to be read aloud because that really clears things up for you" (Rifenburg and Forester 2018, 58). This cadet understands orality a bit differently than Logan in that he connects it with reading his own writing alone and hearing sentence-level infelicities. For this cadet, reading his work aloud leads to stronger writing. This technique is commonly used in high-school and university writing centers where the tutors ask the writer to read sections of the paper aloud. Logan, on the other hand, doesn't stress reading his work aloud to improve his prose. For Logan, writing should be read aloud because that is how ideas are best communicated. The words on the page are not the final product for Logan. Instead, in a dialogic fashion, these words on the page lead to spoken-aloud text between the author and the audience. This orally transmitted process is the final product.

Logan's definitional paper appeared at an important moment in Logan's literacy development. This paper was the last one he completed during his first semester at UNG and his first semester as a member of the Corps. Three days a week, he woke between 0530 and 0630 hours for physical training. He made his way through his first semester of Military Science classes and labs. At the same time, he completed his first semester of civilian classes: environmental science, information technologies, psychology. I may not see Logan in this paper because it was written at a new point in Logan's literate life. As I write at the beginning of this chapter, the first year of college is a transformative period (psychologically, socially, scholastically) for students. This paper marked the midpoint of this transformative period for Logan. It was a result of Logan's rapid immersion into military life and college-level thinking and writing. It's telling that as Logan reached the midway point of his first year of college as a student and a cadet, the stylistic conventions that shined forth in his essay (distancing, masculine tone, rhetorical questions, oral elements) are those most related to Army writing.

*

The calendar pages turn, the spring semester begins, and the wintry mix of sleet, snow, and ice creeps over the Appalachian Mountains and onto campus. Less than four weeks into the semester, the twisting, narrow roads leading into campus are covered with a hazardous mixture of frozen mud and ice. The university cancels classes for three days. Students meet in the drill field—a large expanse of grass in the middle of campus used primarily for intramurals and Corps activities—for frenzied snowball fights. Snowmen with lopsided grins, droopy carrot noses, and mismatched mittens and scarves pop up as temporary campus denizens. A snow angel here. Another snow angel there. While professors fuss over revising syllabi, students live for coffee, snowball fights, and Netflix.

Then the snow and ice melt. Classes began again. Logan and the sixteen thousand other UNG students return to their schedules. The snowmen and snow angels gone.

Logan enrolled in fifteen hours:

- ECON 2015H: Honors Macro Economics (3 credit hours)
- ENGL 2131: American Literature I (3 credit hours)
- MATH 2400: Elementary Statistics (3 credit hours)
- MGMT 3661: Fundamentals of Management (3 credit hours)
- MILS 1100: Introduction to Tactical Leadership (2 credit hours)
- MILS 1105: Physical Readiness Leadership and Exercise Physiology (1 credit hour)

ENGLISH 2131: AMERICAN LITERATURE I

American Literature I gave Logan the most trouble because of his increased immersion in the Corps of Cadets and the genres and conventions found within the Corps. Two weeks into the semester, Logan sits in my office lamenting fifteen more weeks of American literature: "It's already killing me," he tells me without a hint of exaggeration one would expect with such hyperbolic language. "Not the grade but the course material. I've expressed before how much I don't like analyzing literature, and every week that's what I got to do. I write reading responses. And it is just very, very in depth."

English 2131: American Literature is one of ten different literature classes students can complete to satisfy portions of their general education requirements. In the course objectives found on the syllabus, the instructor offers broad questions with which the class will engage:

> What was it like to be an American before there was an America? When America was in its infancy? When the future of the American union was in doubt? Early American Literature gives us an opportunity to learn the answers to these questions through the words of Americans struggling for self-definition and fearing for the future of the American experiment. In this class, students will become acquainted with key works in our national history and will gain insight into the perspectives of early Americans, as well as continue to develop analytic and writing skills.

Under the section on the syllabus titled "Methods of Instruction," the instructor tells students they will be expected to

> read carefully; to interact with that reading by asking questions of it and noting its methods and assumptions; to recall details about readings during discussion; to raise issues from their interactive reading in discussion and respond to ones brought forward by their classmates; and to write clear, well-developed analyses of what they have read.

The reading responses, mentioned by Logan, were key to writing these "clear, well-developed analyses." After completing the assigned readings, students are directed to the reading-response questions posted on DesireaLearn, UNG's course-management software. Logan and his classmates were assigned twenty-three reading responses for the sixteen-week semester. The instructor asked students to complete "10 satisfactory responses to get a 100 for that part of the grade." In addition to the reading responses, students completed three papers.

Logan struggled with the reading responses early in the semester. I saw this struggle in his reading response to Anne Bradstreet's poem "The Author to Her Book." Logan wrote a one-page response. Out of the ten sentences in his brief response, I identified four that move beyond summary and into analysis, and one of these four sentences is the final sentence that acts as a summation of Logan's analysis. The first line of analysis on Logan's part appears midway through the response. After walking the reader through the narrative of the poem, Logan writes, "This demonstrates to the reader that not only is Bradstreet characterized as a poor mother, but a de-motivated, powerless one." The vague "this" leading the sentence refers to lines twelve and thirteen in Bradstreet's poem: "Yet being mine own . . . / blemishes amend, if so I could." Following his stilted analysis, Logan reverts to summary. He starts a sentence with "To summarize . . ." He then adds several more sentences that seem to run the reader in a circle.

Though he received high marks on the responses, the instructor kept pushing him to think more deeply about the text:

> [The instructor] really enjoys, really, really in-depth analysis of, I guess, symbolic meaning. It's not enough to say the room was blue. You gotta say the room was blue because. No, he didn't write the room was blue because he wanted it to be blue but because of some imagery of him being sad or some really abstract meaning. And that's always been a struggle for me because I have always been a numbers guy and take-it-for-what-it-is.

As I read through the response, I could understand Logan's frustration as he learned that what writing for literature classes entails ("really, really in-depth analysis of . . . symbolic meaning") stands in contrast to his early assumptions about Army writing. For Logan, writing for literature is *not* writing for the Army. He explained what Bradstreet is expressing, but he struggled mightily with explaining *how* Bradstreet expresses herself. The rhetorical work of poetry eluded him. He was not engaging with the vocabulary of prosody. He struggled with the generic conventions of literary analysis and with the necessary content knowledge. He had a good handle on his audience in that he knew what the audience expects and does not, but he struggled with genre and content knowledge. Therefore, Logan wrote sentences like this one in his response: "To summarize, 'The Author to Her Book' essentially serves as Bradstreet's apology to her child and a synopsis of her failures to readers." I am not sure of the purpose of the adverb "essentially," but I do see what Logan is working through in this sentence. As he worked from the "take-it-for-what-it-is position," he understood his task as explaining the poem's purpose to the reader. With his summation sentence, he accomplished the goal he gave himself. But Logan found this summation sentence occurred a bit too early in his paper and added two more circular sentences to his response.

Yet Logan displayed maturity as a young writer and started adopting some of the generic conventions of literary analysis. He was beginning to see disciplinary conventions at work. Logan was butting up against disciplinary conventions, not the whimsical taste of an individual instructor. Logan struggled to arrive at knowledge in the discipline of literature.

David R. Russell and Arturo Yañez (2003) draw on activity theory and North American genre theory to articulate why students may struggle in university-required general education courses. They paint a rich picture of a student named Beth, an aspiring journalist, who was struggling in an Irish History course. Beth struggled with understanding the relevance of the Irish History course to her career objectives—a common struggle for many students as they make their way through the general education curriculum. She was struggling with writing a book review, which she had written before, but found that a book review in a history course was a much different writing assignment. In her interview with Russell and Yañez, Beth said, "I felt really frustrated. Kind of mad" (346). Russell and Yañez are not advocating for the dismantling of general education. They, instead, use activity theory and discussions of genre pathways in and through disciplines to argue for greater attention on the part of instructors (and I add advisors and additional staff in student affairs) directed toward highlighting for students how the writing practices within one discipline lead into and inform the writing practices of another. They submit that "teachers might be able . . . to help students see genre pathways for expanding into a discipline or, using a discipline's critical tools, expanding into other systems of activity, civic, personal, or professional" (358). Here I appreciate Russell and Yañez thinking beyond the here and now of curricular writing to capture how disciplinary writing may lead to a fruitful literate life. Logan, soon, would connect the writing practices animating his curricular classes to the writing practices animating his self-sponsored writing.

Logan didn't express anger as Beth did, but he did admit the American Literature I class was a "struggle" and "killing [him]." The move to writing in different disciplines and in various rhetorical situations across college curricula is one of the biggest struggles for inexperienced writers. Logan, however, navigated this disciplinary boundary leap with his writing and began penning stronger pieces of literary analysis later in the semester.

In late April, just a week before final exams, Logan merged a reading response on Emily Dickinson with one on Edgar Allan Poe. Through his twelve hundred-word response, Logan engaged with elements and terminology of literary analysis, elements and terminology absent in his Bradstreet response written early in the semester. In his second sentence, he linked Dickinson and Poe: "Dickinson utilizes various poetic elements including repetition, simile, and metaphor while Poe opts to utilize vivid imagery and symbolism to highlight the overall characteristics of the mind in the face of death." The verb *utilizes* strikes me as clunky and a bit too much—why not just write "uses"—but I read this sentence as Logan's adopting the disciplinary conventions of literary analysis and moving his writing in a new direction.

His second paragraph moved away from the lengthy summary found in his Bradstreet response and into analysis. The closest Logan came to summary was in his opening sentence, where he wrote that both Dickinson's poems "340" and "355" and Poe's short story "The Tell-Tale Heart" are texts in which "the mind is the subject and death is the environment." Such a statement—though it provides narrative summation—is still a more sophisticated take on summary than we find with Logan's summary of Bradstreet. The Bradstreet summary read as an unfolding series of linear events: first this happened, then this, then this, and finally this. The material Logan authored late in the semester struck a balance between summary and analysis. One would agree that both the Dickinson and Poe texts are about the mind and death. But not all would agree that the mind is the subject and that death is the environment. That difference of opinion is a good thing in the disciplinary conventions of literary analysis. Analysis offers a reader's interpretation of a text grounded in a theory or approach and strengthened by a close reading of the text with textual evidence. In other words, even Logan's summation sentences are more sophisticated later in the semester.

In the second paragraph of the Dickinson and Poe response, Logan focused his attention on Dickinson:

> [Dickinson] writes, "Kept beating-beating—till I thought my mind was going numb" (Dickinson line 7–8). These lines demonstrate the first characteristic of a dying mind which is its tendency to pick up a sensory rhythm. Repetition of the word "beating" helps indicate this and gives readers a sensory experience in imagining what a "beating" mind feels like.

Logan drew the reader's attention to Dickinson's prosody. He linked this rhythm with sensorial imagery. More important, Logan linked these poetic elements with what he believed to be a central focus of the poem: a dying mind.

In the third paragraph of his response, Logan turned to Poe's unsettling short story. Logan drew attention to the obsession the narrator developed over an old man's eye. The narrator, a disturbed and untrustworthy narrator typically found in Poe, is driven mad by this eye and kills the old man in a violent fury. Logan looked at a specific quote from the text:

> Poe writes, "He had never wronged me. He had never given me insult. For his gold I had no desire. I think it was his eye!—yes, it was this!" (Poe 691). In this passage, the old man is a representation of death. Poe refers to death in itself (the old man) as something that has never done him any harm, but

the eye (one's own death) constantly irritates him. He describes the eye as being "the eye of a vulture—a pale blue eye, with a film over it." (Poe 691). The description of the eye, namely the word "film" indicates a kind of cloudiness linking to the obscurity of one's death, but still identifiable.

Logan provided his American-literature instructor with what he described as "really, really in-depth analysis of, I guess, symbolic meaning." He mused on what Poe *really* meant when he dropped the word "film" in the spooky narrative. He offered the old man as a representation of death. He modeled the rhetorical and conceptual moves of literary analysis at a level high enough to satisfy a general education requirement. Logan received an A in American Literature I. He completed the one literature class he needed.

He learned what Army writing is *not*.

As he did during his first semester, Logan received an A all his classes. Over the summer, he planned to complete an education abroad in Italy, where he planned to take classes related to his business management major. Yet, life has a whimsical way of changing one's plans suddenly. Logan didn't go to Italy. He was offered the opportunity to go to Army Airborne School under the direction of the First Battalion, 507th Parachute Infantry Regiment. Rome, Italy gave way to Columbus, Georgia; *al fresco* dining to indoor mess halls; red wine in full-bodied glasses to water in metal canisters. Logan went to Fort Benning, Georgia, a muggy, humid fort in southwest Georgia to jump from a C-130 or C-17 plane at 1,205 feet.[2] He jumped five times. He received the Parachutist Badge, a silver pin with wings encircling an open parachute.

NOTES

1. RC/WS scholars roundly critiqued *Academically Adrift*. *College Composition and Communication* published a series of reviews on the book. The titles of the reviews signify the authors' varied critiques such as Richard H. Haswell's (2012) "Methodologically Adrift" and Carolyn Calhoon-Dillahunt's (2012) "Important Focus, Limited Perspective." But *Academically Adrift* sent a shock wave through US higher education and led to further research and actionable items. In short, we learned (again) that we needed to do something.

2. Fort Benning is named for Henry L. Benning, a brigadier general who fought for the Confederacy during the Civil War. The 2021 National Defense Authorization Act established a bipartisan committee to rename nine Army installations. One of these is Fort Benning. A recent *Army Times* news article (Webb, February 2, 2022) outlines the steps of this bipartisan committee, termed the Naming Commission. The commission will deliver their recommendations to Congress by October 2022 with the Secretary of Defense tasked with implementing these renaming decisions by January 2024.

6
OPERATIONS ORDERS AS A BEGINNINGS OF ARMY WRITING

Dahlonega campus. The Brooks Pennington, Jr. Military Leadership Center is named after Pennington, who attended what was then North Georgia College in the 1940s, fought in World War II and the Korean War, and went on to a business and political career. A thick triangle of black and gray stone decorates the walkway to the MLC. The cadet honor code is chiseled into the stone: "A Cadet will not lie, cheat, steal, plagiarize, evade the truth, conspire to deceive, nor will he/she tolerate those who do." Visitors enter the MLC through the atrium, where commissioning ceremonies are held throughout the year. Hallways lead to classrooms and offices. Cadets and uniformed officers roam the halls, throwing lines of conversation back and forth while gripping sheets of paper. Bulletin boards are covered with memos, sign-in sheets for commuters, an updated Order of Merit List. A visual Army chain of command decorates another wall: pictures of suits and soldiers. A picture of Donald Trump, then-president of the United States, at the top. Underneath him, James Mattis, then-secretary of defense, and Mark Esper, then-secretary of the Army. The Colonel Raymond C. Hamilton Rifle Range adjoins the MLC. Inside the range, members of UNG's NCAA rifle team take aim at fifty yards away, tallying scores with Sius Hybridscore electronic targets and scoring system.

Military Science (MILS) 1000: Leadership and Personal Development is the first of four MILS classes Logan will take. The instructor, an Army officer, provides the following assignment early in the semester. The scenario in the assignment sheet is intense. I include the complete handout below with all stylistic conventions in the original:

> Cadets will use the elements of thought to consider and solve the included moral dilemma. The Cadet will need to identify and articulate their solution in a coherent paragraph. They will then explain their solution using each of the elements as a building block with a supporting paragraph each. While there is no size restriction, Cadets should try to keep the explanation to fewer than two pages.

You and a dozen other people, two of which are your children (a seven month old baby girl and 12 year old son) are hiding in a basement. You are all the targets for genocide in a country with an oppressive regime. Enemy soldiers are searching the ground level of your house for people like you and the people you're hiding with, and will be drawn to any noise. Fortunately, your basement door is hidden from view. However, the walls are not soundproof, and any moderately loud sound can sufficiently travel through to the soldiers.

Suddenly, your baby bursts out crying, but luckily the soldiers didn't hear the first outburst. However, if the baby keeps on crying it will alert the soldiers to your presence. Would you smother the baby to death to silence its cries or would you allow it to cry and alert the soldiers? A third choice is knocking the baby unconscious.

Conditions:
-If you smother the baby, the soldiers will NOT find you and the other 10 people.
-If you don't, the soldiers will definitely find your group, and take you to a concentration camp. There, all of you will be tortured to death, including the baby and your son.
-If you knock the baby unconscious, it has a 50% chance of dying. If it lives, it will live the rest of its life with permanent brain damage and will never gain the mental capacity to even recognize its name.
-You MUST either knock the baby out or kill it. No loopholes like covering its mouth only and leaving its nose uncovered.

Logan authored 350 words in response to this scenario. He began with stating his decision: "Given the conditions that have been placed upon me, I feel like the best option in this situation is to smother the child, making it unconscious." About midway through his paper, Logan offered his reasoning: "The main reason this solution is better is because it minimizes the psychological damage on the survivors. If the baby dies, it is accidental, and if it lives, all the better regardless of mental handicaps."

As I look again at Logan's written response and the assignment sheet, I find myself more drawn to the assignment sheet. This assignment sheet is one of the first he received in his MILS classes that had cadet-produced writing as the end goal. Additionally, the writing required in the assignment illustrates the form of writing the Army privileges. Just as a biology lab-report assignment or a history or sociology paper asks students to replicate the genres, conventions, exigencies of the given discipline, so, too, does an assignment in a MILS class. This assignment sheet offers a pressing and serious scenario, a life-or-death situation demanding quick, individual decision-making that carries ramifications for all parties involved. The exigency of this rhetorical situation, then, replicates combat exigencies cadets may encounter.

The assignment sheet does not ask for the cadet to use a certain number of scholarly outside sources or a certain format. Yet, it does ask that

"Cadets should try to keep the explanation to fewer than two pages." The assignment privileges short, declarative statements, not long ruminations weighing the sanctity of human life and the ethical quandary of killing in self-defense. Here is how writing for the Army is portrayed for Logan. Here is what writing for the Army is. If the Army does indeed privilege quick thinking and brief writing, one can understand how Logan struggled with lengthy expositions of Anne Bradstreet's puritanical prosody.

Logan received full credit for his ethical-dilemma paper. He received an A in MILS 1000.

*

It's early December. Students balance the joy of a forthcoming winter break with the stress of final exams and final grades. Cars in the residence-hall parking lots are stuffed with suitcases. Class schedules fixed for the first sixteen weeks of the semester change to accommodate two-hour final-exam periods. Each day of final exams, fewer and fewer students fill the campus as they pile into the cars, drive away from the angst of grades and into the freedom of a long break.

Logan is sitting in my office. He is dressed in civilian clothing, a privilege for cadets during finals. He is sitting up straight and still. Only his eyes move; they bounce around the room rarely meeting mine. His first semester as a college student and member of the Corps is complete. He is midway through the all-important first year, a year so important campuses across the country create programing for it, a journal is named after it, a survey is given nationally to students who are preparing for it.

"I was surprised how easy it was to do well in college," he tells me when I ask for his reaction to the first semester. He continues,

> I was expecting for me to be stressing out a bit more and freaking out about things and actually having to study. It really didn't challenge me as much as I thought it would. And I don't know if that was due to my major and the course work that's involved or I was just better prepared I high school than I thought I was. But that was really the main thing. The academic course workload was just interesting to me.

I ask about his Computer Science class. Logan entered the class with little background in computing, and he had previously expressed worry over the class:

> I was surprised how simple it would be to pass that class because I knew nothing about computers before coming in here. That was easy. It was almost like a high-school class. Psychology felt like a high-school class.

There is not a class that felt like what in my mind I thought college classes would be like except the English class and my Environmental [Science] were really the only two significant changes.

"Are you just telling me that because I am talking with you?" I ask with a wry smile.

In typical Logan fashion, he doesn't engage my attempt at banter. He responds with a forced "ha."

"No. Ha. You really do take a different approach to teaching composition writing than all my other instructors have."

I note to myself that he says "different approach," not "better" or "effective" or "helpful." *Different?* I think to myself.

I ask him about writing in MILS classes and what he anticipates having to write next semester. He tells me there is "very little writing" in MILS classes, but he does anticipate writing operations orders (OPORDs):

> Next semester, I believe I might start writing those OPORDs because next semester, according to what I have been told, is when we start the tactics and all the technical stuff that is supposed to be soldiering because part of soldiering and being an officer is writing down those plans and writing out how something is going to happen. I foresee practicing structuring op orders and something like that.

In my mind, I make a note about the oddity of Logan's answer. "Very little writing" in MILS classes, yet "part of soldiering and being an officer is writing." I don't push him at this point; I want to chart his understanding of writing, the fluidity of this understanding as he immerses himself more and more in the Army. I am trying to capture these understandings and offer them up as elements of literacy development. Instead of pushing back at his prognostication, I ask if he anticipates struggling with OPORDs. "I think I might have a few hiccups at first," Logan tells me, "because it is a different type of writing, but after I get the hang of it, I think it will be pretty simple. It will just be more tedious than anything because it is so, so detailed."

I then ask if he has heard an **OPORD** delivered.

LOGAN: I got to participate in the reading of one. A guy gave one and the operation itself was very, very simple. He was just telling his troops how they were going to run a route and what was going to happening for the next two weeks. And it took him close to twenty minutes to explain the route they were going to run.

MICHAEL: Was he reading that the whole time?

LOGAN: Yes. It is very, very detailed. You gotta talk about your main route, your alternate route. This, that, and the other. And you had to have a model of the school out on the floor and draw all sorts of pictures.

MICHAEL: A model?

LOGAN: Terrain model. Just got cardboard buildings. Colored in roads and stuff. Little toy soldiers and yarn.

MICHAEL: Did you help out? Were you involved?

LOGAN: I had to be a demonstrator for what uniform they had to wear. Telling them what they were going to wear isn't sufficient enough; they had to have the visual. It's just for redundancy so everyone knows.

Modeling is a critical element in Logan's literacy development. No surprise there. Writing researchers and learning theorists have long pointed to modeling or some version of it as instrumental to learning, from toddlers watching how an adult holds a spoon and then mimicking this action to novice engineers mimicking the writing style of professional engineers. But often this modeling, especially at more advanced levels, is not directly taught. Instead, amateurs need self-motivation to seek out a model. The Army's chain of command builds in scaffolding by which junior and senior cadets walk first-year cadets sequentially through knowledge and practice steps. This chain of command continues once the cadets commission. Though Logan does seek out examples of OPORDs on his own (he tells me he has Googled them before on his phone), the Corps will walk Logan through the steps of writing and delivering this new genre of writing.

What also stands out to me is the use of props to visualize the future embodiment of text. The goal of OPORDs is synchronized physical action, be that action delivering supplies or storming an enemy position. As OPORDs lead to this synchronized physical action, props and tangible representations of the OPORD are central to the teaching and learning of the OPORD. These props provide cognitive stepping stones for cadets who need to take a static written OPORD and prepare to embody and perform the orders in a garrison or field environment. I make a note to learn more about terrain models and to see how props like yarn and rocks may provide physical stepping stones into the world of Army literacy learning.

I ask Logan if he accomplished what he wanted to this semester. He admits he did: "I wanted to get contracted. I wanted to start getting paid. I wanted to do well in the Corps and make sure people know I am not normal. I want to get somewhere. And really stay on top of things and not fail college and be a statistic."

He tells me he signed up to go through the Noncommissioned Officer Academy run through the Corps of Cadets. He describes it as "going to classes and taking tests and things to make sure I am qualified for that promotion." The academy is designed to teach cadets about various leadership roles they have the opportunity to assume, like leading Drill and Ceremony, Flag Detail, and completing developmental counseling forms on subordinates. He is proud of the work he put into the semester but also reflects on the semester with a checklist mentality: I did this, I did this, I did this. He finished the semester with an A in his seven classes and appeared on the President's List. But he doesn't appear to draw satisfaction from his work, just a simple acknowledgment that he did what he set out to do. When he talks about his semester, I remember back to his narrative about middle school and devising a checklist to get into a military service academy.

Logan tells me his plans for next semester. He wants to rush a fraternity, not necessarily for the camaraderie, the philanthropic activities, and all the intangibles offered as reasons to rush. Logan wants to rush because he receives points for doing so on the Campus Order of Merit List (OML). These data points then feed into the national OML. According to USAAC Regulation 145-9 (2016), the Campus OML is based on three factors: "ROTC program participation, campus activities, and academic performance" (3). Cadets' data within these three factors are inputted as they near graduation, and the OML is displayed in the MLC. The specific weight assigned to each factor and what activities are included within each factor change every year. Hearsay and rumor among the ranks drive individual cadet decision-making, such as whether to accept or decline a sorority or fraternity bid, continue with or change a major, head on a study abroad trip during the summer, or work an internship. "Supposedly, a fraternity gives you more points than special units here on campus," he tells me. Special unites are voluntary, extracurricular units of the Corps, such as the Blue Ridge Rifles, Color Guard, and Aggressor Platoon. In addition to rushing, Logan was elected as vice president of the Swing Club and will be teaching swing-dance classes every Friday. He tells me of plans to start a Ballroom Dance Club.

We wrap up our chat. Logan stands and shakes my hand. Outside, the sharp winter wind whips. Bare trees stand like sentries in the raw air. I turn on my screen to finish grading.

SECTION 3

Year Two, Cadet Sergeant First Class

The North Georgia Ballroom Dance Club was formed to give students at the University of North Georgia a chance to discover the thrills of ballroom dancing. The primary goal of this constitution is to address the official name of our organization, provide clear and concise elaboration on the goals of the organization, and provide instruction on administration of the organization.

—Logan Blackwell's written Preamble to the
North Georgia Ballroom Dance Club's Constitution

7
FINDING 2
The Lamination of Literate Activity

Data collected from this academic year lead me to argue my second finding in response to the research question driving this book: *How does Logan Blackwell leverage the resources offered through the ROTC curriculum to learn the doctrinally defined Army writing standard and key Army genres with which he will engage upon commissioning as an officer in the US Army?* If the first year of Logan's work at UNG helped him understand what Army writing is *not*, year 2 helped Logan understand what Army writing *is*. He learned this not from undertaking Army writing assignments but through seeking out self-sponsored nonschool writing spaces and immersing himself in his self-sponsored words. He learned this from the laminations of his extracurricular and Army writing that helped him hone a writerly agency.

The Order of Merit List (OML) gives points for "extracurricular activities." Therefore, as a someone who attends to rankings and points, Logan turned to self-sponsored nonschool writing, which helped him develop a writerly agency he brought to bear on his curricular writing. This year, Logan wrote for *Odyssey*, a blog popular with millennials, found a ballroom-dance club, and authored a constitution and bylaws; he joined a fraternity and authored documents for his fraternity in his role as treasurer. He took two military-science classes and completed the academic writing that comes with those classes. By linking together various textual engagements, Logan illustrated what Prior and Jody Shipka (2003) refer to as the chronotopic laminations of literacy development. Laminations attends to "dispersed and fluid chains of places, times, people, and artifacts that come to be tied together in trajectories of literate action" (181). While I am bounding much of the focus of this chapter by Logan's second year, chronotopic laminations of literate activity help us see how Logan's work did not just occur during this one year of his undergraduate experience. Sure, he only contributed to *Odyssey* for this one year. But to write for *Odyssey*, he drew on a host of technologies and knowledges and artifacts fashioned across his literate life, and he continued to draw on his experience with *Odyssey* long after he formally ended this relationship. After his second year he dropped *Odyssey* over frustrations with how the editor adjusted his prose. During his fourth year, he began writing a novel but decided to not purse publication because he didn't want someone to meddle, again, in his prose. His literacy practices during his second year, then, stretched beyond just this one year and were entangled with his past and future engagements with writing. He told me he initially contributed to *Odyssey* because he heard through the cadet rumor mill that publishing raises one's place on the OML. Laminations of creative, extracurricular writing and Army writing were a part of his second year at the University of North Georgia. Both flowed together to constitute his literate becoming.

I see the writerly identity that he forged during this year as central to his becoming a writer. This disposition helped him focus on what he wanted to author, what he wanted to create, and he authored and created in response to exigencies he felt, saw, imagined. When his writerly agency was disrupted, as was the case with writing for *Odyssey*, he left that writing space. In his words, "They [*Odyssey* editors] were putting content out there on my behalf that wasn't mine. The basis was the same but that is not how I write. So, I didn't like that too much." Through developing a writerly agency, Logan grew more sophisticated in how he understood what writing is, how it is accomplished, and how it serves purposes in varied rhetorical situations. He brought this stronger and more nuanced understanding of writing to bear in his academic classes. We cannot isolate his literacy development to just school.

He developed this disposition by stepping out of the academically sanctioned classroom space, by seeking out extracurricular writing opportunities, engaging with these opportunities, and even turning away from these opportunities. The all-important OML, a literal checklist guiding the path of cadets who move through ROTC, pushed Logan out of the classroom and into new and multifaceted literacy experiences that shaped—in ways he recognized and did not recognize, in ways I recognize and did not recognize—his literacy development, that shaped his way of being, that shaped him. A laminated representation of literate becoming.

8
FLIPPED CLASSROOM AND INCREASED MORALE

One year into his college career, Logan finds himself with fifty-five credit hours: thirty-one hours from UNG and twenty-four hours coming from AP credit or College Level Exam Program testing. He is a semester ahead of his fellow second-year cadets. Logan "got a little bit of a bump," as he puts it, and is an S-3.[1] In this capacity, he works operations at the battalion level to coordinate PR (physical-readiness training) throughout the week and physical-readiness lab (simply termed *lab*) held on Mondays.

As he sits in my office in mid-September—the cool air coming down off the mountains and pushing away the humidity of another Georgia summer—he reflects on his time at Fort Benning, where he completed the Basic Airborne Course under the direction of the First Battalion, 507th Parachute Infantry Regiment. Logan isn't one for bombastic storytelling, replete with gesticulations and hyperbole. He is direct: "Jumping out of airplanes is pretty fun" is as close as Logan gets to an engaging sound bite about his three weeks in South Georgia. He describes the three weeks as "learning how to fall; learning how to fall some more; and operate your parachute." He didn't suffer the broken, sprained, or twisted ankles soldiers can often experience (resulting in leaving jump school and "recycling" or heading back to Benning next summer to give it another go). He made five jumps from 1,250 feet and received his pin. Sitting in my office, I notice he isn't wearing it. He tells me he can still go to Italy next summer, but he also wants to get SCUBA certified.

We were one month into the semester by the time Logan and I found a time to sit down and talk. He was registered for fifteen hours:

- ACCT 2101: Principles of Accounting I (3 credit hours)
- BUSA 2108: Business Communication (3 credit hours)
- ECON 2106: Principles of Microeconomics (Honors upgrade) (3 credit hours)
- MILS 2000: Innovative Team Leadership (2 credit hours)
- MILS 2005: Physical Readiness Leadership and Exercise (1 credit hour)
- MKTG 3700: Principles of Marketing (3 credit hours)

I start this chapter with a focus on Logan navigating the world of concise, professional communication. This writing style aligns with the Army writing standard. However, Logan didn't see this alignment. During the academic year, Logan would spend a great deal of energy struggling to adapt to his Business Communication instructor's pedagogy.

BUSINESS 2108: BUSINESS COMMUNICATION

The instructor implemented a flipped-classroom approach. This approach asks students to engage with lectures and instructional material at home and complete work in the classroom. In the classroom, the teacher rotates around, lending personal attention to students working on a task. This pedagogical approach is different. Logan had to adjust. In our interview, Logan thought through his experiences:

> He [the instructor] has decided to do a flipped-classroom approach. It is different for me—not getting a lecture in class because that is what I am used to. He basically gives us a quiz every week at home on D2L [the course management software used at UNG]. We take it. And we come into class and do, I want to say, it is almost set up like a writing lab. You pick something, a topic, and then he helps us modify it, and we will have an assignment due. For instance, we brought in a draft of a resumé of ours and he went in and showed us some stuff that was good and bad with resumés. And he is real big into group work, too. We did mock interviews in class. It's has been a nice change of pace. I can say that. But it's still weird not having a traditional lecture because that is how I learn. I learn in class not out of class because I am so busy. But it's been good.

Logan's response carried several starts and stops. I could hear him going back and forth: *it's different but I like it, kinda; it's different but* . . . I tried my best not to interrupt and let him talk through the class.

The instructor was explicit about the flipped-classroom approach in the syllabus. The instructor wrote, " **This semester, I will be using a 'Flipped Style' classroom, which involves students reading, listening, or watching course content outside of class and taking a quiz over the material prior to coming to class. Class time will largely be spent on activities, discussion, and exercises.*"

For Logan, the delivery of the material overshadowed the material itself, occluding his entrance in the knowledge and practice of business communication. The delivery of the material was so different Logan didn't see the commonalities between business communication and Army writing. I see pedagogical delivery of writing (i.e., how writing is taught) as a potent force in how Logan understands and approaches writing. Pedagogy acts as a gatekeeper wherein Logan first must adjust to *how* an individual instructor teaches writing before he is ready to engage with the writing itself. Logan went through a similar adjustment in American Literature I. Yet what is different between American Literature I and Business Communication is Logan struggling with the literature teacher's grading and what she was looking for in literary analysis. Logan struggled with how his Business Communication teacher even got to the writing assignment. Logan struggled before words were even typed across the screen.

The content of the Business Communication course was in line with what one would expect from a standard business communication curriculum. The instructor emphasized writing, presentation skills, and intangibles I wonder how an instructor assesses, such as "learn how to send positive & negative messages in the workplace." Throughout the semester, Logan completed six written assignments: a self-analysis paper written after taking the Myers-Briggs Personality Test; a chapter report; a recommendation report and presentation; a cover letter; a resumé; a rejection memo. He assembled a final portfolio to encapsulate his work for the semester.

I turn to his first written assignment: a two-page single-spaced paper based on his Myers-Briggs personality test. The instructor termed this task a *self-analysis assignment*. Logan completed it less than a month into the fall semester. In the final section of this paper, Logan wrote,

> Between the three assessments I took, I confirmed a few strengths I have and found some weaknesses I wasn't completely aware of. I know now that I am [a] high monitoring INTJ driver who is strong-willed, assertive, efficient, rational, dominating, apathetic, task-oriented, and a perfectionist by all counts. I struggle with developing and keeping relationships, sparing the feelings of others around me, and tolerating imperfection. I am pleased with my strengths, but now I know what I should work on to become a better communicator and a better leader and have developed goals to keep me on the path to a better version of myself.

Playing arm-chair psychologist for a moment, I appreciate Logan reflecting on his strengths and weaknesses. It stands out to me that he admits to struggling with "developing and keeping relationships" even as he is social chair of his fraternity and has recently started a student club. Yet these two activities may result from his task-oriented personality. He admitted to me on several occasions that he selects activities that will help him reach a predetermined goal and not because his gets joy out of them. Remember, this is the individual who made a checklist in seventh grade to physically prepare for matriculation at West Point.

Two weeks after Logan's self-analysis assignment, he turned in his resumé and mock cover letter directed toward a program-management-specialist position at Fjord-Atlanta, a global design and innovation consultancy. In his resumé, Logan highlighted his experience with the Corps, specifically his current role as a junior leader in the operation department, and his founding of the ballroom-dance club. He concluded with a long list of his "Activities & Awards." The list does not appear to be in any particular order. He started with "Dean's List"—a noteworthy achievement certainly—but Army Airborne School Graduate and landing in the top 5 percent of cadets in the Senior Leadership Course are buried in his long list.

Logan's Business Communication writing was succinct. He produced precise documents aimed at specific audiences in reaction to existing exigencies and seeking clear results. I see such writing traits in the work he provided me from his MILS classes.

MILITARY SCIENCE 2000: INNOVATIVE TEAM LEADERSHIP

Taught by what Logan describes as "active-duty guys," MILS 2000: Innovative Team Leadership focuses again on leadership. When Logan and I spoke in September, he had recently completed a report on Confederate Army General Nathan Bedford Forrest. During our interview, Logan expressed fatigue with the leadership emphasis in the class: "It's a double-tap. Bored of it. We [cadets] already have leadership skills and know what's going on." What excited Logan was putting these leadership skills to use. After our September conversation, Logan emailed me documents he had recently written. Many came from his Business Communication class. He also tossed in a MILS report he wrote in early November.

Titled "North Georgia Corps of Cadets: Increasing Morale within the Ranks," the four-page single-spaced report—complete with a cover page and reference page—was directed to Colonel (Ret.) James T. Palmer, who, at the time Logan wrote was the report, served as Commandant of the Corps at UNG. The report focused on low morale among cadets, a historically common problem for militaries.

Before articulating the problem, Logan opened with a brief two paragraphs. I quote the second paragraph in full:

> This report presents information accurately defining the problem in the North Georgia Corps of Cadets, three possible solutions to mitigate the problem, and a recommendation based on my analysis of the problem.

The next section outlined the problem as Logan came to understand it based on "personal interviews" and a brief reading of journals, including

Military Psychology. He did clarify in this section that "not all cadets are experiencing low morale." Based on this perceived problem, Logan overviewed three potential solutions: "Development of Privileges Policy Letter"; "Individual Privilege for Individual Achievements"; and "Adoption of Individual Physical Fitness Training Days." Logan closed with a "Conclusion and Recommendation" section, which I quote in full:

> In order to increase personal morale of cadets, we must start providing individual privileges for individual achievements. The work to attain these achievements can be stressful, so if we can alleviate some of that stress to raise morale, we should do so. Although exempting any cadet from curfew can be risky, it is a necessary step towards a more motivated Corps that rewards hard work.
>
> In conclusion, I recommend we utilize Alternative 2 and begin rewarding our Dean's List cadets with exemption from curfew and other individual privileges by the Commandant's Staff.

Like Logan's one-page cover letter written to Fjord-Atlanta, his MILS report was directed to a specific audience and sought a particular response. Logan drew on his own ethos to buttress his position. He told Fjord-Atlanta that he accomplished a lot of great things; he told the commandant he had "gathered opinions from first through fourth year cadets" and "studied articles." He moved into descriptive adjectives when describing the "problem." Fjord-Atlanta needed a new program-management specialist who was a "charismatic leader with initiative, passion, and communication skills." Logan met those needs. Low morale within the ranks leads to "increased apathy," "acute disregard for Corps policies and procedures," "heightened sense of distrust," and "overall pessimistic outlook"—and Logan had a solution.

Though Logan told me he didn't "see a lot of pen and paper writing going on" in his MILS classes, the report he authored gives a glimpse into writing for the Army and parallels writing for business and writing for the Army. As a business management major, Logan will write text governed by the genre of business communication. As I forecasted Logan's literate future, I was heartened that the two genres in which he would be most commonly writing—military and business communication—share commonalities.

At the same time, I found it odd that Logan had yet to mention these similarities to me. This may have been because of what I cover earlier in this chapter concerning the Business Communication class. In this class, Logan struggled to adapt to the flipped-classroom approach. The pedagogical approach was so startling for Logan I am not sure he ever spent time reflecting on the content to the degree he did in his American literature class. As I relistened to my recorded interviews with Logan, I was struck by how frequently he returned to his experience in American Literature I and to the style of literary analysis. He did talk from time to time about the readings from this course, but my impression was that the genre of literary analysis made the greater impact on him. Even in our September interview, American Literature I completed roughly four months ago, Logan returned to this class (the ellipses in the excerpt below signal pauses on the part of Logan, not my elisions):

> Because it wasn't . . . my writing wasn't questioned as far as style and mechanics or anything. She was more concerned with content and me being able to pull out stuff from the text. So long as I did that, the grammar and mechanics and how I write didn't really matter.

Logan struggled to find the vocabulary to talk about it; he tried to give voice to genre and distinctions in genres between disciplines. Often, when students struggle with writing for one class but excel in writing for a different class, a reason is genre. Genres reflect epistemological differences between disciplines. A literary analysis and chemistry lab report are different genres. The genres of a literary analysis and a chemistry lab report carry different writing styles, different understandings of what counts as evidence, and different expectations for how knowledge will be conveyed to readers. A student may talk of learning to write for a teacher, but such language reveals a student attempting to formulate an understanding of the differences in genre expectations among the many—sometimes divergent—classes students navigate. Logan said it wasn't "style and mechanics or anything." He was right. The struggle wasn't style and mechanics, but these issues are nested inside genre and how one writes the genre of literary analysis. This experience struggling with genre stayed with Logan. He was now on the lookout for writing differences across academic classes, but he could not see similarities yet.

*

In the spring semester, Logan registered for sixteen hours:
- ACCT 2102: Principles of Accounting II (3 credit hours)
- ASTR 1010: Astronomy of the Solar System (3 credit hours)
- ASTR 1010L: Solar System Lab (1 credit hour)
- BUSA 2810: Legal Environment of Business (3 credit hours)
- FINC 3440: Principles of Finance (3 credit hours)
- MILS 2100: Foundations of Tactical Leadership (2 credit hours)
- MILS 2105: Physical Readiness Leadership and Exercise (1 credit hour)

According to Logan, the Legal Environment of Business class was the only class in which an instructor would ask him to complete assessed writing assignments. The instructor wrote that one of the eleven topics to be covered during the semester was "Written Communication." To this end, the instructor asked students to complete article reviews: "The purpose of the article review is to heighten your awareness of the interrelationship of business and law . . . the Instructor is looking for an expression of your insightful reflection upon the article, not merely a summary of the article itself." The instructor did assign an essay portion of the test, but the article reviews were stand-alone writing assignments.

A few weeks into the semester, Logan wrote an article review on the *New York Times*'s coverage of a recent Supreme Court decision on class-action lawsuits. In a paragraph, Logan offered an overview of the case and majority decision and offered his support of Chief Justice John Roberts's dissenting opinion. Logan wrote, "This scenario is very similar to trying to sell a car for its book value. The purchaser (defendant) is willing to give the entire book value, whereas the salesman (plaintiff) refuses to accept because he *feels* like it's worth more." I haven't followed the case under consideration here and do not have a head for legal decisions on business matters. But I spend much of my commute to work listening to oral arguments I downloaded from the Supreme Court's website. As a rhetorician interested in oral arguments and as a teacher invested in helping students generate better questions, when I listen to oral arguments, I listen to how the justices ask questions. I'm surprised by how often they form their questions as hypotheticals. Associate Justice Stephen Breyer, especially, likes to pose questions this way. In *Hurst v Florida* (2015), Breyer asked the solicitor general of Florida to agree, hypothetically, that details of a case and the jury's decision-making processes are known through "mental telepathy." In a case about the federal government regulating marijuana growers, *Ashcroft v. Raich*, later decided as *Gonzalez v. Raich* (2005), Breyer wondered aloud about tomato children (yes, Breyer did use this descriptor!) invading Boston. My training in rhetoric makes me think these hypotheticals are a way for Breyer to test the limitations and malleability of an argument and, by extension, a decision the Court may order. Logan, too, drops a hypothetical. I taught Logan for a year and have closely followed his writing since. This was the first time I had seen him implement this rhetorical device. I didn't count this occurrence as a coincidence but instead saw Logan adopting a rhetorical device unique to the legal field and giving it a run in his writing. Logan was trying to think like one training in law school. He was doing what we ask students to do when we introduce them to a new field—to think like those in that field.

The instructor for Logan's astronomy class offered writing as a method for internalizing course content. The astronomy instructor provided students with a list of close to a hundred discussion questions. The questions followed the trajectory of the course starting with section 1 on "Fundamental Concepts" and extending to section 5 on "Worlds of the Outer Solar System & Space Debris." Each of the five sections contained roughly twenty open-ended instructions or questions, such as, "Describe the concept of the Celestial Sphere and the various points and lines defined on its surface" and "What is precession? Does it have any effect on time or the seasons as they are defined?" from section 1. Section 5 included, "Describe the general interior structure of Jupiter and the other Jovian planets. How have we determined the interior structure of these worlds?" The instructor suggested students answer the questions based on the information provided during the lecture. These prompts invited students to illustrate comprehension of course material, and the completed responses became the study material for the tests. While the instructor did not grade the discussion responses, they used the discussion responses to facilitate class learning. Writing was a vehicle to arrive at class content.

Logan struggled academically this semester more than his previous semesters. He received Bs in Astronomy, Legal Environment of Business, and Principles of Finance. He received an A in his other three classes. Grades only paint a small portion of the picture of Logan as a writer. While he was writing about Jupiter's interior structure and Supreme Court decisions, he was writing for *Odyssey*, writing an online social-content platform, and authoring bylaws for a ballroom-dance club he started. Writing was prompted by class assignments and sought out by Logan's love of language: school and nonschool writing coming together in a choreographed dance of literate becoming. The next chapter returns to Logan's second year at UNG and peeks at his world of self-sponsored writing that existed alongside writing on the interior structure of Jupiter.

NOTE

1. ROTC follows the Army with the designation S-3. An S-3 is a federal designation in which the *S* stands for the job description and the *3* stands for pay grade. For the Army, an S-3 is often an assistant chief of staff, operations officer. To learn more about the writing practices of an S-3, see Rifenburg (2019), in which I trace the writing practices of Lieutenant Colonel Brian Forester, who, at the time I collected data, served as an S-3 at his then-rank of major.

9
DANCING WITH EXTRACURRICULAR LITERATE ACTIVITY

Settled into student and cadet life as a second-year student, Logan turned attention to extracurricular literate activities. He started seeking out opportunities to write more. Drawing together these extracurricular experiences with the curricular experiences described in the previous chapter, Logan collectively constituted his literate becoming. The laminations of school and nonschool writing led to his writerly agency. He would take this specific disposition with him into upper-division MILS classes.

RC/WS scholarship examines how literacy development hinges on the interplay of all writing experiences—those occurring in officially sanctioned spaces, like classrooms, and those that occur beyond these spaces. This scholarship yields robust constructs of literacy, robust theories for conceptualizing literacy and its place in school. According to Katherine Schultz and Glynda Hull (2002), such research has been "pivotal in reshaping the field" (11). By way of example, consider the Stanford Study of Writing (SSW). Under the leadership of Andrea Lunsford and Stanford's upper administrators, the SSW launched in 2001 with the goal of tracking the writing development of incoming Stanford students. All incoming students were invited to participate. Over five years, Lunsford and her research team interviewed students, collected curricular writing and extracurricular writing students elected to share, and administered an annual survey. To date, the SSW has digitized over fifteen thousand artifacts of student writing. One outcome of this large-scale longitudinal study was a coauthored article on the SSW by Jenn Fishman, Lunsford, Beth McGregor, and Mark Otuteye (2005) in which they draw attention to how participants often tied extracurricular writing to theories and practices of performance. They argue that writing performances, like slam poetry and theatrical presentations, "play a role in early college students' development as writers" (226).

While the SSW looks at hundreds of students, Kevin Roozen (2008, 2010, 2020) turns attention to broader meaning-making acts that serve as foundational blocks for erecting a literate life by studying one student:

Charles, an African American undergraduate enrolled in Roozen's basic writing class and published writer, stand-up comedian, and spoken-word poet. For Charles, stand-up comedy, open-mic night, and other opportunities to display publicly his literacy development informed his academic course work. Reading his original poems during the African American Cultural Center's weekly readings and performing jokes at his university's open-mic night "enhanced [Charles's] speeches" (Roozen 2008, 24) for Speech Communication 101, a course Charles was failing midway through the semester but finished with a C (24). Such connections between school and nonschool literacy allow Roozen to argue that "extracurricular and curricular literate activities . . . are so profoundly interconnected that it becomes difficult to see where one ends and others begin" (27).

If we agree with the broader exigencies and arguments arising from studies like these, and I do, RC/WS must look beyond the classroom to understand how writers develop as writers. We must get beyond officially sanctioned literacy practices like blue-book essays written in no. 2 pencils and definitional arguments in 12-point Times New Roman font. Sure, school-sanctioned curricula profoundly shape literacy development, as the Lifespan Writing Development Group (Bazerman et al. 2017, 2018) argue. But we also must follow writers where they go; we must get away from writing as alphabetic text only and look toward inscriptions, semiotics, and embodied meaning-making process; we must get away from just-in-school writing and follow the trajectory of literate becoming as it jumps across spaces and times. To trace writing development, we must follow writers and go where they go. For me to capture the dynamic moments of Logan's literacy development, spatially bounded by just his four years at UNG, I had to read ballroom-dance bylaws and blog posts on fashion, siblings, and cadet life.

Early in his time at UNG, Logan got involved with the swing-dance club. He taught lessons and assumed the position of vice president of the club. His love of dance and his ambition to continue amassing experiences that would help shape his anticipated Army career led him to forming his own dance club: the North Georgia Ballroom Dance Club. Logan enlisted me as faculty advisor. He then wrote a constitution, a required document to become an official student club and receive funding through the student government association. The full preamble read as follows:

> The North Georgia Ballroom Dance Club [NGBDC] was formed to give students at the University of North Georgia a chance to discover the thrills of ballroom dancing. The primary goal of this constitution is to address

the official name of our organization, provide clear and concise elaboration on the goals of the organization, and provide instruction on administration of the organization.

In Article II, Logan provides six purposes of the organization. Many of these purposes covered intangible benefits such as "To encourage social bonding"; "To foster confidence"; "To offer a tension relief for all students from academic and military commitments." Article III, Section ii offered duties of the president, a roll Logan assumed. I quote in full:

> Presidential Duties: supervise ballroom classes. If qualified, teach ballroom classes at various levels. Hold officer meetings and preside over Ballroom Instructor boards. Be accountable for all actions of club members and ensure university policies are being enforced at club activities. Set up recommended dress code for classes and ensure all instructors are professional, yet relaxed and entertaining at all times. Arrange for guest instructors (professionals) to visit NGBDC and teach master classes for instructors and members alike. Ensure all equipment is functioning and music is prepared for class.

The club held dance lessons twice a week with roughly forty students attending.

Logan was also an active contributor to *Odyssey*, an online social-content platform founded by two students at Indiana University. The site is directed toward millennials and has over thirty-five hundred active writers. He contributed blog posts to a section titled "500 Words On." He wrote "I Am My Sister's Keeper" (2015a), in which he described his relationship with his sister. He wrote blogs titled "The 7 Professors You Meet At UNG" (2015b) and "7 Students You See At UNG" (2015c).

When Logan and I talked at the end of the fall semester, he was writing for *Odyssey*. He was proud of one of his recent posts, which garnered much attention at UNG: "7 Students You See At UNG." This piece was humorous and light-hearted, full of self-deprecating humor in which readers could see their friends, roommates, and classmates in Logan's categories. One of the seven types of students he identified are what he titled the "The Freshman-Froggy" in line with the language of the Corps's FROG week:

> The "recruit" is probably one of the friendliest cadets on campus. You will ALWAYS find this freshman in a uniform and he can be seen everywhere around campus greeting just about everyone in a uniform. He's a little awkward the first few weeks of school and is intimidated by his non-cadet classmates (especially girls). He is also known to have a buzz-cut and will never be out past 8 p.m.

Almost as quickly as he picked up *Odyssey*, he dropped it.

Logan's reasons for leaving *Odyssey* are important to understanding how he was developing as a writer; he grew frustrated over what he perceived as lack of authorial control. *Odyssey* isn't just directed to UNG students. It's a large-scale digital-media platform based in New York and targets millennials as readers and content providers. College students read the site and churn out the content; they have the freedom to pursue their own topics but must leave final edits and decision with editors, who are not college students. Logan told me writers email their content to an editor, who may or may not make amendments to the content. The editor then posts the content without seeking final approval for the writer.

According to Logan, his editor "was some lady up in New York." He emailed his content to her, she made changes, and then she posted his content. Logan grew increasingly frustrated with her changes: "Whenever I got comments back from the editor, I didn't really like the edits she was making. And [the edits] kinda destroyed some of the value of it. She really butchered up the writing conventions-wise; she is not a skilled editor. There is some grammar and conventions, and I was surprised she was an editor because there are some terrible mistakes in there." Logan looked over his published pieces and compared these pieces to what he submitted. He often found discrepancies between the two and thought the changes reflected poorly on him. The editor would "mess with [his] titles or put commas where they don't need to be or change around sentence structure." The editor did not like the oxford comma, for example, and Logan did. He penned a piece on his frustration about going to class in the rain and titled the piece "Rain and Suffering," intending to play on the phrase "pain and suffering." Once published, the piece was retitled "Pain and Suffering in College." "I know it sounds miniscule," Logan told me, "but I don't like my titles changed." As he understood, the editor was not posting his writing: "They were putting content out there on my behalf that wasn't mine. The basis was the same but that is not how I write. So, I didn't like that too much."

I see the oxford comma dispute between Logan and the editor as Logan's lack of understanding of specific generic conventions. Newspapers largely avoid the oxford comma, and no matter how much ethos the columnist Gail Collins may have, she isn't getting the *New York Times* to publish a sentence with a comma before a conjunction in a list. The title issue, too, unfortunately results from Logan's lack of awareness of how text is generated within a specific community. In the academic community, I largely have control over my titles, especially with journal articles. But when I worked for newspapers, I didn't. The copyeditors would read over my piece and pen a title that fit the piece but also fit in the space on the page without leaving too much white space. Titles are a marketing thing, sometimes best left to copyeditors and marketing personnel. But Logan did say, "They were putting out content on my behalf that wasn't mine."

Logan also struggled to conceptualize his audience. To the page, he brought a very limited understanding of who would access his content other than his editor. Logan believed he was writing to just UNG students. His editor often made alterations to this writing so what he was saying was accessible to readers beyond UNG: "I think she was trying to clarify things to readers so the whole community would understand. But I was writing for UNG. So, I would say something in my paper which would make perfect sense to everyone here, but she would add something in my paper to explain to the general public what it is and it just took away from the voice of the writing."

I understand his frustration over *Odyssey* "putting content out on [his] behalf that wasn't [his]." But talking with him, the examples he provided sounded like common challenges faced by writers and editors, Logan's lack of awareness of his audience, and how writing works within *Odyssey*. But at this point in Logan's literacy development, I was drawn to how Logan saw himself as needing authorial control. He was confident enough in his writing and knowing how he wanted to be read to sever a writing opportunity that didn't sit well with him. Logan was a strong-willed writer.

One last point about Logan's leaving *Odyssey*. When he talked about his frustrations with lack of authorial control, I couldn't help but think of Army writing and whether Logan anticipated having this level of control. Did he not want or expect his Army writing to be edited as it moved up or down the chain of command? Even though it is common for OPORDs, memos, correspondences, and 9 Line MEDEVAC reports to be reused and reformatted by multiple writers, Logan did not voice concern: "Most of the stuff I will be writing will be operation orders. So, I will get an operation order down from higher, and then I am going to have to do what they call 'flip it': take out the parts that apply to my people and write my own. There's really nobody below me that needs to flip it or change anything in it. I am kinda the sole writer of that operation order for my platoon, so I don't really see anything like that."

Logan offers many ideas in this response. First, he is not thinking about writing OPORDs as a second lieutenant. He is thinking about the here and now of cadet life. With this perspective, he is correct. He is quite low in the proverbial chain of command, and there will not be people below him who will also need to "flip" the OPORDs. Second, the phrase "flip it" stands out to me. With this phrase, Logan speaks to how documents are repurposed within the Army community; text is adjusted to meet the needs of the immediate audience. Just as the editor with *Odyssey* took Logan's work and adjusted it to the readers, so, too, will Logan adjust OPORDs for his platoon. In this sense, Logan's rumination that he is the "sole writer" doesn't stand up, as multiple voices can rise in the document.

With *Odyssey* dropped, Logan turned his attention to his remaining extracurricular activities. His fraternity, Delta Chi, promoted him to treasurer, and he authored a fifteen-page financial-policy document he declined to share with me. While he declined to share this document with me, he did tell me his Business Communication class, which he took the previous semester and in which he struggled with the instructor's teaching style, "did teach me some things." He told me he specifically drew on these "things" when writing the financial document for his fraternity.

I see here Logan consciously drawing together his extracurricular and curricular writing experiences. His Business Communication class offered strong connections to Army writing, connections Logan somewhat saw, but he was more focused on the differences. He received an A in the class but did not speak well of the class and even expressed strong dissatisfaction with the professor, a sentiment I had not heard Logan utter before. To turn the conversation in a positive direction, I asked if there were connections between business writing and Army writing. Logan was ambivalent: "Yes and no. Yes, in the technical aspects. Business writing is clear and concise much like military writing. The difference is in the way it is taught. Military is not so much about form as they are about function. In business, they are more articulate." He continued, "The military—they want you to have good grammar and just typical conventions, but they don't really focus on like persuasive pieces for instance, they don't really focus on sentence structure and stuff, making things persuasive. They just want the facts put down and everything acknowledged. They are not really focused on 'what will make this more persuasive is if you put this down and move this here.' Where in business they were fixing this and fixing that. So, they were a lot more focused on, I guess, the way the document is outlined."

Logan was a strong-willed and adventurous writer. He jumped from genre to genre and from discipline to discipline. He was a student who in two years wrote for his honors FYC, for honors economics, for American Literature I, Business Communication, and history; he was a cadet who wrote an award-winning essay on censorship and a piece of flash-fiction horror, who wrote constitution bylaws for the ballroom-dance club, a financial report for his fraternity, and blogs for a digital platform targeting millennials. This was just the writing he shared with me. Yet despite all these many genres through which Logan filtered his writing, Army writing seemed to stand off in a corner cloaked in distinct characteristics, a wallflower denying a dance to other genres.

Prior and Shipka (2003) help writing researchers see how the lamination of writing and textual production across spaces and across times leads to literate becoming. RC/WS has the theories and methods to make these claims and the findings to bolster these claims. But what of our students like Logan? How do we, how do I, help him see that all of his engagements with writing, however we conceptualize writing, inform who he is as a writer? From my privileged researcher position, I saw how the fraternity and the Business Communication class and the blog posts and the OPORDs all drove toward his literate becoming. But Logan? He kept moving forward, at times noticing connections among his many spheres of communicative activity, at times not, but trusting the OML, trusting the ROTC curriculum, trusting the general education curriculum at UNG, trusting that these structures in place would prepare him for life as an Army officer.

Intersection 2

STAYING THERE
Storying Our Data Collection and Analysis in Longitudinal Research[1]

> *In my own work, which is never my own but linked to many people, it has never been enough to ask an interview question, record it, code it, and report what I perceive to be the meaning underneath what is said. That sequence should smack of individualized hubris; it does to me.*
>
> —Leigh Patel

The epigraph comes from Leigh Patel's (2019) "Turning Away from Logarithms to Return to Story," in which she argues for stories over logarithms.[2] Patel asks readers to embrace qualitative literacy research as an unfolding story in which the researcher is just one of many characters. I find Patel's argument apt for considering how researchers collect and analyze data found in a research moment. Specifically, I find it apt for considering how we build and offer knowledge with our participants. Too often our scholarship offers these logarithms of research Patel cautions against. Too often we opt for offering a tidy, seemingly objective description of research methods instead of inviting readers into the messy story of making knowledge with others.

Book-length longitudinal studies in RC/WS often provide these tidy research details privileged as pinnacles of knowledge making. For example, Sternglass's (1997) longitudinal study of "a multicultural, urban population" (xiv) at City College of New York is complete with an appendix detailing the study design and providing interviews and demographic questionnaires; Herrington and Curtis (2000), after telling rich stories of four student writers, also offer their study design and "other details of the study" in an appendix. Chiseri-Strater (1991) provides reflections on ethnography, her research approach of choice, also as an appendix. Conversely, Carroll (2002) engages with the challenges of research design and representation in an early chapter, even confessing that "to represent participants in a qualitative research project is an endeavor fraught with opportunities for misrepresentation" (35). These discussions of method, methodology, context, and representation are in line with what the qualitative-research handbooks and primers tell novice and experienced researchers alike about how to collect and analyze data.

But, along with Carroll, what I offer is an entrance into the messy moments and messy questions that come with conducting an ethical study, that come with acknowledging one's own positionality, acknowledging concerns about influence and representation, and demonstrating a deep respect for the research participants. Too often, the data-collection and analysis sections of methods sections feel too tidy, too clean. Research, instead, is mess made organized for a reader. When we look to story our research and invite readers into the messy process by which we coconstruct knowledge with research participants, our data collection is not mechanical (to borrow from Stornaiuolo, Campano, and Thomas [2019]), not logarithmic (to borrow from Patel [2019]).

In this Intersection, I consider how current and future researchers might story data collection and analysis and invite readers into the messiness (Law 2014), the serendipity (Goggin and Goggin 2018), the interruptions (Ruecker and Svihla 2020) that constitute working with and researching writers. I limit my focus to just storying data collection and analysis because these are the areas of the research process that handbooks and primers describe as the most linear and definitive. These handbooks and primers offer data collection and analysis as fill-in-the-blank templates, whereas knowledge coconstruction is not.

One way we story our data collection and analysis is by adopting what Amy Stornaiuolo, Anna Smith, and Nathan Phillips (2016) and call an "inquiry stance." Doing so helps researchers account for their role in "unfolding activity" (76). An inquiry stance "routinely *questions* [a researcher's] own assumptions and positionalities while remaining *sensitive* and *open* to multiple interpretations" (76; emphasis added). Notice the words I emphasize in the quote: *question, sensitive, open.* These words disallow a tidy and clean path of data collection. These words connect to stories, as stories are communally crafted narratives serving an audience and a need for a specific time and specific moment. Stories shift according to the when and where and why of the storytelling; rhetor and audience alike shape and shift the unfolding story for that moment. Stories carry meaning and accomplish meaning. Stories are fluid and ever changing for biological reasons as our memories fade, for rhetorical reasons as our audience changes.

Because I had four years with Logan, my data collection changed. Some years, I observed his classes; some years I asked him to sketch scenes of his writing space; some years, I spent more time reading over and thinking about his self-sponsored fiction. I followed the trends in published scholarship. For example, I asked Logan to draw his writing space after I came across Hannah Rule's (2018) work describing the importance of one's writing space. I remained open to serendipitous moments that moved me in a new direction, such as requesting and conducting an interview with General Townsend after he happened to make an appearance at a conference I was also attending. I frantically applied for a modification to my IRB application to allow me to interview Townsend before deciding to classify my interview with him as an oral history and thus exempt from IRB review under the revised interpretation of the Common Rule. My writing on Poland appears after a chance visit with the chief research officer at UNG, who encouraged me to visit UNG's international military partners, which again led me to writing a new IRB to include qualitative interviews with Polish Army officers. I hope my book comes across as tidy and structured; it's no fun to read a messy book. But data collection and data analysis are messy. I modified my IRB application three times over four years.

Through holding an inquiry stance over four years of data collection and two years of writing about my data, I found myself able to return to Stornaiuolo, Campano, and Thomas's (2019) important point: "what is at stake and for whom" (194). These two questions should hover over qualitative studies of writing and writers.

By eschewing logarithms of research and by embracing the unfolding activity of working with writing and writers, we story our work. We invite readers into the challenging and messy rhetorical decisions that come with qualitative research. But at some point, we leave the mess and articulate our findings. We must articulate what we—working in partnership with our research participants—learned. I do so in Intersection 3.

NOTES

1. In this Intersection, I draw from a research partnership with Brad Jacobson. As I was drafting the conclusion to this book, Brad and I coauthored a chapter for an edited collection on longitudinal research. Brad and I wrote through what storying research might mean by drawing on our two individual research projects: Brad's study of a research participant named Jain and my work with Logan. Thanks to Brad for reading a draft of this section and the feedback he provided.
2. In her book, which predates this article, Patel (2015) writes that "research is a fundamentally relational project" (48).

SECTION 4

Year Three, Cadet Second Lieutenant

Little toy soldiers are actually pretty popular. The little ones you see in a toy store. People glue those down and set them up. And yarn is very popular to mark different color routes. I have seen people use cardboard and make 3D structures. It really is like Legoland except with different materials.

—Logan Blackwell describing the construction
of an Army terrain model

10
FINDING 3
Offloading Cognitive Tasks

Data collected from this academic year leads me to argue my third finding in response to the research question driving this book: *How does Logan Blackwell leverage the resources offered through the ROTC curriculum to learn the doctrinally defined Army writing standard and key Army genres with which he will engage upon commissioning as an officer in the US Army?* My third finding is that Logan offloaded the cognitive challenge of authoring OPORDs onto external tools provided by ROTC and tools Logan developed himself.

With little writing for his major, business management, the writing Logan undertakes at this point in his academic career is for his MILS classes. ROTC helped Logan develop external tools to offload the cognitive challenge of authoring various Army documents. He received some of these external tools directly from the Corps, such as the terrain model. Logan described the terrain model as a "Legoland except with different materials." It sits in the corner of a classroom in the Military Leadership Center. A square wooden box propped up waist high holds sand cadets shape into the topography of a given field operation. Plastic toy Army soldiers and plastic jeeps and helicopters dot the sandy landscape, as do plastic miniatures of walls and rocks and barbed wire. Cadets move the sand to raise mountain ranges, pave roads with their forefinger pressed into the pliable sand. Measurements written along the side of the terrain model keep the work to scale. Before committing soldiers and supplies to an operation, cadets engage with these physical manipulatives; they visualize and play and think through inscriptions in the sandbox.

Logan also developed external tools on his own to support the cognitive challenge of writing. He used his own money to purchase what he called "a little field book." With a yellow string, laminated paper, grid paper, topography maps, Rite in the Rain paper, plastic protractor, and operations order (OPORD) templates, the durable notebook is an effective tool for Logan to gather and arrange the various strands of information that go into an OPORD. Many cadets and soldiers create such a field book with their own resources.

Logan worked in a tradition of Army personnel assembling tools like these to aid writing tasks. While writing this book, I observed the writing of an Army major who oversaw the operations at Fort Wainwright in Fairbanks, Alaska (Rifenburg 2019). For two days, I sat in Major (now Lieutenant Colonel) Brian Forester's office while he wrote emails, drafted memos, held synchronization meetings with his subordinates, and developed PowerPoint presentations for higher headquarters. Forester carried a small green notebook in which he kept handwritten notes. The whiteboards in his office were covered in a color-coded timeline for upcoming operations, and the large table in the center of his office held several Excel spreadsheets taped together. Across these three physical writing platforms (the notebook, a whiteboard, and a spreadsheet), Forester coordinated the upcoming actions of over four thousand soldiers stationed in the interior of Alaska. Moving further up the chain of the command, the then-commanding general of training and doctrine command, General Townsend, whom I introduced in the opening passages of this book, also keeps a small green notebook about the size of an iPhone in the pocket on his left ankle. During my interview with him, he told me he had kept this kind of notepad since he was a second lieutenant. He prefers grid paper and opts for a writing device that is both a pen and pencil; he prefers blue ink. Like Forester, and like many people who use writing to accomplish work-related tasks, Townsend was specific about the tools he needs to accomplish writing. He did tell me, "I am also a modern solider, so I have my electronic device." To illustrate, he pulled a black iPhone from the pocket on his right ankle. But for reviewing and sending documents, he "prefer[s] the hard-copy technique." From cadets at UNG to a four-star general, there is something about physical material as a tool for aiding the writing that drives forward the Army's work. A cadet, a major, and a general created material objects to aid in their work. But the Army and the Corps also provide—even require—cadets to use collectively sourced and doctrinally approved external objects like the terrain model.

Scholars across a range of disciplines have traced the interdependent relationship between the mind and external objects for facilitating cognitive activity (Angeli 2019; Hutchins 1995; Malafouris 2013). This scholarship falls under various labels, like distributed cognition or extended cognition; however, the general thrust remains the same: a study of how the paired labor of mind and objects facilitates cognitive activity.[1] By way of example, consider Edwin Hutchins's (1995) work. He studies the cognitive activity of docking a ship. This activity is not isolated to the mind of the captain, but the captain draws on external objects like a nautical slide rule, map, and geographical landmarks to perform the all-important action of docking. Elizabeth Angeli (2019), in her work on the communicative practices of emergency medical services (EMS) professionals, describes the role memory and distributed cognition play when EMS professionals arrive on a scene. Angeli argues that EMS professionals observe a scene, which jump-starts memories, which, in turn, help them respond to the scene: "The external environment facilitates memory in an unpredictable workplace . . . collaborative, professional, and individual memory work together to help communicators manage changes in information and location" (141). Worth noting is that Angeli is invested in tracing the communicative practices within what she calls "unpredictable workplaces." For her, EMS serves as her case study for these locations. But she also identifies the military as an unpredictable workplace (147).

What we learn about distributed cognition from a study of ROTC is how some external cognitive aids, like terrain models, are required components of a required heuristic. We see the idea and practice of distributed cognition as an explicit part of a curriculum. Cadets use terrain models to visualize operations prior to and even during the authoring and circulating of OPORDs. As I show in chapters 13 and 14, the military decision making process, an Army approved doctrine for critical thinking, requires cadets and soldiers to use the terrain model to brainstorm an operation.

By seeking out tools to offload challenging cognitive tasks, by developing tools on his own and engaging with collective tools, Logan moved from reading about OPORDs during his first year as a cadet to brainstorming, writing, and circulating OPORDs during his third year. After shaping writing dispositions during his first two years, cadet Logan Blackwell was coordinating with people and tools to accomplish common Army genres.

NOTE

1. For a helpful overview of extended cognition, particularly in relation to how it has informed RC/WS theory, practice, and research, see the introduction to *Contemporary Perspectives on Cognition and Writing* (Portanova, Rifenburg, and Roen 2017).

11
"A LITTLE FIELD BOOK," OPORDS, AND CORDON AND SEARCH TACTICAL TECHNIQUES

Another fall in the north Georgia mountains. Another start to the semester at the University of North Georgia, founded in 1873 and now witness to another new semester of cadet and civilian students. Logan has ninety credit hours, enough to apply for an officer position even though he is only a junior. Logan sends a memorandum to the Second Delta Platoon Company command leader requesting a platoon-leader spot and lands the job. He now oversees about forty cadets broken into smaller squads and proudly displays a black dot in the center of his occupational camouflage pattern that signifies his position. It's a tiny detail disappearing into the visual cacophony of the camo, but for cadets and soldiers alike, these insignia carry much weight.

In his new role, Logan tells me, "I oversee everything they do. Making sure there are no issues. So, I got one guy who works directly under me. He is called a 'platoon sergeant.' And, basically, he tells me any issues or anything that goes wrong. Like if someone is not doing well with school or if they are not doing well physically or anything like that. So, I just talk to the commander. So, I am just a link between the commander and the enlisted side."

Like the semester before, Logan registers for sixteen hours. At this point in his plan of study, all his non-MILS courses are for his business management major:

- BUSSA 3110: Statistics for Business (3 credit hours)
- BUSA 3120: Operations Management (3 credit hours)
- BUSA 3130: Business Information Systems (3 credit hours)
- MGMT 4665: Human Resources Management (3 credit hours)
- MILS 3000: Adaptive Team Leadership (3 credit hours)
- MILS 3005: Physical Readiness Leadership and Exercise (1 credit hour)

We talk early in the semester before he feels the weight of sixteen hours and the demand of overseeing forty cadets. His mind is still roaming around Italy. After cancelling his trip to Rome last summer to attend jump school, he finally made it to the Eternal City for an education-abroad trip. Logan describes his time in Italy as a "cleansing from the institution for a little bit." He continues, "I kinda got to be a normal college student for a few weeks. It was weird though because I could still feel myself in that military kind of mode. I was not really fully carefree. I still had my head on a swivel. I was still trying to do the things I was trained to do, more or less."

He stayed in the Trevi neighborhood, named after the famous Trevi Fountain, where legend holds if one throws a penny in the fountain waters, a return trip to Rome is slated in the thrower's future (my penny hit the water in 2014; I am still waiting for my return trip). He took two classes: ART 1100: Art Appreciation (Honors) and BUSA: 2528: Travel Abroad/International Experience (Honors). He roamed the city, taking handwritten notes on the architecture, visiting businesses. Eurorail sped him off to Munich, then London, over the weekends. "It was really fun," he says, "and I think it opened up my political perspective and just global understanding. The world is a lot bigger now, I guess." He kept a blog, displaying his penchant for weaving informative, self-motivated writing into his life as he did when he authored blogs for *Odyssey*. He wrote thirty-seven blog posts detailing his experience. His first, titled "Buongiorno from Rome," opens directly: "I've decided to create a blog for my time here in Europe. I've never been out of the country before, and I'm not much for writing to get other people's approval, but I figure that my family and a few friends might be legitimately interested in what I'm doing." His military training comes through in his second post, titled "Boots on the Ground: My First Few Hours in Italy." Describing his experience with the baggage check in Italy, he writes, "I made my way through customs and baggage check, no issues. Throughout this whole ordeal, I wasn't really amazed at anything yet, just watching. I was observing patterns and I didn't even know it yet." In his final post, "Final Reflections," written back on US soil, Logan looks back positively on his experience: "In seeing Rome, Bracciano, Perugia, Tuscany, Munich, and London, I believe I have gained cultural perspectives that I never could have learned in a classroom. Being in these places helped me better understand the world economy, the intricacies of global political cooperation, and gain an overall better understanding of why our global neighbors possess the attitudes and prejudices that we see so often. Although there were several headaches throughout this trip, including filthy roommates and long airport lines, the money paid for this trip was well worth the experience." His words illustrate what education-abroad proponents highlight: an opportunity to gather global experiences that refigure how one approaches domestic experiences.

With his final reflections written, Logan turned attention to the most demanding year for cadets: the third year. When I first met Logan during his first semester as a first-year student, I broached the topic of spending four years together reflecting on how he learns to write standard Army genres. He agreed, but he did stress, even back then as a first-year student, that he didn't anticipate writing for his MILS classes until his third year. He anticipated that in the third year, he would move from being a receiver of information to a conduit of information. As a third-year cadet, he is now faced with learning the OPORD. These written texts are delivered to subordinates for the purpose of executing an operation. When authoring an OPORD, cadets and soldiers alike adhere to the Army writing standard: "Effective Army writing is understood by the reader in a single rapid reading and is clear, concise, and well-organized" (US Army 2020c). Learning, and writing, delivering, and enacting an OPORD is the focus of Logan's third year.

To learn this genre, Logan will make use of two external tools: a little field book of his own construction and a terrain model provided by ROTC. One tool is self-sponsored and one tool is a part of the Army doctrinal approach to critical thinking and authoring OPORDs.

OPERATIONS ORDERS: ABSORBING AND REMIXING TEXT

The Army is designed to undertake operations in a garrison or field environment. OPORDs are the textual vehicle for accomplishing operations. As written documents that are delivered orally, OPORDS flow down the chain of command, with each link in the chain responsible for receiving the order and then, to use Logan's words, "flipping it" to the link immediately below. On and on the OPORD goes, flipping its way down the chain until all necessary parties are briefed. OPORDs begin as textual documents with a strict form, almost a template of sorts, for collecting and arranging pertinent information. Cadets and soldiers deliver OPORDs orally, one party briefing another. The receiving party writes down the OPORD and then delivers it to the next party. Such a cycle continues until all necessary parties are briefed. The most fundamental purpose of the Army is predicated on the accurate and rapid collection and circulation of text in physical and oral form. Effective writing forms the foundation of the Army.

Prior to his junior year, Logan had not written or flipped any OPORDs. He did sit in on "two or three" and spent his free time browsing digital

UNCLASSIFIED//FOUO

Copy ___ of 14 Copies
B/1-34 AR, 1st BDE, 1st IN DIV (M)
FT. RILEY, KANSAS
091700JUN06

OPORD 06-06 (SD STX, 12-15JUN06)

References:

a. Map, Series: V778SFTRILEYMIM, EDITION 6-NIMA
b. FM 3-20.15 Tank Platoon NOV 01
c. ARTEP 17-237-10-MTP Mission Training Plan for the Tank Platoon 02
d. FR Reg 385-12, Range and Training Safety, 14JUN04
e. 1-34 AR CO/TM TACSOP NOV 05
f. 1/1ID OPORD 06-40 OPN VOLTRON
g. 1-34 AR OPORD 06-23 (OPN WHIRLWIND, 5-23JUN06)
h. B/1-34 AR OPORD 06-05 (OPN WHIRLWIND, 5-23JUN06)

Task Organization:
HQ/B/1-34 AR   1/B/1-34 AR   2/B/1-34 AR   3/B/1-34 AR
MAINT/B/1-34 AR   4/B/1-34 AR   5/B/1-34 AR   6/B/1-34 AR

1. **SITUATION.**

   a. Enemy Forces:

   (1) General. CIA sources indicate a Former Regime Element (FRE) loyalist cell is responsible for recent IED and Small Arms attacks against Coalition Forces along MSRs in AO CENTURION. Host Nation sources collaborate intelligence that FRE are operating from nearby villages with sympathizer support. The local population does not actively participate in the attacks against Coalition Forces but allow them to happen in order to prevent reprisals against their villages from FRE.

   (2) Specific. 3-4 man teams of FRE continue to operate independently with monetary and resource support operating throughout the AO. Over the past two weeks, insurgents have employed roadside IEDs and conducted small arms attacks along MSRs and ASRs, focusing on soft targets and logistics convoys. FRE insurgent teams are equipped with AK47s, RPGs and mortars. Recent reports describe military aged males utilizing Jawa motorcycles to transport, hastily emplace, and egress from the IED site. IEDs are additionally concealed in roadside debris and in construction material alongside construction sites.

   b. Friendly Situation: TF 1-34 AR occupies FOB CENTURION vicinity PJ 945 336. TF 3-34 AR, will conduct a TF cordon and search in the town of Keats vic PJ 978 441, targeting and IED cell reportedly possessing EFP technology. 3-34 AR shares a common boundary with F 1-34 AR along RTE PUCK vic PJ 961 433. Movement into 3-34 ARs AO requires prior coordination.

2. **MISSION.** B/1-34 AR conducts a combat logistics patrol, securing a logistics convoy from FOB CENTURION to a Logistics Release Point vic PJ 970 339, IOT allow logistics vehicles to conduct re-supply operations.

3. **EXECUTION.**

UNCLASSIFIED//FOUO

Figure 11.1. The first page of an unclassified OPORD provided by Lieutenant Colonel Brian Forester. At the top of the OPORD is the UNCLASSIFIED designation and the acronym FOUO, which means "for official use only."

examples. To prepare, Logan used his own money to purchase "a little field book." This "little field book" is more accurately a book cover, about the size and thickness of a five hundred-page paperback. A zipper secures the field book. It is dark green, and Logan bought it online. He tells me, "I spent quite a bit of money putting this together." When he zips it open, the two sides fall part. The inside cover shows the name of the company that manufactured the book: Tactical Notebook Covers.com. Unzipped, the left side holds a mechanical pencil and **OPORD** templates Logan printed on individual sheets of paper and then slid into clear plastic protective pockets. The right side of the field book holds around twenty sheets of Rite in the Rain paper in a greenish hue. Rite in the Rain is a common paper used by the military, hunters, and construction workers for, as the name suggests, writing in adverse weather. Some Rite in the Rain sheets of paper are broken into grids. I also notice templates for 9 Line MEDEVAC reports. A yellow string floats loosely in the middle of the field book, as does a plastic protractor. Logan uses both external tools to chart points on a map and write down navigation coordinates. Logan tells me some cadets prefer using the side of a sheet of paper for measuring coordinates. He prefers the string. Tucked into the pockets are more external tools: additional cards, detailing troop leading procedures, and cards reminding Logan "doctrinally how [they] are taught to do things." Logan didn't anticipate needing to compile such a compact field book: "I was actually surprised by the amount of field-craft things I have learned how to do." This field book serves as Logan's self-initiated and self-designed external tool for offloading and then facilitating the cognitive demands of a key Army writing task.

All material in the field book is designed for rapid use and reuse. Logan tells me, "We always like to keep things laminated in plastic because we take these little map pens, write on them, and wipe them off with alcohol wipes for next time. A big part of doing missions is being, you know, [able to] reuse our stuff and get it down quickly." A pencil is preferred over a pen. More, not less, paper is preferred because you "never know when you need paper out there." The **OPORD** prepares cadets and soldiers for the "out there."

In brief, an **OPORD** makes use of the long-dominant five-paragraph structure for conveying information (see fig.11.1). As Logan says, "Five paragraphs but it might as well be an essay." Each paragraph has a label, and the total template for the **OPORD** in Logan's book runs twenty pages. When receiving an **OPORD**, he fills in five sections:

- Situation
- Mission
- Execution
- Service and Support
- Command Signal

Situation is the setting. Even before telling troops the mission, an **OPORD** states where the mission will occur. Logan will describe the anticipated weather and terrain and identify obstacles, the area of interest and operation, potential places for cover and concealment, lines of sight for fire, and ways to get to the area of interest. Additionally, situation asks the writer to detail the opposition's status, which requires reconnaissance. This subsection of the situation reads like an audience analysis: How are they organized? What is their attitude and political or religious motivation? What is their strength, and what have they been doing? What is their most probable course of action (COA)? What is their most dangerous COA? What is the worst they can do to us? Finally, situation specifies adjacent forces and civilian considerations: What other friendly or oppositional forces are nearby, and what civilian concerns need to be accounted for? In total, the template for situation tallies over six pages in Logan's field book.

At this point, the receiver of this OPORD has yet to hear the mission. In Logan's words, the "mission paragraph is actually pretty small." The mission includes the task and purpose and is orally recited twice. It's the details surrounding the mission that add length to an OPORD.

When moving through the Situation and Mission sections, Logan talks with confidence and alacrity. I hardly keep up as he flips his pages and rattles off acronyms. At one point, I set my pen down and let my recorder do the work; I just listen. Logan's confidence wanes with execution. He speaks in ellipses: "I can tell you there is going to be so many acronyms in this that nobody is . . . and the rest of these papers are very much execution."

Logan does show me execution includes the commander's intent, purpose, key tasks, concept of operation, and most decisive point. For most decisive point, Logan interjects unsettling clarification, which reminds me that though we are looking at quotidian military documents, these documents lead to physical harm: "They want you to say something along the lines of 'OK, when we assault this part of the objective, this is kinda like our no turning back.'" Following the decisive point, the writer includes information on the scheme maneuver. According to Logan, scheme of maneuver is the most important subparagraph to the OPORD. Scheme of maneuver entails ten points. Logan says,

> This is going to tell you how you are going to move there, all your compass coordinates, how you plan on getting eyes on the objective beforehand, how you are going to occupy the objective, how you are going to let people know it is time to move onto the objective, how you are going to shoot, what kind of control measures there are going to be if something goes wrong, actions on the objective, how we are going to reorganize after attack, how we are going to get out of there? What are we going to do if we get compromised and can no longer put up a fight?

The scheme of maneuver also details the scheme of fire that tells artillery soldiers which unit has priority to fire first. Who is pulling the trigger and where? Who will be watching to make sure the objective is accomplished? Finally, scheme of maneuver also details the casualty evacuation plan. In Logan's words, the casualty evacuation plan describes "how are we going to get people out of there? Stuff we need other units to do. Our lower-level units. As a platoon leader, I might cast out to a certain squad to be on prisoner detail or something like that."

The next subsection details coordinating instructions. Here the writer puts together a timeline. The writer then details service support (i.e., logistics) and then details command and control (i.e., if the leaders get injured, who is next in line? Where are other units? Where is the command post? What are all the frequencies and call signals?).

As Logan walks me through the twenty laminated pages of his OPORD template, I feel my mind pulled in two directions. For one, as a writing teacher, I've held a long and firm belief in the importance of writing and that writing and textual delivery are foundational for building and sustaining the work of what it means to be human: our government, private and public businesses, entertainment, and religion are grounded in written text. But I find myself nodding along and not at all surprised the Army uses written and oral text for directing all of its operations—from practicing squad maneuvers on base to securing machine-gun bunkers on foreign soil. But on the other hand, I find myself wondering whether the emphasis on written text might open the Army to additional criticism as politicians and the general public reflect on missions that did not go according to plan. If a successful operation, say the United States storming French beaches during World War II, finds genesis in written plans, so, too, don't failed operations? The template form of the OPORD does not leave much room for improvisation, for adjusting rapidly to a changing situation. I ask Logan if he could browse through his mental rolodex of military history and point to a time when a faulty OPORD led to a disastrous mission. He shrugs off my question but offers one of the more sustained points during our hour-long chat. I provide it in full:

> It's never really a blame game when things go wrong. You saw how many contingency plans we had. It's combat; things are going to go bad. The only thing I can say about an operations order is when its briefed, the people below you are probably going to catch some mistakes before you do because you gotta take it in the context of "I've been doing this stuff for probably a year or less at the point I'll be briefing it to them and some of those guys will have been in the military ten to fifteen years." So, if I brief them a route

plan that they think is completely and utterly stupid, they will be like "Sir, we gotta refine this thing." And that is part of the troop-leading procedures we use. Those are important. The last step in the troop-leading procedures, there is eight of them, right after the op order is given, are the words *supervise* and *refine*. And so, after the plan is briefed, you can kinda take some feedback and then modify the plan. Just because you briefed the op order doesn't mean it is set in stone. Most of the times, the people below you are going to catch those mistakes. Or at least, that's what I have been told.

I then ask about problems. If something goes wrong during battle, I ask, do commanders trace back the problem to how an OPORD was written? Can poorly written text take the blame? Logan says *no*:

> You can't trace it back to individual documents. But what I can say is that commander's intent paragraph, you know when we went into Iraq and Afghanistan, or when we first went to Iraq for sure, we kinda messed up on the whole civilian consideration thing. We had a lot of learning to do when we went into Iraq. And we are doing the Gulf Wars and Iraqi Freedom and everything. There was a big learning curve there. These guys that were writing all these orders and doing these things, they were just going off their commander's intent. You can't trace it back to specific documents, but that commander's intent really does play a part in the method in which the people below the commander make their plans.

Logan's musing offers many points. He anticipates the old maxim that the best-laid plans go to waste and trusts those below him to *supervise* and *refine* a given order. He also acknowledges the need for flexibility in an OPORD: "Just because you briefed the op order doesn't mean it is set in stone." Logan has not seen combat, so he cannot speak to how he has experienced an OPORD shifting because of a changing situation. But even though OPORDs give the appearance of a static document, the kind that demands the writer fill in blanks and adhere to a strict format, Logan, though a novice, sees areas within this genre for flexibility, adaptability. For novices, genres appear as fixed, unmalleable forms. For experts, genres appear as suggested templates. Though a novice, Logan understands an OPORD may not be "set in stone." Logan developed a sophisticated notion of this genre in a limited amount of time through a variety of resources provided by ROTC: toy soldiers, yarn, cardboard, and practice after practice after practice.

LEARNING AN OPORD

Logan offloaded the cognitive challenge of authoring OPORDs onto external tools provided by ROTC and external tools he developed himself. As I work with Logan to tease out how he learned and is still learning to compose this genre, he spends a great deal of time qualifying his remarks. Logan is in training, working on the periphery of the Army. When Logan works on OPORD, he works under a different learning context than a commissioned officer training with her soldiers at, say, Fort Bragg in Fayetteville, North Carolina, or even soldiers penning OPORDs at a forward operating base in Abu Ghraib. Logan delineated between what the "real Army [does] versus what we do here." One distinction between OPORDs in these two spaces, for example, is that the Army does not type out OPORDs because "in the field, you aren't going to have a typewriter or anything out there." Logan was also responsible for constructing his own terrain model to brainstorm operations. This three-dimensional topographical model includes route plans and enemy and friendly forces represented by a variety of found objects. In the "real Army," operations staff create the model. Finally, Logan works under a different set of deadlines. He is not rolling through the raucous world of war. Instead, he can take his time to write and polish. His OPORDs are due by the close of business on Friday. The deadlines in the field are within a couple of hours of when the assignment is given.

Once a week, Logan briefs an OPORD to whomever is in charge of the squad. As a platoon leader, Logan oversees three squads. Logan starts by reminding me again that an OPORD is "a mouthful":

> We have to brief one of these operations orders every week to whoever is in charge of the squad. So, they get briefed accompanying the op order the night before and they will have to put out a warning order (WARNO) within fifteen minutes. A WARNO is basically just the situation, mission, and general and specific instructions. A "Hey, get ready to move." Within a couple of hours, in the real word, you will have to have that op order done, but for us we got to be done by close of business Friday. So, we will get it Thursday night and it needs to be done Friday.

In addition to writing, cadets build a physical representation illustrating the where and how of an OPORD. This physical representation is called a *terrain model*, which is made for a specific purpose at a specific moment. Like the "so practical, so modest, so pervasive" inscriptions Latour (1990, 21) notes are crucial for developing scientific text, the inscriptions Logan builds in the terrain model are foundational for the OPORD he will author. The road built through mounding the sand, the tree line represented with string, the people represented with plastic toy soldiers from Walmart—all these tools become the inscription that leads to an OPORD (see fig. 11.2). The material objects are often reused but not the complete model itself because of the amount of detail specific to COA. Cadets make use of a variety of objects to add necessary detail.

"A Little Field Book," OPORDs, and Tactical Techniques   151

Figure 11.2. An ROTC terrain model at UNG sits in the Military Leadership Center on the Dahlonega campus. Photo by author.

> Little toy soldiers are actually pretty popular. The little ones you see in a toy store. People glue those down and set them up. And yarn is very popular to mark different color routes. I have seen people use cardboard and make 3D structures. It really is like Legoland except with different materials.

With a terrain model provided and the OPORD complete, a cadet flips the order. Logan receives an OPORD from the company and flips it for his three squad leaders below him. This process, in Logan's words, helps "bring it down to the context of your level" to "make it relevant to our guys and then put it out to our squads." Logan stresses, "We always have to brief it in a way that makes sense to the people below us."

Then the oral briefing begins:

> And we have to brief this thing orally. We don't get to just sit there and read from the paper. You are reading to whatever unit you are doing the mission. You are reading to someone below you. When we graduate, we are all going to be platoon leaders, essentially, which is what I am now in the cadet world. I mean we have bullet points, but we can't just type this thing out. That is one thing that they just will not let us do—type them—cause in the field I am going to have to sit here and fill this thing out and brief from this basically. And they basically grade us on how well we brief. A key point is it's got to be detailed but it also needs to make

sense like you are telling a story; they absolutely hate when people are robots reading from paper. And it's kinda funny because it does relate to public speaking really, really closely.

The building of a terrain model, the writing of an OPORD, the flipping of the OPORD for a new audience, and the speaking of the order clearly is "the meat and potatoes of what they want us to learn." Additionally, Logan says OPORDs are not disconnected from larger Army training goals: "Getting good with this operations order helps your confidence with the actual tactics, and if you don't know the tactics, then it will be kinda hard to write an operations order, too. Because that is going to help."

I ask Logan to describe an OPORD he helped with that did not work out well. He has a ready response:

> Our first one that we did, we did it together and we decided that we were going to fill in our movement plan (how we were going to get to this mythical objective with grid coordinates), so we were rattling off seventeen golf zero delta one, one, two, six, seven, eight, six. And we put out four or five of these grid coordinates to brief our place. And in that instance, he said we were way, way too detailed. "Why don't you give me one starting grid point and then say what direction you are doing and then be done with it." We were way too detailed with that. We were reading from the paper, and our terrain model was bland. There was no color to it to mark different types of landscape. You want green for grass and black for the roads and stuff like that.

As we are wrapping up our conversation before Logan heads to class, I ask him to reflect on his view of writing and how his experience with OPORDs has affected this view. His definition of good writing has remained largely consistent since he pondered my question many semesters ago in an honors English 1101 course. He tells me, "Good writing is being able to put something together on paper that can either inspire somebody and have an influence over somebody's life and it's also something that, when delivered orally, can really have a psychological effect on somebody. At least that is what I think."

I follow up by asking if the Army was teaching him this form of writing:

> They are not specifically doing it, but I think they have inspired a little bit of desires for me because they are writing so technical. For me to add some of my own writing I've learned from other sources and just like kinda not change the way they do things but really change the way people listen to the writing I've put out with an Army style. I think changing some of my language might help, changing some of the language might help people be able to understand and conceptualize the Army writing more. I know the first time I was given an operations order, it was, you know, I was racing to copy everything down because the guy spoke so fast and was so

dry; I just couldn't understand him. So, me being able to add that human element back into an op order might help people understand it more.

With these reflections in place—reflections on what works in OPORDs and what does not; reflections on how he might adapt the generic conventions of OPORDs and also incorporate a "human element" into the genre—the calendar page turns yet again. The north Georgia mountains will face their mildest winter since Logan's boots hit the ground as a first-year student. Spring will come early with daffodils poking their heads out of the loam and waving their yellow petals before the spring semester begins in full. The spring will see a new president assume a seat in the Oval Office, a new secretary of defense, two new national security advisors—all of whom will shape the Army for which Logan prepares. The spring will see Logan change his commissioning plans; the spring will see Logan shed commitments and delegate more responsibility to those serving underneath him.

But all that will come. For now, Logan looks over his grades for the semester (an A in every class) and rests.

*

Logan begins another semester:

- MGMT 4655: Advanced Operations Management (3 credit hours)
- MGMT 4667: Small Business Management (3 credit hours)
- MGMT 4668: Seminar in Management (3 credit hours)
- MILS 3100: App Leaders in Small Unit Ops (3 credit hours)
- MILS 3105: Physical Readiness Leadership and Exercise (1 credit hour)
- POLS 2401: Global Issues (Honors) (3 credit hours)

I'm sitting in the back row of MILS 3100: Applied Leadership in Small Unit Operations. A divider runs down the middle of the classroom. Five long rows of tables further divide the space populated by thirty cadets and one instructor. I arrange my laptop on my table as the instructor, Major Williams (a pseudonym), pulls up PowerPoint slides. Cadets chat, scroll through their phones. I rub my chin as my laptop powers up; for the first time in many months, I dragged a razor across my face, and the softness of my chin feels out of place. Army Regulation 670-1 allows a mustache on men, but I decided against that. I walk up to Williams, offer my hand, and introduce myself. He is cordial and direct. He knew I was coming. I had to clear my presence with my dean and then with Williams's immediate supervisor. Williams has a commanding presence. Logan said he is "highly, highly decorated." He's a veteran of multiple deployments and Army training programs: airborne, air assault. He came to UNG from the 75th Ranger Regiment. As I am returning to my seat, his sharp voice cuts through the soft din of preclass chatter. Last names shouted by Williams are followed by a "here, sir" from the cadet. I see two Polish cadets from the General Tadeusz Kosciuszko Military University of Land Forces. In two years, one of these cadets, Jacob Pochodaj, will give me a tour me of his home campus.

The walls are sparsely decorated. The few posters present seem to have been placed many years back and then promptly forgotten. In one corner is a map of Fort Knox, a location that becomes prominent during class discussion. Behind Williams hangs a poster designed and printed by UNG cadets; it's titled "Cultural Understanding and Language Proficiency" and looks like a class research project. Behind me are two official Army recruitment posters. The first reads "Army Officer" in yellow font. Below the yellow font, text reads "Inspiring strength in others." The other poster offers the simple and well-known phrase in all caps: "ARE YOU ARMY STRONG?"

Williams ends roll and provides a class overview with specific learning objectives. The class is running a practical exercise (PE) on tactical call-out. Williams encourages cadets to listen because this information will be tested both in the cadet world and after commissioning, for those who commission. He asks cadets which mock scenario they want to run. A few mumble a response. I think I hear the word *Iraq* as the answer. Williams leaves to make copies and asks a cadet to step up to the podium and remind the class of the scenario. The cadet pulls up a new PowerPoint and begins.

The PowerPoint is labeled "January 2017 IPR Brief." My fingers scramble across my keyboard to capture the information. No one slows down for the civilian researcher in the back row. I'm trying to stay afloat in my first cadet class, an upper-division class that has already met for twelve weeks. I'm jotting down the acronyms to look them up later: PE, IPR. About four minutes into the brief, I get a feel for what is going on.

This upper-division class is studying counterinsurgency techniques, specifically how to move to a location, enter the location, and secure the high-value target (HVT). This HVT is often an oppositional force (i.e., a bad guy), a person with intelligence sought by the Army. In Army language, they are running through a PE on tactical call-outs with an emphasis on cordon-and-search techniques. The PowerPoint is an in-process review (IPR) of a mock situation based, it seems, on the imbroglios in Syria and Iraq. The cadet running the brief toggles between PowerPoint slides and an aerial image showing a village of roughly fifteen buildings huddled together. A road runs vertically through the village. On one side of the road sits a large forest. For this mock exercise, this aerial view shows a village in the fictional country of Atrophia. Two fictional oppositional forces are working in tandem against the Army's presence in Atrophia: Ariana and SAPA forces. The former is an officially sanctioned, but now rogue, branch of the Atrophia army; the latter are guerilla forces.

The PowerPoint details the tactics and procedures used by these two forces and the weapons they favor: a belt-fed, 7.62 × 54 mm, medium machine gun with an effective range of one thousand meters. The next series of slides provide an update on the current situation. On each slide, the date appears at the top, and then there is a direct statement of action followed by results statements in italics:

> 10 Feb 2017
> Three vehicle convoy ambushed
> *Ambush result of heightened border patrols*
> *May have also been an attempt for ambush training*

The PowerPoint concludes, and Williams returns with handouts. He begins again by turning off the projector, taking up a black marker, and writing in all caps "ATP 3-06.20." He tells cadets to Google it. I do later. The field manual is titled *Multi-Service Tactics, Techniques, and Procedures for Cordon and Search Operations*.[1] During my years of research, every Army publication or joint publication I have looked up has been freely available as a pdf through the Army Publishing Directorate. During an interview with Logan, I learned the military-science instructors at UNG do not provide hard copies of any publication but ask cadets to locate digital copies.

In the middle of the board, Williams begins an outline. He again stresses the need to remember this information because it will be tested in camp for cadets and tested again for those commissioning. After a few moments, Williams's outline is complete:

> Cordon and search (company-level operation)
>   *Cordon and knock*
>   *Tactical call-out—might do this because safety to soldiers or unknown*
>   *Cordon and enter/kick*

He emphasizes security. Counterinsurgency drives a wedge between locals and the rebels, who often use villages and towns as strongholds. For Army soldiers to reclaim rebel-held territory, they work with and gain the trust of the local civilian population. Williams stresses that the first and most important step for gaining this trust is through offering security. If the locals feel safe under the watch of the Army, they offer aid; fear, on the other hand, is fodder for rebel strength.

With this background information, the class exercise begins. Williams hands out paper copies of the aerial image of Atrophia. I later learn the image shows an actual location at Fort Knox designed to mimic an Iraqi village. Williams draws a circle around a building with a white roof in the middle of the village. He points to it and tells cadets to design a company order cordon-and-search tactical call-out for locating and capturing the HVT located in this building. In the Army hierarchy, a company is one notch above a platoon. For this exercise, a company contains three platoons, sixteen to fifty soldiers each. The cadets need to place two platoons; the third platoon needs to be briefed on the actual operation. In groups of five, Williams gives the cadets fifteen minutes to develop a plan and then brief the class on their plan. As cadets work, Williams calls out reminders, such as using FM 1-02, *Operational Terms and Graphics* (now *FM 1-02.2, Military Symbols* 2020d) to illustrate their plans with the appropriate symbols.[2]

Groups in camo gather over the tables. One enters into a discussion full of expletives directed at each other, the opposing forces, and the location of this fictional operation. In the front row, I see Logan working with a group. I notice the terrain model in the corner of the front of the classroom. It's a large, elevated box full of sand. String crisscrosses the box and breaks the space into grids. Williams shouts out more reminders, asking cadets what they plan on doing with women and children, where they will locate their first platoon, their second and third. What is the withdrawal plan? Are they going in at night or during the day?

Williams picks Logan's group to brief first. Logan and four cadets make their way to the front. The screen displays the aerial view of the village. One cadet takes a black marker and begins marking the image, but the cadet is not using the proper symbols. Williams jumps on this teaching moment to stress graphic control measures found in FM 1-02. Williams draws the symbol set below on the whiteboard:

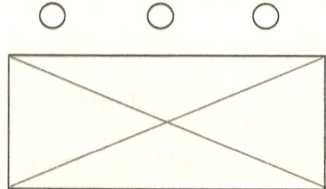

The rectangle shape is the foundation of this symbol set detailed in chapter 5, "Unit Symbols," of FM 1-02 (US Army 2020b). The rectangle, or *frame*, represents a friendly force. A hostile force is signified by a frame tilted, a neutral force is a square, and an unknown force has a frame resembling a cloud. The branch or functional symbol is inside the frame. For the example above, the X shape symbolizes infantry branch. The final detail Williams includes in the class demonstration is a symbol to convey the size of the infantry branch. He places three dots above the top of the frame representing a platoon-sized, friendly, light infantry branch. This is the echelon area of the symbol and can include thirteen different symbols that detail thirteen different sizes of forces according to table 5-6 in FM 1-02. The entire FM dedicated to graphic control measures runs over five hundred pages, and though the first one-third is a dictionary of sorts that offers what the field manual terms "doctrinally-accepted definitions" (vii), Williams only touches on the symbols of most immediate use to the cadets who, for this exercise, need to place three infantry platoons and then execute a cordon-and-search tactical call-out.

As the group briefs their plan, Williams and other cadets offer questions:

> Do you have to clear buildings en route to the target building? Gotta think if it is worth disturbing additional civilians.
> Are you going at night or during the day?
> Who is patting down all the women and children?
> Where is your interpreter standing?
> Where is your clean area (i.e., the area where civilians who have been patted down are temporarily held)?
> Do you have time and security to pull out a whole village?

The group finishes and sits. Williams heads back to the board to emphasize more graphic control measures. He sketches a friendly infantry platoon and then draws a lightning-bolt shape pointing to the top of the board and another pointing to the bottom of the board. The lightning bolts coming from the platoon symbolize the physical movement the platoon will take. During a cordon-and-search tactical call-out, two platoons are standing guard. But they are not standing still. Instead, the lightning bolts symbolize the paths the platoon will patrol. Williams then draws a straight line down the middle of the road that cuts vertically through the aerial photo and draws a line perpendicular to the first, which cuts along a ditch behind the village. He stresses the need to locate boundaries for each platoon and to use easy-to-recognize topographical markers or buildings to mark these boundaries. One platoon will patrol the road and the other will patrol south of the village. Class is reaching an end when Williams hits a somber note. He points to data reporting that most Army deaths occur during the first ninety days or last ninety days of deployment. Soldiers are either too green or too comfortable.

Later, my mind still lingering around issues of counterinsurgency and the ongoing civil war in Syria and conflict in Iraq, I find myself browsing for updates on Syria. I read that Syria's largest dam partially burst, that Syria threatened to launch Scud missiles at Israel, and that a year-long Syrian refugee-relocation program in Canada is reaching an end. For the many students I teach at UNG, these developments are literally and figuratively thousands of miles away from the pressures of forthcoming final exams and summer vacation plans. But for the cadets I shared a classroom with, these developments are and will continue to be the catalyst driving their classroom activities.

A POSTSCRIPT

As I was finishing this chapter late in the spring semester, UNG faculty and staff received an email from UNG's president, Bonita Jacobs. The subject line read "Alumnus killed in action." I reprint the full email below:

> Dear Faculty and Staff:
>
> It saddens me to share that U.S. Army 1st Lt. Weston C. Lee, a 2014 University of North Georgia graduate, was killed Saturday in Mosul, Iraq. Lt. Lee, who is from Bluffton, Georgia, earned a Bachelor of Science degree in criminal justice and commissioned as a U.S. Army infantry officer from UNG in December 2014. He was assigned to the 1st Battalion, 325th Infantry Regiment, 2nd Brigade Combat Team, 82nd Airborne Division, Fort Bragg, North Carolina and was supporting Operation Inherent Resolve.
>
> Lt. Lee made the ultimate sacrifice in service to his country, and our hearts and thoughts are with his family and friends at this difficult time. Funeral arrangements have not yet been announced.
>
> Sincerely,
> Bonita

Lee is now buried in Arlington National Cemetery and was posthumously awarded the Bronze Star Medal, Purple Heart, and Meritorious Service Medal. Lee is the eighth UNG graduate to die on active duty since the Unites States was attacked on September 11, 2001.

Lee died in early 2017. In May of 2018, Logan Blackwell will take off his black graduation gown, raise his right hand, and recite the Oath of Enlisted Officers. Upon completion of the oath, Logan will be a second lieutenant in the Army.

This time next year, Logan will be on active duty, eligible for deployment to Iraq, Afghanistan, or any other foreign theater of war.

NOTES

1. According to the Army Publishing Directorate, Army Techniques Publication (ATP) 3-06.20 was published on August 8, 2016. But it was "rescinded" by Army Training and Doctrine Command on October 9, 2018. Therefore, while the ATP can still be found floating around the web, it is not officially housed on the Army Publishing Directorate's website, where I found all additional Army publications referenced in this book. Curious readers can locate ATP 3-06.20 with a simple Google search. More interesting, however, is why TRADOC rescinded it. I twice emailed my point of contact at TRADOC for a response. I did not receive a reply.
2. FM 1-02 was superseded by Army Doctrine Publication 1-02, *Terms and Military Symbols*. ADP 1-02 has since been superseded by FM 1-02.2, *Military Symbols*. This is the third different publication on symbols I have worked with since I began this project. As is often the case with the scores and scores of armed forces publications, one publication may be absorbed into a new publication to streamline the flow of information. While FM 1-02 and ADP 1-02 can still be easily found online, all official Army sites only provide a pdf of FM 1-02.2. Therefore, I include the reference and link to FM 1-02.2.

12
SELF-SPONSORED WRITING AND A PRESIDENTIAL ELECTION

In 2007, Barack Obama defeated John McCain, and the United States welcomed its first African American president roughly one 142 years after Abraham Lincoln stubbornly and rightly pushed through the Thirteenth Amendment, fifty-three years after the Supreme Court rightly and unanimously ruled in *Brown v. Board of Education*, and forty-three years after Lyndon Johnson rightly signed the Civil Rights Act.

The power in Washington swung from the Republicans under George W. Bush to the Democrats under Obama.

Logan was almost twelve years old when Obama placed his right hand on the Bible and recited the Oath given by Chief Justice John Roberts. Logan reached maturity under an Obama presidency. He enrolled at UNG and signed paperwork to commission into the Army under an Obama presidency.

Upon graduation, Logan will have a new boss: Donald Trump.

November 8, 2016, was shocking. Just a day earlier, Real Clear Politics aggregated data that showed seventy out of seventy-five polls predicted a Hillary Clinton win. Nate Silver gained popularity for correctly predicting forty-nine out of fifty states in the 2008 presidential election and all fifty states in the 2012 election. Data on his blog, *FiveThirtyEight*, gave Clinton a 71.4 percent chance to win and an 87 percent chance after the third debate.

What *was* to happen doesn't matter. What *did* happen does. Trump won, and on a wet and mild January afternoon, Roberts administered the oath of office to Trump as stipulated in Article II, Section 2, Clause 8 of the US Constitution.

When Logan left UNG and commissioned into the Army, he would enter a different geopolitical situation governed by a very different type of leader. Just as businesses and immigrants were adjusting to a markedly different president, so, too, were the armed forces. Logan trained under one president and would enter the service under another. We had a record of accomplishment for how Obama shaped his foreign policy. We were not fully sure how Trump would, but the call for increased troop levels and the bombastic rhetoric directed toward even the most innocuous of nations (Australia, for example) signaled Logan would enter the service under a decidedly more hawkish president or, at the very least, a more hawkish presidential cabinet.

As the commander of the armed forces, the president of the United States leads our military. Though Congress alone has the power to declare war, a president's fate is often inextricably linked to their handling of foreign (often more than domestic) affairs. George Washington rose to prominence through his role in the US Revolution; Lincoln is remembered for guiding us through the Civil War; Ulysses S. Grant got the White House because of his success as a general during the Civil War; Franklin D. Roosevelt got four terms because of World War II; Dwight Eisenhower got the White House because his success as supreme allied commander during World War II; Johnson, even with signing the Civil Rights Act, is historically packaged with the imbroglio that was Vietnam; and it may be increasingly more challenging to separate both Bush presidencies from Middle East conflict. My history colleagues may cringe over the generalities above, but a president's use of military might crafts his legacy. A president's foreign policy, and how they use or do not use their military powers, affects how the world sees and interacts with the United States. Even though Logan was not yet an officer, a president's decisions trickle down to the Corps, the ROTC, and the curriculum used to guide a person from a civilian to a solider.

Just two years and one month after winning the White House, a young and optimistic Obama stepped up to the mic and delivered his Nobel Prize Lecture in the Oslo City Hall. He was the recipient of the Nobel Peace Prize, just the fourth sitting US president to receive the honor. Foreign-policy analysts point to Obama's speech that December as an early glimpse into his foreign policy. Campaign promises are one thing, but when he was settled in the White House, the realities of ongoing conflict in the Middle East and documented torture practices at Guantanamo Bay rested heavily on the shoulders of the former senator from Illinois as he delivered his talk.

Obama (2009a) began by addressing understandable criticism directed at his winning the award. True, he said, he was a receiving a peace prize while also overseeing a war: "I am the Commander-in-Chief of the military of a nation in the midst of two wars. . . . I'm responsible for the deployment of thousands of young Americans to battle in a distant land. Some will kill, and some will be killed. And so I come here with an acute sense of the costs of armed conflict—filled with difficult questions about the relationship between war and peace, and our effort to replace one with the other."

After musing on the long history humankind has with armed conflict, he offered a "hard truth": "We will not eradicate violent conflict in our lifetime. There will be times when nations . . . will find the use of force not only necessary but morally justified." He continued by offering an openness to the power of nonviolence: "As someone who stands here as a direct consequence of Dr. [Martin Luther] King's life work, I am living testimony to the moral force of non-violence. I know there's nothing weak—nothing passive—nothing naïve—in the creed and lives of Gandhi and King."

Fred Kaplan (2016), writing for *Foreign Affairs*, quotes Benjamin Rhodes, Obama's deputy national security adviser for strategic communications: "When people ask me to summarize [Obama's] foreign policy, I tell them to take a close look at that speech."

Obama approached foreign policy as a realist, maybe even a cynical realist. He believed in the inevitability of conflict. Amid this inevitable conflict, he focused on the possibility and power of nonviolence.

In the summer of 2013, Obama brought his words spoken in Norway to action.

Syria happened.

In the wake of the Arab Spring, protests broke out in Syria, much to the consternation of Syrian President Bashar al-Assad, who responded by killing protestors. Again, the United States found itself cautiously watching an unfolding conflict in the Middle East. Obama publicly warned Assad about using chemical weapons against the protestors. Obama committed to airstrikes if Assad crossed the proverbial red line. At this point, the conflict escalated to a point at which the rhetoric changed. *Protestors* became *rebels*. Obama's warning were met with deaf ears. On August 21, 2013, rocket shells of sarin gas blasted rebel-held territory. Fifteen hundred people died. Both Kaplan (2016), in *Foreign Affairs*, and Jeffrey Goldberg (2016), in the *Atlantic*, provide an in-depth look into this pivotal moment of Obama's presidency, and though it's too early to declare a verdict on how effectively Obama handled Assad's unthinkable actions, we do know Obama did not sign off on US airstrikes against Syria; we do know Assad agreed to turn over his chemical weapons to Russia for destruction; and we do know the tumultuous climate of Syria fostered the development of ISIS, which now uses Syria as a headquarters.

As Goldberg writes, "Obama understands that the decision he made to step back from air strikes, and to allow the violation of a red line he himself had drawn to go unpunished, will be interrogated mercilessly by historians." However, Obama spoke highly of his decision in an interview with Goldberg: "I'm very proud of this moment . . . for me to press the pause button at that moment, I knew, would cost me politically. And the fact that I was able to pull back from the immediate pressures and think through in my own mind what was in America's interest, not only with respect to Syria but also with respect to our democracy, was as tough a decision as I've made—and I believe ultimately, it was the right decision to make" (76).

With a mind trained at Harvard Law School and a commitment to nonviolence, Obama's decision (or nondecision) lines up with his speech in Oslo. Depending on what side of the aisle you find yourself, Obama either backpedaled on his word or flexed the muscles of nonviolence. Obama's pivotal decision during the summer of 2013—and the tremors still felt as a new president entered the Oval Office—may rumble for a long time. Goldberg uses a poker metaphor to draw comparisons between George W. Bush and Obama: "Bush was also a gambler, not a bluffer. He will be remembered harshly for the things he did in the Middle East. Barack Obama is gambling that he will be judged well for the things he didn't do" (90).

Looking over his two terms, Obama preferred drone strikes to deployment of troops. He ordered the strike that killed Osama bin Laden, a venerable boogieman to the American people who eluded the second Bush. He also made great strides in overhauling long-held military social policies. Now, gay and transgender members serve openly, women serve in combat roles (for the first time, two women completed Army Ranger School), and same-sex couples receive military benefits. On January 3, 2017—just days before Trump swore the presidential oath—the Army approved hijabs, turbans, and beards for observant Sikh soldiers. But Obama is also the only president to serve two full terms with troops deployed to combat zones for his entire presidency.

When Obama left the White House, the *Army Times* (Altman and Shane, January 8, 2017) surveyed over sixteen hundred active-duty troops regarding his role as commander in chief. Only 18 percent reported a "very favorable" view of Obama; 29.1 percent held a "very unfavorable" view, 71 percent of respondents said the military needed "more personnel," and 41 percent believed Obama's transgender policies hurt military readiness. These data reported that many active-duty troops were most disappointed in his decision to shrink the military. On the other hand, Trump promised to raise troop levels. His first proposed budget detailed a $54 billion increase in defense spending. His confrontational and bumbling approach to foreign affairs suggested our country might need this additional funding, as he found himself embroiled in conflict instead of engaging in diplomatic talks or leveling sanctions. Regardless of the paths Obama or Trump trod, Logan grew up under one presidential view of the armed forces and would enter the armed forces with a different presidential view.

When we talked in my office a month after the presidential inauguration, I asked Logan how cadets were reacting to the new president:

> I would say most of the commissioning cadets were not satisfied but they were excited—not necessarily about the president-elect—but about his secretary of defense pick [General James Mattis]. Because he was an actual active military-duty person himself. I mean General Mattis is renowned for being, you know, he is a great guy. He didn't play politics and people look him kinda like a man of the people. So that is really where most of the discussion was. They were really, really excited about General Mattis coming in as a secretary of defense.

The "Policy" section of the US Department of Defense Directive 1344.10 "Political Activities by Members of the Armed Forces" (2008), encourages "members of the Armed Forces . . . to carry out the obligations of citizenship." However, the directive adheres to the "traditional concept that members on active duty not engage in partisan political activity." Logan and his fellow cadets were not active-duty members of the armed forces, but the UNG Corps of Cadets encourages their cadets to see themselves as representatives of the uniform, and, as such, follow this DoD Directive. As the presidential election coverage was escalating, and then in the wake of the Trump win, I asked Logan if the Corps instructed the cadets on how approach the election results.

Logan told me, "We had a visiting colonel come by and he told one of our commanders, 'One of the biggest things you need to tell your troops is you need to be apolitical.' He says, 'You need to encourage them to remember that they are representatives of the uniform, whether they are active or not, about not openly endorsing or not endorsing a certain candidate.' But other than that, people didn't really make a big deal out of it. Because it is not as prevalent for us being in college."

I wasn't sure what to make of Logan's last statement: "It is not as prevalent for us being in college." He might be misusing the word *prevalent*, but I try not to be pedantic when interviewing. I asked a follow-up question, trying to gain a richer sense of how cadets felt about the incoming president, a future boss for many of the cadets:

"People talk," Logan says. "A lot of it at this college level is humor based. They like the character of President Trump and think it's, they think it's kinda comical, the way he goes about doing things. And they just love the rhetoric that goes along with it. They just think it is funny, the general disregard for people's feelings. I mean, being the type A personalities we are, it's kinda funny to see people bend out of shape about a few harsh words."

In a sense, Trump's personality revealed through the presidential-election cycle, nomination, and general-election win typified a military personality: brash, bold, driven, full of "harsh words" and a "general disregard for people's feelings," to borrow two phrases from Logan. These elements of Trump's personality resonated with Logan and his fellow cadets. But where Trump as president struggled were areas in which the military excels: collaboration, teamwork, and unity. As Logan mentioned, most of the talk about Trump among the Corps was "humor based." The brash, egotistical Trump was the one that grinned for the cameras; the one who made easy fodder for news headlines. These were the headlines—and soundbites—that reached Logan and his fellow cadets and the ones that also made easy fodder for barracks banter. When I talked with Logan about his future boss, he didn't show any concern about Trump's struggle with establishing partnerships and instilling a teamwork mentality among his administrators—both of which are at the core of what the Corps does.

But I might have been pushing Logan into an area where he was not comfortable, and I might have been reading too much into his words. Logan shrugged off most of my concerns about the new presidential administration. In a sense, he expressed sentiments like Obama's in his Oslo talk: problems will always persist; we just need to keep moving forward. Changes will certainly filter down through the ranks. Trump promised a strong military and that promise, if made manifest, would certainly affect the daily life of Logan as he moved from cadet to second lieutenant in the Army. But Logan tempered his excitement and tempered his prognostications about what might come to pass under a Trump presidency:

> I'm not entirely sure if there is excitement or not because when they do troop-increasing levels, you know with us, we are talking about officer corps, so it is a different selection. We don't necessarily see the change right away. I can tell you if anything there hasn't been really any change yet. I think the changes will come but it will be a little slower on our end. You won't be seeing those kinds of changes right away. But there is definitely an anticipation building. Especially if another large-scale war breaks out, I think we will see a lot of standards for commissioning change and they will approve a lot more waivers and there will be a lot more officers allowed to enter that previously would not have been let in. I think those are the changes we will be seeing.

Logan's words stayed with me after he left my office. They stayed with me as the calendar page turned to the new year, as the winter left and spring came. The northeast Georgia mountains washed in color—the pink of the azaleas, the white of the dogwood, the pale pink of Indian hawthorn, the green of the grass, and, of course, the yellow of the pollen. I was looking over my calendar for another time to sit and talk with Logan when an email came my way. It was from Logan. He wrote,

> Dr. Rifenburg,
>
> It's been a while since we've chatted, but I remember you asking for some samples of writing last time we spoke. As you may remember, I told you I didn't free write much anymore, but recently I've gotten back into it a bit. Attached is a copy of two creative pieces I worked on within the past 3 months. . . . Feel free to ask questions about either, along with critiques. I enjoyed writing them, but creative isn't always my strong suit.
>
> Enjoy,
> Logan Blackwell

He attached two documents to the email. In the portion of Logan's email I redacted, he asked that I keep one of the stories private, the first time he had made such a request during our three years together. I printed the second story, titled "A Faux Pas of the Soul: The Fable of the Gilded Prince." I sent Logan an email back, and we set up a time to talk. I headed outside into the colors of spring to read about three thousand words about a prince and why he is gilded.

Logan divided the story into five chapters with an opening paragraph before chapter 1, which serves as a prologue. This prologue provides the etymology of *faux pas* and a tease for the rest of the narrative: "A faux pas lends itself to the idea of an accident, or a blunder. But for the Gilded Prince, it was much more than that. It was one of the greatest tragedies in his entire being." The narrative follows Timothy Deham, an everyday person with aspirations to live the life of a jet-setting aristocrat. When Timothy moves off to "University," he surrounds himself with lavish clothing, spinning yarns with classmates about his "estate in the rolling hills of the plantation wood." Timothy acquires a benefactor of sorts, a Mrs. Diedre Robinson and dear but subservient friend, Phillip Devreaux, and is seeking romantic female companionship at the close of Logan's unfinished tale. Timothy, the titular Gilded Prince, finds his perfect woman at "the lounge of an upscale dining establishment," but he cannot contact her. The narrative ends with the Prince waiting for "his Daisy" to come back: "So, for the next year, our Prince sat at that same lounge, sipping the same drink, every Friday until she returned."

The story came to Logan "out of thin air." He says, "I kinda got bored one day and had some free time. I recently watched the movie *Café Society*. It was a Woody Allen film. And I was like 'Man, I wish I could tell a story like that.' I've been wanting to really like write something longer for a while. I don't know. I threw on some music and put something together. Some kind of piano jazz stuff, real soft stuff in the background."

He wrote it in the barracks and typed it in 10-point Bookman Old font, fully justified the margins, and adjusted the ruler on Microsoft Word to condense the amount of text that fits onto one page. I typed these words on Microsoft Word. With standard margins and a 12-point font, I fit around sixteen to nineteen words per line. Logan adjusted the layout so he fit around eleven words per line. Logan was mimicking a novel, the look and feel of a professionally published book. His three thousand-word story printed off at ten pages, but the text covered only a quarter of the printed page:

> I've written a lot of stuff over the years, but I feel like I haven't gotten to put significant time into a piece of work before, to really push it out there. I don't know. I just wanted something longer. I was thinking in my head, after reading the books I've read, "How do these authors spend so much time getting all those pages together and writing something that long?" So, I decided to give it a shot.

He wanted to return to the story and see where else he could take it. But he was worried he was borrowing too heavily and too directly from *The Great Gatsby*:

> There is definitely more that could be added to it for sure; it is just whether I want to finish it or not. I go back and forth with it. I reread the chapters a couple of times. The only thing I worried about with it was it being too similar to other works. I didn't really want to be caught plagiarizing or anything. Because it is written in the style of other works I've read. It clearly has references to *The Great Gatsby* and some of those other pieces that I've looked at. And I didn't want to get in trouble, even though it is my own ideas.

Writing fiction, for fun, in the barracks, during the afternoon while listening to jazz and piano stuff on Spotify is a part of who Logan is and how writing is woven through the tapestry of his world. He sees this sort of writing as a necessary counterbalance to the required writing he undertakes for his classes and the Corps:

> Because I am so used to writing school papers and stuff like that, I wanted to branch out and get better at it. Ever since you have known me in your class, you know I like to write stuff that moves and pushes people. I felt

like fiction was one of the few ways to do that. I can only write self-help and tell people to do stuff before they get tired of hearing the same old advice. I think it will be a part of my life [writing fiction], but I'm just not sure where it will fit in yet.

He also believes his continual drive toward self-sponsored writing sets him apart from his fellow cadets. So, too, does his predilection toward ballroom-dance and interest in Italian art, architecture, and Woody Allen films:

> I'm an oddball in the Army. At least here. I got a, I don't want to say a fully romanticist view of life, but I tend to be a little bit more optimistic and a little bit more into the arts than some of my companions. I feel they don't really appreciate literature and stuff the same way I do. They always see it as work. You don't see many guys in uniform writing for pleasure.

Logan, in uniform or out of uniform, in Italy or in the barracks, wrote for pleasure.

As this year and this chapter reached a close, and as we looked toward Logan's final year as a cadet, I was left with a deep impression of Logan as a literate person with a kaleidoscope of interests. On my desk, I was surrounded by his words—written and spoken. I had his blog entries from Italy, his bylaws for his ballroom-dance club, a five-page paper on the United Kingdom's decision to leave the European Union written for an honors section of Political Science, a seven-page paper written in a Business Management class on W. Edwards Deming's fourteen points of quality, and "The Fable of the Gilded Prince." Taken together, these texts formed the activity system in which Logan constructs and reconstructs his literate identity. Throughout the semester, he moved through the spaces in which each of these writing tasks occurred. Some of these tasks overlap with similar cognitive demands. For example, the management paper on Deming and the Political Science paper on Brexit overlap. During our second interview of the semester, I asked Logan how he moved through different classes. To explain my odd question, I took a piece of paper from my yellow legal pad and drew three circles. I wrote "Poli Sci" in one circle and "MILS" and "Advanced Ops" (his management class) in the other two. Pointing to each circle, I asked Logan what goes through his head as he moves from a 2000-level honor Political Science class to a 4000-level management class to a 3000-MILS class. True, literacy development occurs as people move across and through these various communicative spheres. But, as Prior and Shipka (2003) note, the notion of chronotopic lamination attends to the ways "multiple activity footings are simultaneously held and managed" (182). In other words, Logan's writing practices across poli sci, business management, and MILS collectively informed his literacy development, they were laminated, but they were also distinct and demanded that Logan hold these separately in his head and manage them effectively according the dictates of the class syllabi and the instructor's guidance. I asked Logan how he "simultaneously held and managed" these classes:

> I don't necessarily segment them. All three of them have similar elements of, almost, I'm trying to come up with the words for this, all three you just kinda have to go through and figure out. Like Advanced Ops is a highly technical class. We know that. Military Science is a technical class, as well, for the most part. You have sat in class; you know there is tactics involved and methods. And Global Issues is most theoretical. But all three of these classes kinda talk about strategy, which is kinda interesting if you think about it, and a lot of business classes are strategy, as well. So, if there was a common link, that is kinda really how I put it into perspective. Every single class I take is a strategic approach to some kind of area of study. That's the only common link I can find between all of them. Because they are all very different in their own way. But they have that same element involved. It's not something I've had a crisis about. I just know I go to class; I take the test, make the grade, and move on.

He moves on, yes. But he keeps bringing himself back to writing, just as Kathleen Blake Yancey (2008) describes, through broad historical examples, how people return again and again to writing to make sense of the world.

In her National Council of Teachers of English keynote address, Yancey (2008) takes her audience through a brief history of people's habitual drive toward self-sponsored writing, despite and maybe because of, extenuating outside circumstances. In other words, as Yancey notes, even though paper was expensive and ink was messy, people wrote; even though military personnel were deployed and found themselves in the squalor of trenches, people wrote. The reoccurring thread woven through her powerful and oft-cited address is, "And still, *outside of school, people composed*" (320; emphasis in original).

I find evidence for Yancey's assertion when I watch my three-year-old daughter, who won a prize at Zoo Atlanta for completing a scavenger hunt. Out of the prize bucket, she didn't pick the neon light-up ring but the notepad of paper. On the way home from the zoo, she fell asleep in her seat, her small right hand clutching her notepad, her small left hand clutching a pencil. Through the night, she held her notepad (my wife and I decided to take the sharp pencil from her when we placed her in her bed). That next morning, she asked for her pencil and began, in her words, "making a list." I don't think my daughter is unique in this regard. We all are born with an innate drive to write, to compose, to create.

I find evidence of Yancey's assertion as I look over Logan's third year at UNG. Even with increasing demands from the cadet world, Logan wrote. Even with increasing academic demands, Logan wrote. He sought out self-sponsored writing when he voluntarily wrote bylaws for the ballroom-dance club he founded and when he volunteered to write documents for his fraternity. When he found free time in the barracks, he put on some jazz and wrote fiction. As our nation transitioned from one president to another, as our new president brought jingoistic rhetoric to the Oval Office and demanded increased defense spending, increased troop levels, as our new president bombed Syria, bombed Afghanistan, flexed his muscles at Australia, Logan wrote.

SECTION 5

Year 4

Rank: Cadet Second Lieutenant

The only thing I worry about, honestly, is if I go into the Chemical Corps, the kind of things I will probably end up seeing at some point when I get deployed. I just don't know what the aftereffects may be after seeing that if it comes to that.
—Logan Blackwell reflecting on the possibility of deploying

13
FINDING 4
The Military Decision-Making Process

Data collected from this academic year led me to argue my fourth finding in response to this book's overarching research question. This year, he gained knowledge of the military decision-making process (MDMP), a specific critical-thinking heuristic. Then he received word he would be slotted for active duty and assigned to the Chemical Corps branch of the Army. This branch assignment told Logan *how* he would apply the MDMP to guide writing as an Army officer. If the third year was about the OPORD template, then the fourth and final year was about the MDMP.

Sitting in MILS 4000, Logan spent sixteen days learning the MDMP, roughly half the semester dedicated to learning what FM 5-0 (US Army 2022) describes as an "iterative planning methodology to understand the situation and mission, develop a course of action, and produce an operation plan or order" (5-1). The MDMP is the collectively agreed upon heuristic for preparing an action at the platoon level or above. Embedded within the MDMP is an understanding of what Army writing is and what it seeks to accomplish. These understandings were internalized by Logan, particularly during his first two years as a cadet when he learned what Army writing is and is not. The specific activities one undertakes when moving through the steps in the MDMP include war gaming, which makes use of terrain models and the maps and templates found in Logan's little field book; during his third year, Logan gained proficiency in war gaming with the terrain model and with offloading challenging cognitive tasks to these external tools. Taken together, the MDMP draws on the cognitive and physical activities of writing that constituted the first three years of Logan's cadet experience. But the MDMP is empty without specifics. A heuristic is a heuristic of something. Logan gained this specificity when he learned he would be slotted active duty and branch Chemical Corps.

With his branch assigned, Logan could approach the MDMP with this lens. The first step, receipt of mission, would be a defensive chemical mission. Maybe ensuring the territory the infantry or artillery soldiers will soon enter is not contaminated by radiological waste. Maybe ensuring the tools and people arriving to check contamination levels are arriving on time and at the same time. Because he received—before he even graduated—his job description, he could begin molding the MDMP to the specifics his job would entail. The Army ROTC program is designed so cadets receive detailed training on the MDMP process during the same semester they begin receiving specifics on their future assignments following graduation. They are taught *how* to think and then given details on *where* they will think. Logan received instruction on how to think through sixteen days on the MDMP. He then learned that he would apply this thinking to the Chemical Corps during a Basic Officer Leader Course at Fort Leonard Wood and at his first duty post at Fort Stewart.

14
THE MDMP AS A CRITICAL-THINKING HEURISTIC

Logan's final semester began in the dusk of a total solar eclipse, the first in ninety-nine years. On August 21, the moon completely covered the sun, and for a few brief moments, in the middle of the afternoon, the day went dim. With my children and wife, I watched from my driveway. The automatic streetlights turned on; crickets and frogs sounded a greeting to what they mistakenly believed to be the coming night. Astronomers hyped the "path of totality," areas of the United States where people could see the moon cover the sun and cast the globe into darkness until the paths of the two heavenly orbs disentangled moments later. This path of totality ran coast to coast across the United States, with portions of the path landing just a few miles north of UNG.

August 21 was also the first day of fall classes. The provost initially cancelled classes. Then he retracted and delayed classes until 4:00 p.m. The Office of University Relations sent an email with the subject line "Eclipse safety information," reminding readers to only purchase "ISO 12312-2 certified" safety glasses. Ineffective eclipse glasses flooded the market. I emailed my astronomy buddy to verify the pairs I bought for my family at Ace Hardware. The eclipse came, and we were captivated. Then, like Christmas trees the day after Christmas, discarded eclipse glasses littered the campus the following day when classes began, and astronomers turned their eyes at once upwards to the sky and downwards to their formulas to prepare for the next celestial phenomenon.

Logan started his final fall semester as a cadet with twenty-six credit hours left to complete before graduating and commissioning. Over the summer, he completed the ROTC-required Advanced Camp at Fort Knox. Day 0 of a thirty-one-day immersive training and leadership experience at United States Army Cadet Command (USACC) Advanced Camp began with in-processing: checking in, finding one's barracks, getting settled. Days 1 to 31 were filled with soldiering: land navigating, seven-foot rappelling, twelve-mile road marching, cultural-awareness training, drug testing. Graduation landed on day 31, a morning ceremony complete with marching.

The USACC (2021) website provides the mission of Advanced Camp. At the top of the site, we read "The mission of the Advanced Camp is to train U.S. Army ROTC cadets to Army standards and to develop leadership and evaluate officer potential. This is accomplished through a tiered training structure using light infantry tactics as the instructional medium." A mission driven by the measurable verb *train* and followed with a clear description of how this training will be facilitated. All cadets with hopes of commissioning must complete Advanced Camp. A cadet's performance here is a key data point in the all-important Order of Merit List (OML).

During the thirty-two days, Logan "wrote to [his] girlfriend a lot" and spent "twenty nights out in the woods [and the] other ten [nights] out in the building." He told me it was a "rough time. I lost about 10 to 12 pounds from being out there."

When he returned to UNG, he registered for 13 hours:

- BUSA 4527: International Business (3 credit hours)
- MGMT 4669: Organizational Behavior (3 credit hours)
- MILS 4000: The Army Officer (3 credit hours)
- MILS 4005: Physical Readiness Leadership and Exercise (1 credit hour)
- MKTG 2005: Consumer Behavior (3 credit hours)

When Logan and I found time to talk, a late October afternoon when the thick summer air finally gave way to a cool autumnal breeze, he was waiting on the last piece of his Army future to fall into place. Logan entered UNG with a goal of graduating and commissioning. He signed a contract with the Army to that effect at the beginning of his college career. But he worked and studied and trained and waited without more specifics than that. Still to be decided? His duty slot: active duty, reserves, or national guard. Still to be decided? His specific job, what the Army calls a *branch*, of which there are seventeen, such as infantry, chemical, aviation, field artillery. Still to be decided? Where he would be stationed. But as the months fell off the calendar, Logan learned more and more about how he would fit into the world of roughly seventy-eight thousand officers in the Army.

When we talked in October, Logan had received word that he was slotted for active duty—not a given for any cadet but a high probability for cadets like Logan with strong grades and strong performance in various camps and Army schools. The Army, as one would expect, has a formalized and structured process by which the senior cadets are placed into duty slots and branches: *accessions*. In Logan's words, accessions are "what they name the process for us, getting put into the system, getting points, getting ranked, and figuring out our components and branches." Not all senior cadets go through accessions; federal service academy cadets, like the cadets at West Point, do not. Nor do the cadets who do not plan on commissioning. Simple math: out of thirty-thousand total senior cadets, four thousand attend West Point and twenty thousand do not commission, which leaves six thousand senior cadets who will move through accessions and shore up the supporting-officer roster of the Army. The OML model guides accessions. According to USACC Circular 601-19-1 (US Army 2018):

   a. The purpose of the OML Model is to provide an objective, consistent process that enables Cadets/commissionees to better equate specific performance measures with their OML standing. The OML Model calculates an Outcome Metrics Score (OMS) for each Cadet/commissionee.

   b. The OMS is computed based on performance in three main categories: Academic Outcomes (both general studies and Military Science), Leadership Outcomes, and Physical Outcomes that generate a merit-based ranking (highest to lowest) of the Cadets to be used in determining Component Selection and Branching. (33)

The circular then provides percentages for these three categories based on the FY18 model: academic outcomes (40 percent); leadership outcomes (45 percent); physical outcomes (15 percent). Each category comes with additional explanation for what counts in that category. While the circular provides guidance and insight into the accessions process, specifics are still vague and the OML model changes slightly each year to keep cadets from gaming the system. Logan went through accessions under the FY17 model, which offered slightly different percentages but still provided the general emphasis on academics, leadership, and fitness. Logan told me, "Rumors of what scores higher and what doesn't score as high . . . it changes every year." As he talked through this ever-changing OML, I thought back to our conversation two years ago when he decided to join a fraternity because, so the rumors at the time went, such a move would score high on the OML. Logan then described one specific change to the OML: "The fitness scores, for example, have decreased over the past years because they are more concerned with what is up here [points to head] because the Army is having issues with people [not] having critical-thinking skills and things like that." Ultimately, according to Logan, the whole OML and weighted percentages were "a guessing game" for cadets. He continued, "GPA, fitness score, extracurricular activities, I don't know if they took it out of accessions, but they call it 'Command Interest Items,' so oral and written publications—the number of times we have been published in the newspaper or magazine." Logan did well in this category: "I maxed out on that category when they had it in there. And you can get points for this logic and reasoning test we take over the summer; it is called the CLA+. I got a pretty good score on that. That gave me 3.5 extra points. I think I had 70 total points." He received five points for completing airborne school and received high marks for his performance at Advanced Camp.

The national OML model for all senior cadets planning to commission is an aggregation of local OMLs. UNG's ROTC compiles its own data, which feeds into the national OML. Logan explained the process of sitting with a staff member and plugging in data about his academics, leadership, and fitness: "We go in and tell the HR lady who does all our paperwork. We go in and tell her, 'Hey, I had so many journal articles that I wrote and got published' or 'so many debates or public-speaking opportunities.' And she just plugs them in and take us for our word. For the most part. But I had to provide evidence for the written things."

Logan received Distinguished Military Graduate (DMG) because he landed in the top 20 percent of all gradating cadets on the OML. He then received word that he got slotted for active duty: "No guard or reserve for me," he told me with a smile. But he downplayed his slot: "At this school, it is not as big of an issue cause the PMS [Professor of Military Science] can put anybody on active duty that he wants. There were only one or two people who got reserve components who requested active. But they were not just very good people."

He knew he would be active duty; he knew he would graduate and commission in May. He was still waiting on branch and first duty station. That information would come in mid-November. Logan, though his future was coming into shape, needed to finish his courses. In MILS 4000, he would work through the MDMP for two weeks. The MDMP forms the foundation of Army critical thinking, which, in turn, forms the foundation of the Army writing standard. Though he was months from leading a platoon as a second lieutenant, that semester Logan would learn how to think through a doctrinally defined heuristic.

MILS 4000: MISSION COMMAND AND THE ARMY PROFESSION

The fall-semester syllabus for MILS 4000 includes a two-paragraph description; MS III refers to cadets with credit hours equal to the class rank of junior, MS IV for cadets with the class rank of senior. The first paragraph of the course description reads as follows,

The MILS 4000 course transitions the focus of student learning from being trained, mentored and evaluated as an MS III Cadet, to learning how to train, mentor and evaluate underclass Cadets. MS IV Cadets will learn the duties and responsibilities of an Army Officer and apply Mission Command, Training Management, Composition Risk Management and the Military Decision Making Process (MDMP) in order to plan, prepare, execute and assess training events.

The second paragraph of the course description includes additional specifics on course content. Worth noting in the paragraph above is the emphasis on the verb *apply*. MS III cadets operate in the passive position at the beginning of the course description; they are *being* trained, they are *being* mentored, they are *being* evaluated. The subject in the sentence is hiding because MS III cadets receive instruction from various points. Then MILS 4000 shifts the sentence structure so MS IV cadets are the subject of the sentence. The action they accomplish is high-level cognitive action: applying ideas "in order to plan, prepare, execute and assess training events."

Following the course description, the syllabus offers a course objective: "The overall purpose of this course is to provide guidance and opportunities in planning, analyzing, evaluating and leading operations." Though my colleagues with expertise in curriculum and course design may cringe at such a vague objective (How does one assess "provide guidance and opportunities"? And isn't this objective really about what the instructor will do and not the student?), I appreciate the move toward creating opportunities in which cadets will gain authority and autonomy in direct preparation for their future job as an Army officer.

The syllabus continues with traditional course policy on office hours and attendance and the like. Cadets learn how they will be graded and find that 20 percent of their final grade hinges on a "Decision Briefing," which, according to page 3 of the syllabus, is where "Cadets will use the Military Decision Making Process to deliver a decision briefing to MS IV Instructors." The syllabus concludes on page 4 with a "Course Agenda" in which cadets find the class will spend sixteen days on learning about MDMP, working in groups on their decision briefs, and then delivering their decision briefs.

According to FM 5-0, *Planning and Orders Production* (US Army 2022), the MDMP process is an "iterative planning methodology" (5-1). Through applying the MDMP, leaders arrive at decisions through "thoroughness, clarity, sound judgment, logic, and professional knowledge" (1-9). Seven steps guide the MDMP, with each step leading directly to the next.

FM 5-0 dedicates an entire chapter to the MDMP. In brief, the seven steps are

1. Receipt of mission.
2. Mission analysis.
3. COA [course of action] development.
4. COA analysis.
5. COA comparison.
6. COA approval.
7. Orders production, dissemination, and transition. (5-1)

In the subsections below, I walk through these steps. I highlight the role of writing and oral delivery and weave in Logan's narrative description. While the MDMP is covered in multiple Army and joint forces publications, all quotes below are from the most recent edition of FM 5-0. When I began this study, the Army worked with a 2005 version of FM 5-0; during final edits to this manuscript, the Army updated FM 5-0. I quote from this May 2022 version. Finally, as FM 5-0 specifies, one step often leads seamlessly into another step so that it may be unclear where one step ends and another begins—such is the case when developing a heuristic for cognitive activity.

Receipt of Mission

The process begins with "receipt of a mission from higher echelon headquarters or in anticipation of a new mission" (5-14). To prepare for mission analysis, the staff gathers the necessary tools for developing COAs and deciding on a specific COA. These tools include maps of the area of operation (AO), appropriate field manuals, and other required materials and products. Staff also develop a generic planning timeline, allocating percentages to each step of the MDMP. The last task in this step is to issue a warning order (WARNO), a common Army genre in which subordinates and supporting units receive a brief overview of the anticipated type of operation and supporting details, such as the general location of the operation and movements to initiate.

Mission Analysis

Of the seven steps covered in the MDMP, FM 5-0 devotes the most length to mission analysis. This step consists of three tasks (key inputs, sub-steps, and key outputs) that collectively help commander and staff arrive at the purpose of mission analysis: "understand the situation, problem, and mission" (5-29). Logan also spoke of the importance of this step for helping him better understand the problem he was faced with: "The funny thing about MDMP is that they always taught us during this mission analysis you will sometimes find that what you thought was the problem to start with actually isn't the problem. And you have to refine it." Because mission analysis often leads to reseeing the initial problem or objective, one of the final tasks is writing a restated mission. FM 5-0 specifies that "a mission statement is a short sentence or paragraph describing the organization's essential task(s), purpose, and action containing the elements of who, what, when, where, and why" (5-71). Five elements constitute a mission statement:

- Who will execute the operation (unit ororganization)?
- What is the unit's essential task (tactical mission task)?
- When will the operation begin (by time or event) or what is the duration of the operation?
- Where will the operation occur (AO, objective, or grid coordinates)?
- Why will the force conduct the operations (for what purpose)? (5-71)

A mission statement is condensed into abbreviations and, ideally, a single sentence for ease of recall and transmission. Below is an example mission statement taken from FM 5-0 in section 5-71. The parenthetical, bolded text appears in the original and is used for Army educational purposes. During a tactical exercise, the bolded content is removed:

> Not later than 220400 August 19 (**when**) 1st Brigade (**Who**) secures ROUTE SOUTH DAKOTA (**what or task**) in AO JACKRABBIT (**where**) to enable the movement of humanitarian assistance materials (**why or purpose**).

The mission statement begins with due date, not later than, and then offers the day, time, month, and year: the 22nd at 4:00 a.m. on August 2019 day of the month: the third of July. The "1100Z" specifies the time in a twenty-four hour clock in Zulu time, which is a universal time zone. Finally, after "JUL," the 03 specifies the year, 2003. All together the action calls for something to happen no later than July 3, 2003, at 1100 hours Zulu time. "1st Bde" is first 1st Brigade is directed by the measureable verb "secures" and is directed what to secure and for what purpose: secure and area of operation to help humanitarian aid move to its destination. These are the five elements of a mission statement in one sentence.

The mission analysis is briefed to subordinate commanders attending in person or via video teleconference; the mission is approved; a new WARNO is written and delivered.

COA Development

Missing from the succinct mission statement in the example above is a clear *how*. How will this armored division support this infantry division? Staff develop multiple COAs to achieve the unit's mission. The COA "includes the tasks to be performed and the conditions to be achieved" (5-92). These COAs consider five screening criteria: is the mission feasible, acceptable, suitable, distinguishable, and able to be completed. COAs are captured in sketches. These course of action sketches are one-page documents in landscape design with two columns outlining all key details of a COA.

In an ideal situation, staff have time to develop several possible course of action sketches. Like the previous step, this step in the MDMP leads directly to briefing the commander. Staff brief the commander course of action sketches. Staff members then begin COA analysis if the commander approves one or more COAs.

COA Analysis

During COA analysis, staff war game. FM 5-0 describes war gaming as "rules and steps that attempt to visualize the flow of an operation" (5-138). War gaming is often a "manual method, often using a tabletop approach with blowups of matrices and templates . . . the most sophisticated form of COA analysis (or war gaming) is computer-aided modeling and simulation" (5-138). Logan described this computer-aided modeling and simulation from his experience:

> The way we learned with was with a deckmat program. It is some kind of statistical software that puts weights to different evaluation criteria. It plays out different scenarios where you change the weights of each and get values for each course of action. And you get like "this course of action is advisable because it scores high on feasibility and high on this, but it is bad on cost effectiveness." It is just doing trials with different weights and just figuring out what is going to give you the most effective decision.

Through war gaming possible COAs, staff provide commanders with more effective information.

COA Comparison

Based on war gaming outcomes, the staff decides on which COA, or COAs, to recommend to the commander.

COA Approval

In a decision briefing, the staff recommends a COA. However, a commander may nix all COAs. Logan said,

> You can make this decision based off these numbers [from war gaming] but ultimately in step 6 [COA approval], going back to the commander, he can look at your numbers and just say "we are not going to do that." Just because he can, but that is the job of a good S-3 [officer rank position who coordinates training and operations] and XOs [executive officers]. They can convince the commander and say look at my numbers; this is going to work.

The commander then approves a COA.

Orders Production, Dissemination, and Transition

In the final step of the MDMP, "The staff turns the selected COA into a clear, concise order with the required supporting information" (5-203). These orders are briefed to subordinates "in person or by other means including radio, telephone, or video teleconference" (5-209).

In sum, the MDMP is doctrinal planning process that helps "Commanders with an assigned staff . . . organize and conduct their planning activities" (5-1). Woven throughout this heuristic are key moments when staff author text, deliver oral text, circulate text up and down the chain of command, and revise text based on statistical analysis, ever-shifting human situations, and unfolding events in the capricious world of war. The MDMP is a way to think, a way to arrive at communally driven action toward a communally agreed-upon objective with communally agreed-upon tools. Inside the MLC on the eastern edge of the UNG Dahlonega campus, Logan and roughly two hundred additional senior cadets were under the tutelage of military-science instructors, all male, who bring with them a wealth of combat experience. Now as MS IV cadets, they are learning how to think, to transfer this thinking into text, and to transfer this text into leading a platoon.

*

Logan's MILS instructors spend two class periods working through the MDMP with MS IV cadets. Then the cadets have their knowledge of the MDMP tested through receiving a group scenario and briefing the MILS instructors on a proposed COA for the scenario. Logan described the scenario to me: "The problem was [what is] the most effective way to prepare entering MS IIIs for precamp." Precamp is a training program organized by UNG ROTC instructors to prepare junior cadets for Advanced Camp held annually at Fort Knox (see fig. 14.1). Cadets who

Figure 14.1. UNG cadet Joshua Lasley writing during precamp. Image by UNG's University Relations. Used with permission.

plan on commissioning or are scheduled to commission must complete Advanced Camp. Not all ROTC programs offer such a preparatory course. The problem that formed Logan's scenario, then, was driven by current ROTC exigencies.

As Logan told me, "All the precampers this year were having lots of trouble keeping up. Their PT [physical training] scores were not very good. They were not in very good shape." In groups, cadets developed possible COAs. "So, we war gamed and selected evaluation criteria and matched each course of action." Following the MDMP steps, the groups delivered "a brief on what we thought would be the best way to do it. Gave the brief to the whole class." Logan didn't remember what his group recommended, but he described the general thrust: "The main thing we came up with was figuring out a way to get them in better shape as MS I and II before they get to their third year." Nor did Logan remember the feedback his group received, if any. But sitting in my office a few weeks removed from the two-week immersion into the MDMP, he could rattle off the steps, with particular attention to war gaming and considering possible COAs based on war gaming outcomes. What he remembered opposed to what he did not struck me as more helpful for down the road when he would face a platoon of roughly twenty soldiers now under his leadership.

With the midpoint of the semester behind him, Logan reflected aloud in my office about his personal life and his extracurricular activities. During his sophomore year, he found himself engaged in a variety of extracurricular activities. Some activities he chose because he believed they would enhance his OML rank; some he chose from pure interest. He joined the honors program, step-dance club, and a fraternity. He founded the ballroom-dance club and wrote for *Odyssey* and for himself and found his work published in UNG's literary magazine. With graduation looming, he had dropped many of these activities. He still danced (ballroom and step) but "ended up cutting out" of the honors program because, for one, he "got behind on the thesis [requirement]." He went inactive in his fraternity and dropped *Odyssey* though he still wrote fiction for fun. He started a job with public safety in which he drove around in a golf cart in the evenings—"rove around, just make sure everything is A-OK and campus stays safe." He also developed a romance with a woman. Their relationship progressed to the point at which Logan was rethinking a full career in the Army, which would require deployments and relocations, all of which is straining for a marriage, and, if the time comes, kids. He told me, "There has been a lot of changes in my life that makes me want to stay in just for a few years. I am realizing it is not going to be great for family life." His girlfriend was training to be a dental hygienist, and he wanted her to continue pursuing her career.

As we wrapped up our conversation, I asked about the Trump administration's impact on the armed forces. I was talking with Logan in October 2017, roughly a year removed from Trump's shocking presidential election. The year before, weeks after Trump's election, Logan laughed off Trump's braggadocio. He laughed at Trump's unfiltered comments and was pleased by Trump's appointment of James Mattis, a retired Marine general, to the position of secretary of defense. I asked Logan again about his thoughts on Trump's push to increase military spending, push to increase troop levels, push back to conventional force-on-force warfare with near peer adversaries. He told me,

> People [in the Army] still love Mattis and they love that intimidation, and they can see a change in the military recruiting. We are toughing up again because we have to fight the big boys again. Conventional warfare is definitely a concern cause the past ten years we were concerned with asymmetric Iraq/Afghanistan conflicts where you didn't know your enemy, so there was a lot of winning hearts and minds going on. Now, we are going back to the way we fought in the [19]80s. With force-on-force uniform conflict, there is a clearly defined bad guy. And we are really trying to focus on getting back to that level.

I asked him about his thoughts on John Kelly, who, like Mattis, was a retired Marine general serving, at the time of my interview with Logan, as Trump's chief of staff. To my surprise, Logan didn't know who Kelly was. I shifted the conversation a bit and asked a more personal question: Do you think you are now more likely to be deployed because Trump is president? Does that make you nervous?

> Not particularly. It doesn't really bother me just because I was in regardless. And things are going to happen. Especially in the fields [branches of the Army] I have picked, I am not as concerned. For some of those combat arms guys, I would be more concerned. The only thing I worry about, honestly, is if I go into the Chemical Corps, the kind of things I will probably end up seeing at some point when I get deployed. I just don't know what the aftereffects may be after seeing that if it comes to that.

I asked a personal question that I knew, if Logan were to entertain it, might carry some heavy outcomes. And it did: *the kind of things I will probably end up seeing; I just don't know what the aftereffects may be.* These heavy and honest comments lingered in the air as I wondered where to go next in our conversation. What could I, a civilian professor, say in response? What could I, a person sitting across from another person, say in response? I failed to gather anything resembling an appropriate response. I asked if he had seen the television show *M*A*S*H*, a darkly comedic portrayal of the US involvement in the Korean War. The highly acclaimed sitcom captured antiwar sentiment that swept the United States following the Vietnam disaster. He hadn't, and I tried to salvage the interview with small talk before we concluded.

Outside my office window, I saw my colleague start her green Kia Soul. The car's exhaust jumped into the cool afternoon wind, rose, and faded. Logan's comments about what he might see in combat and what he might carry with him after combat hung with me.

I sighed.

*

It's early December. Three days before the end of the semester. Outside, the sun still shines warmly and students shuttling between classes still stubbornly cling to their shorts and t-shirts. I'm back in the MLC observing MILS 4000. I'm the only civilian in a sea of OCPs. With my jeans and beard, I stand out in the back row. From my position, I see Logan walk in and take a seat near the front. His eyes don't meet mine. One cadet takes out an unopened box of Chips Ahoy! cookies, cracks them open, eats two. Little small talk. Most cadets are lost in Instagram.

All cadets in this class are platoon cadet leaders, responsible for leading twenty-five to thirty cadets. Platoon sizes are smaller in ROTC. Once these cadets commission, they will lead a platoon of roughly forty soldiers. The cadets sit behind long white tables: four tables on the right of the room, four tables on the left of the room, with a pathway down the center the instructor uses as he talks through the material.

The time is 1000 hours. Class begins. No words of welcome from the instructor, Major Williams (a pseudonym). With an Excel spreadsheet displayed on the screen, Williams runs through the roll shouting out last names, a cup of cream-colored coffee off to his side. Like other Army spreadsheets I have seen, this one is a dizzying combination of acronyms, names, numbers, and colors. September items are in green; October in orange; November in blue; December in lavender. Attendance completed, Williams toggles to the PowerPoint content for today. The top of the slide reads, "MILS 401 Lesson 33; Awards. Army ROTC." The indicator on the PowerPoint is a generic tag for all Army Cadet Command slides. Below this title is an image of a ribbon rack: seventeen Army ribbons arranged in a square of sixteen with one on the top. Williams stresses the importance of understanding what these different ribbons reference, how and why they are awarded, and how officers recommend a soldier for a ribbon. He ends this brief overview of class by pointing cadets' attention to the Army regulation governing the class content for the day: AR 600-8-22, *Army Awards* (US Army 2019b), which stipulates all aspects of the awarding process.

The class flows freely from there, with Williams asking open-ended questions about the various ribbons. Cadets offer answers that range from confident to silly. Laughter breaks out at various points, with Williams joining. The semester is reaching a close. Many of these cadets will graduate soon, and the atmosphere is relaxed. Williams points out the Good Conduct Medal ribbon, National Defense Service Medal ribbon, Army Achievement Medal, Army Commendation Medal, Mandatory Service Medal, and Bronze Star. He talks of the difference between medals and awards and then brings up a new slide that shows two quotes from Napoleon: "Give me enough medals and I'll win you any war"; "A solider will fight long and hard for a bit of coloured ribbon." Williams asks for responses to these words spoken by a military genius but a military genius who, at least according to words attributed to Napoleon, viewed his soldiers as disposable assets. At the height of his powers, he declared to the Austrian diplomat and statesman Klemens von Metternich, "You cannot stop me. I can spend 30,000 men a month."

Williams wants the class to think aloud about the larger role of awards in motivating soldiers. This is the second time I have observed one of

Williams's classes, and he pushes cadets to think critically about the material. He doesn't endorse a position—regardless of whether they are talking about how medals are awarded (as in this class) or the best plan for securing an HVT (as he did in the previous class I observed). As Logan stressed during one of our many interviews, the Army is putting more energy into developing critical-thinking skills in their officers. The Army publications I read through emphasize critical thinking, even creativity and imagination.

Several cadets venture opinions on Napoleon's statement. Williams doesn't offer a definitive stance. He talks of the importance of being awarded for a job well done. He talks of how some Army awards are diluted, given too freely and too often. The discussion quickly turns to rhetoric: how to read the ribbons worn by a soldier. Ribbons are visual markers of where someone has been, what someone has accomplished. Ribbons are visual representations of someone's resumé or CV.

At this point, the curriculum calls for a take-home quiz. Williams elects to work through the quiz in class, aloud. Questions and statements pepper the screen.

- Which of the following is not one of the categories of individual awards?
- Place a number next to the listed US Army decorations to indicate the order of precedence from highest to lowest.
- Which of the following military decorations is only awarded during war time and can be awarded to US Military and Foreign Military but not civilians?
- What is the lowest ranking officer that may approve an Army Achievement Medal during peacetime criteria?

The class responds with mixed results, but Williams shrugs off their minimal knowledge of ribbons. With a few days left in the semester, with a few months until graduation for the cadets in the room, more pressing concerns are at the forefront of their minds. A few weeks earlier, commissioning cadets received their branch and their first duty post. Logan will branch Chemical Corps and attend Basic Officer Leader Course (BOLC) to receive seventeen weeks of training in his branch and training to lead a platoon of soldiers. For BOLC, he is off to a fort in the middle of the United States.

All commissioned officers, once they receive their specific branch assignments, head off to BOLC. For Logan, the Chemical Corps requires seventeen weeks at an Army fort where the Chemical Corps is garrisoned. During BOLC, according to Logan, "They teach you everything you need." After completing BOLC, Logan will head to his duty base. But, in Logan's words, his early trajectory in the Army will be a little more complicated than the tidy sentences I have laid out. His branch detail is chemical, but he will be in the Signal Corps. Logan does his best to explain this odd placement to me during one of our final interviews in late March. He starts with a lament:

> Naturally, because it was me, it was complicated. I am Signal Corps, branch detail chem. So, what that means is that for the first few years of my military career, I'm going to be in the Chemical Corps. They put in the prep work for any chemical, biological, radiological, nuclear, environmental threat. They are the gas-mask people. So, I am getting borrowed by them for a few years. Once I get ready to go to the advanced course, which is how you learn to be a captain and company commander, I will switch branches to the Signal Corps, which focuses on communications. So, my base branch, what I am really supposed to be in and what I will be for the rest of my career as I see fit, is signal, but chemical gets to use me for a little bit because they need lots of lieutenants.

The Chemical Corps defends against chemical, biological, radiological, and nuclear (CBRN) weapons. The verb *defends* is key to the previous sentence, as the United States does not officially engage with chemical weapons on the offensive—though readers may wonder about the Army's Operation Ranch Hand during the Vietnam War when the Army sprayed herbicides and defoliants like Agent Orange across the jungles of Vietnam. These chemicals were designed to destroy flora and fauna—revealing the enemy hidden in the environs—and not harm people; however, we now know of the devastating effects chemicals like Agent Orange have had on civilians and soldiers. From the gas attacks on the western front during World War I to Syria's President Bashar al-Assad gassing his own people in 2013, recent geopolitical history displays devilishly dangerous chemical use. The Geneva Protocol, signed by nations following the barbaric gas attacks in World War I, forbids the offensive use of chemicals. But belligerent enemy forces may not adhere to such a policy. The Chemical Corps, which began as the US Chemical Warfare Service during World War I and then adopted its current name in 1946, is the US military response to such a possibility.

Logan is a business management major, not a chemistry major. I asked him if the Army is concerned about his lack of basic chemistry knowledge. His academic transcript shows he never took a college-level chemistry class. The last science class he took was the first semester of his first year: an environmental science class. "They don't really care," he tells me. "They teach you everything you need to know."

He does not anticipate actively engaging with chemical decontamination or detection as a chemical officer. Instead, he anticipates paperwork more than field work. As he tells me, "I mean as officers, that is what we are supposed to do. Most of the word is *office*." I chuckle at his wordplay. He anticipates being linked with a combat-arms unit:

> Every combat-arms unit—so infantry, armor, field artillery, those kind of guys—every infantry battalion they need at least one chemical officer and one chemical noncommissioned officer. Just because I am chem qualified doesn't mean I will be doing chemical stuff. What happens oftentimes is that I am the chemical officer slash S-3 [staff] assistant. Which means I am going straight to staff to help out the staff officers. So, I can be helping to plan infantry things even though my background in is chemical.

At his duty base, he will learn about decontamination and firefighting. He will learn to detect chemical threats to AOs.

Logan has received his branch and duty post but one more semester awaits him. A final semester. He has enrolled in five classes for the spring semester:

- BUSA 4995: Strategic Management (3 credit hours)
- HIST 2112: US History II (3 credit hours)
- MGMT 4626: Labor Management Relations (3 credit hours)
- MILS 4100: Company Grade Leadership (3 credit hours)
- MILS 4105: Physical Readiness & Exercise Physiology (1 credit hour)

At the close of this semester, Logan will have logged 126 credit hours. He will receive one B in a class and graduate UNG with a 3.8 GPA, a bachelor of business administration, and a major in management.

The Chemical Corps is waiting for him.

15

DRAWING THE SPACES OF WRITING AND THEN GRADUATING

When Logan and I talk in April, just a few weeks from his graduation and commissioning ceremony, he comes with more details about his future work with Chemical Corps. He will be a "tech escort." In this capacity, he will attach himself to "anybody who is going to be going into a chemical environment and [will be] supporting their mission and giving them guidance in dealing with CBRN threats." He knows he will be at BOLC for seventeen weeks. Then he will move to his duty base. But beyond these specifics, his professional future is unclear—such is life with the Army.

But his personal life, he tells me with a rare smile, is coming together. He proposed to his girlfriend over spring break; they plan to sign marriage papers at a local courthouse in September. He shifts excitedly in his chair as we talk about his fiancé. Logan tugs at his OCPs, and I see the three diamonds on the center of his chest, a visual marking of his rank as cadet colonel O-6. It's the highest rank for a cadet.

We wrap up our conversation, our thirteenth audio-recorded conversation. I pull out a sheet of white 8.5 × 11 paper. I push the paper toward Logan and ask if he is up for drawing.

Drawing is an underused but effective tool that can serve learners, research participants, and researchers. Educational psychologist Paul Pintrich (2000) argues that drawing, specifically mapping exercises, provides learners with a helpful metacognitive frame because learners can visualize their thoughts.[1] RC/WS researchers also use drawing to help research participants think through local writing and processes of writing. For example, Prior and Shipka (2003) asked their research participants to "draw two pictures of their processes for [a] specific research project" (182). The first drawing task asked participants to draw their writing space; the second task asked participants to draw their writing processes. Prior and Shipka offer a two-pronged argument for this unique data-collection method: "The drawing . . . is for us a means to another end—a thick description of literate activity. The combination

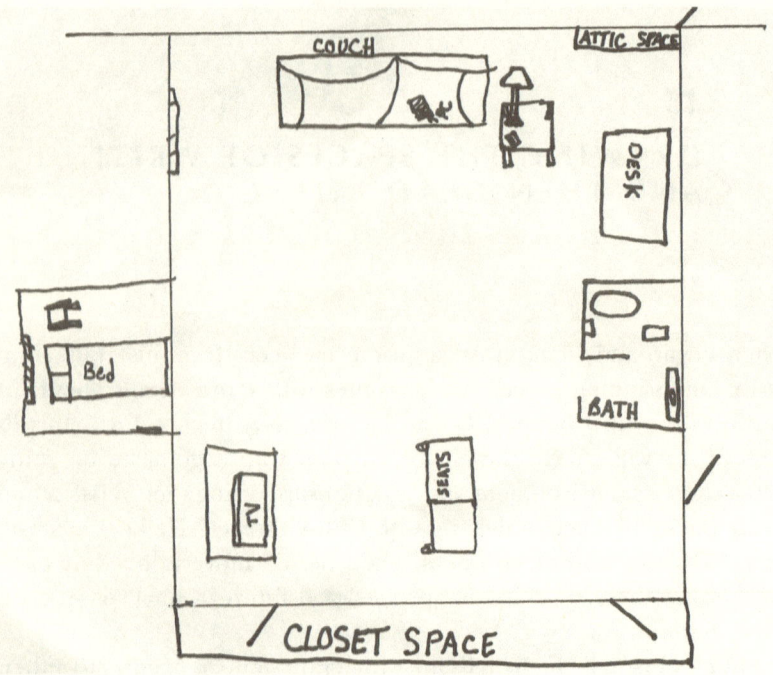

Figure 15.1. Logan's hand-drawn depiction of his writing space.

of texts, talk, and drawings, of participants' accounts and our perceptions, supports a triangulated analysis of these writing processes" (185). Motivated by Prior and Shipka's argument that drawing illustrates a "thick description of literate activity," and motivated by Rule's (2018) work on the importance of space during writing, I ask Logan to draw his preferred writing space. When I slide the paper across to Logan, I explain why I am asking him to draw and what I am asking him to draw. When I start to introduce drawing, I anticipate giving him time and space to draw—maybe slide the drawing under my office door in a week? But Logan jumps into drawing. With a blue pen, he starts. I don't interrupt, and I step out of my office to refill my water bottle.

Logan is particular about his writing space. His ideal writing space, seen in figure 15.1, is his couch in his bedroom in his parent's house in eastern Georgia. In his drawing, he includes his computer, which he labels "PC," on the right sofa cushion. He prefers the couch, which sits next to a lamp. No food or drink appears in Logan's picture. He finds such additions a distraction and tells me, "If I am drinking and eating, I am not writing, and crumbs [get] on the keyboard." He listens to music, which he describes as "jazz and stuff," when writing "something poetic or really like creative or something." He is an evening writer: "8 to 9 p.m. Best work comes out."

Based on my observations of writing at multiple Army forts, I know the Army doesn't strive to create whatever space an individual might find most conductive to crafting effective prose. Army offices are sparse, with few additions provided for whichever individual calls the office home for whatever brief period. When I observed the writing practices of an Army major based in Fort Wainwright, the only personal details in the private office were an iPhone charger and water bottle. I wonder how Logan who, like me and like many writers, is particular about the when and where and tools of writing, may transition to a depersonalized Army office environment. Army officers can't stroll down to the local coffee shop at a time of their choosing, log in, and knock out work-related emails and memos.

After Logan hands his drawing back to me and describes the space, our talk turns to my concern. Logan shrugs it off:

> I have written stuff before in a sleeping bag in the middle of the woods. Because there is not a lot of pressure for the types of writing I am doing, I really don't feel like I have to be locked in a certain space. But if it is something for a grade, something for turning in, as long as I have some kind of quiet, I am generally okay. When I have trouble is when I have people all around me talking and stuff; I don't feel like the quality is there. I am sure I will have an office at whatever post I go to, but I mean, there is plenty of open green space wherever we go. But a lot of our restrictions are that we gotta be logged in with one of those cards [for the Army's internal encrypted network] and things. We are kinda stationary.

I ask about his "not much pressure" comment. He tells me he is describing his current writing tasks for ROTC, which, since he is already slated to commission and has already received a duty and a branch, does not carry much weight. He then metaphorically flexes his muscles: "I'm a little cocky about my writing for the Army because I just think I will be able to create stuff that is different from my peers just because I have just a little bit of a talent for it. I have seen how my peers write versus me, so I say 'oh, I'll be fine.'" As he talks, my mind wanders to his short story "A Faux Pas of the Soul: The Fable of the Gilded Prince," a roughly three thousand-word narrative he wrote in the tradition of *The Great Gatsby*. This isn't the kind of text many other cadets, many other students, many other people, are actively and voluntarily creating during a school year. As I reach to turn my digital recorder off, my mind hits on a final question. I ask, "What is ROTC trying to prepare you for?" Logan's final audio-recorded response highlights his positive four-year experience:

Their goal here is to give us a foundation of leadership to build off of and just get us used to and condition us to how the Army organization works and how the structure works out and, I mean, it has done a pretty effective job. Even though we do a lot of stuff real Army doesn't do or vice versa, they do a very good job of showing us what each individual level of the chain of command in the whole structure does because we get to experience all those levels. Kids at other schools don't get the experience of being a private, a sergeant, a sergeant major, a lieutenant, whatever. For most of them, four years of ROTC and then boom, straight into officer.

For Logan, these four years carry weight because he gained practical experience directed toward his future professional career. Logan and I talk details about his commissioning ceremony, which I plan to attend, and then he leaves my office for the final time.

Earlier in the day, Logan attended the commencement ceremonies for UNG's Mike Cottrell College of Business. He sat through commencement in a black gown, a hat on his head; he crossed the stage, shook the university president's hand, received a diploma, shook the alumni director's hand, stopped for a picture, found his seat again. Near the end of the ceremony, an active-duty soldier asked Logan and the other graduating cadets to stand, take off their caps and gowns, hold their right hands up, and repeat the oath of enlistment. The oath of enlistment is followed by the oath of commissioned officers, repeated in a more intimate setting. This season, Logan is one of roughly seven thousand cadets commissioning into the Army. I didn't make his graduation, but I have seen this ceremony enacted many times for cadets who graduate through my college, the College of Arts and Letters. I attended my college's graduation while Logan attended his. I did, however, make it to his commissioning ceremony held inside the MLC that afternoon.

*

I arrive early to feel the space of the MLC and watch the events upfold. Logan's commissioning is one of roughly fifteen scheduled for the day, and as in a good Army operation, a basic Excel spreadsheet taped to a plastic table outlines the when and where and who of all the commissioning ceremonies. I find Logan's name, the time, the location, and who is conducting the ceremonial oath of commissioned officers (the cadet can choose) and who is giving the first salute (again, the cadet can choose). The person conducting the oath must be any active-duty or retired military officer. The first salute may be rendered by any enlisted military member, active duty or retired. Traditionally, however, the first salute is rendered by a noncommissioned officer because a platoon sergeant, which is an NCO, will be the first person the newly commissioned

Figure 15.2. *Logan Blackwell takes the Oath of Commissioned Officers. Photo by author.*

officer will see when taking charge of a platoon as a lieutenant, and the NCO will be the first to salute the new officer. As tradition goes, during the ceremonial first salute, the officer shakes the hand of the NCO following the salute. The officer slips a silver coin to the NCO as a symbol of thanks for trusting the officer's upcoming leadership.

While I wait for Logan's ceremony, I make my way into the reception room, where family and friends have gathered and are eating the small snacks provided. I recognize the space. It is a military-science classroom, and the terrain model is sitting in the corner of the space. Just a few weeks prior, I heard Major Williams deliver a lecture on ribbons and awards in this space. The dividing wall is pushed away, doubling the space. I find Logan, dressed in his blues, and make my way over. Meet his dad, mom, sister, fiancé. *Mom,* Logan says, *this is the professor who is writing a book about me.* She shakes my hand, and I express my thanks for letting Logan work with me for four years.

The time ticks away. I chat with Logan's immediate family, then his extended family, then the Marine, Master Gunnery Sergeant (Ret.) Tony Howard, who led Logan's JROTC. Howard will give the first salute.

The time comes. As a small group of Logan supporters, we make our way to the MLC's atrium. The group in front of us finishes, and we enter, arranging ourselves against the wall to watch. I stand behind Grandma. The PMS, Colonel Brent Cummings, opens with a few words about Logan's academic and military achievements. A friend of Logan's family—Lieutenant Colonel (Ret.) Charles Schrankel—prepares to administer the oath but first offers a few words about Logan and foreign affairs. Then the oath is delivered and repeated by Logan (see fig. 15.2). The mom, dad, sister, come forward to place the pins on his shoulders that signify his new rank. Logan turns and receives his first salute from Howard. Logan sharply returns the salute. They shake hands and, as per tradition and not regulation, Logan slips Howard a silver coin. Logan turns to face his audience and delivers a short speech of thanks. Done. Eight minutes.

Logan, swept into the small crowd of his supporters and me trailing behind, leaves the atrium and goes into another room for more pictures. I linger in the doorway as pictures snap and snap and snap. Logan with Mom and Dad. Logan with sister. Logan with Mom and Dad and sister. The combinations continue. I don't enter the space. Just watch. And then leave. Don't say goodbye. My last view of Logan is the side of his face, the US flag behind him, looking off in the distance with a mix of tired exhaustion and tested patience as the pictures continue.

Now a US Army officer.

Though we still exchange emails, it was the last time I saw him after four years of steady conversations, his face fading into the bright lights of flashes, the red and blue and white hues of the flag. I haven't seen him since.

NOTE

1. For additional resources on drawing, see Bridget Turner Kelly and Carrie A. Kortegast's (2017) edited collection *Engaging Images for Research, Pedagogy, and Practice*, which provides a wealth of readings on how educational researchers might bring visual methods, like participant or student drawing, into our work as teacher-scholars.

Intersection 3
LEAVING THERE
Articulating Our Longitudinal Research Findings and Implications

> *Being a scholar, in short, means engaging in reflective, well-informed practices that help us accomplish the goals of advancing and sharing our knowledge of what it means to write and be a writer.*
> —Michael Day, Susan H. Delagrange, Mike Palmquist, Michael A. Pemberton, and Janice R. Walker

In Intersection 1, I work through how we enter a research moment, and in Intersection 2, I work through how we stay in a research moment. Here, at the close, I offer how we leave a research moment. I believe that when I leave a research moment, I must take the knowledge and practices honed with my participants back to the classroom and then to the broad public through presenting my research in public-facing and publicly accessible outlets like blog posts, public-library talks, Rotary-club-meeting presentations, newspaper Op-Eds. These outlets connect with readers beyond our disciplinary niche. As I need to be continually reminded: more than just RC/WS people are interested in writing.

In this conclusion, I leave my research moment and show how Logan's documented learning experiences can impact curricular design, classroom practice, and public scholarship. All three outcomes (curricula, classroom, public) constitute areas where we can go upon leaving our research moments. Alongside big data analytics in US higher education (Scott 2017), rich studies of student writers complement ever-emerging pictures of student learning. When we head to committee meetings to make curricular decisions, head to the classrooms where writing theory and research is enacted as writing practice, head out of our academic spaces and into our communities—when we leave our research moments, I invite use to take our findings with us. I invite us to place our portraits of individual writers alongside big data to account more fully for how our students develop as writers.

LEARNING FROM LONGITUDINAL STUDIES OF WRITERS: CURRICULA, CLASSROOM, AND PUBLIC IMPACTS

Reflecting on their three-year study of science undergraduates, Lerner and Poe (2014) write that "we see a continuing need to better understand student learning through *students'* perspectives" because "students' stories of learning and becoming . . . can tell us a great deal about the results of teaching and curricular designs" (60). Like Lerner and Poe, I position this four-year study of Logan's literate becoming against the Excel spreadsheets and endless charts and matrices of student learning that drive what my university often labels *student success initiatives*; my university even has a vice president with this phrase in their title. Through listening to Logan's stories, words, and writings, I offer curricular and classroom implications—as Lerner and Poe suggest studies like this one can do. But I also illustrate how student voices should be at the fore when we engage in public scholarship about writing and writing instruction.

In intersections 1 and 2, I argue self-reflexivity is central to conducting ethical and legal human-subject research. A portion of self-reflexivity is adopting a stance of reciprocity. Just as the required human-subject-research form at my university asks me to detail participant benefits, reciprocity invites researchers to articulate how participants and researchers will develop a mutually beneficial partnership. One way to develop this partnership is through the data analysis and circulation of findings, wherein the researcher may draw from participants' documented experiences to facilitate practical outcomes—like curricular change, a programmatic redesign, a classroom implementation. Through this process, research participants, as Malenczyk, Lerner, and Boquet (2018) argue, become knowledge producers, and this knowledge comes with practical import. I take up two outcomes based on Logan's documented experiences: one outcome on curricular design, one on classroom practice. And I offer how we might go public with our longitudinal studies of writers.

To recap, in this book I offer four broad findings:

- During his first year, Logan dipped a toe into the doctrinally defined Army writing standards and genres with which he would soon engage as an Army officer by learning what they are *not*.
- In his second year, Logan, encouraged by the ROTC Order of Merit List, turned to self-sponsored nonschool writing, which, in turn, helped him develop a writerly agency he brought to bear on his curricular writing.
- During his third year, Logan offloaded the cognitive challenge of authoring operation orders onto tools provided by ROTC and tools Logan developed himself.

- As a senior and preparing to graduate, Logan learned the doctrinally defined Army writing standard and key Army genres with which he would engage upon commissioning by gaining knowledge of a specific critical-thinking heuristic (i.e., the military decision-making process [MDMP]) and receiving his branch assignment that would, in a few short months, provide a more nuanced approach to applying the MDMP to his future writing tasks.

The first and third finding impact curricular and classroom labor.

The Curricula: Articulating the Importance of General Education

My first finding illustrates the importance of Logan's learning what writing is *not* through immersing himself in UNG's general education course offerings and taking classes outside his major and outside his career focus of Army soldiering. This finding stresses the importance of general education courses. My university system, the University System of Georgia, is revising the general education course offerings. A committee composed of representatives across the system drafted a statement articulating the importance of general education, the broad courses that will compose the core, and the need for schools to hold individual autonomy in what they label these courses and how they teach these courses while also designing them in such a manner that students may transfer between system schools and see their core classes count at their new institution. The draft of this statement is floating about thirty thousand feet above my head at conference tables at the system office. I do not have any indication that English 1101 and English 1102, both of which are in UNG's general education, are disappearing. But Logan's voice, Logan's experience, may lend helpful evidence for supporting the need for continued focus on writing instruction in general education and, more broadly, for our students to move through a variety of courses as they deepen their civic, quantitative, and qualitative knowledge, becoming informed and knowledgeable citizens. Sure, we have the big data analytics that show the links that connect passing required math and English courses and retention and one-semester persistence rates. We know passing math and English will keep a student at UNG. For example, during the 2018–2019 academic year, only 60.8 percent of students who received a D, F, W, or I in English 1101 during fall 218 returned to campus in spring 2019. This percent is up from the previous academic year when we saw a 54.3 percent one-semester persistence rate for English 1101. In short, if a student struggles in English 1101, our first step in a required two-step writing sequence, that student may not return next semester. From an economic model, this costs the university money because recruiting new students is more expensive than keeping students. We also know English 1101 and English 1102 produced 29,031 credit hours during the 2018–2019 academic year and English instructors taught 525 sections and 9,872 students. English 1101 and English 1102 are statistically and financially significant courses.

But we can also add student voices to our data points. Here, looking beyond my local context, I wonder how longitudinal studies of literacy development may aid in current and assuredly forthcoming conversations about the need for core curricula. As state legislatures hear their constituents bemoan student debt and push colleges and universities toward clearer paths to graduation, the general education course offerings may get sliced and outsourced to AP and CLEP testing and other testing outlets that will surely arise. I wonder how student voices and documented student learning experiences may offer more evidence for showing students a wide array of courses as an intellectual complement to their majors, their careers, their lives as members of the educated citizenry?

Here are also moments for us to partner with our local institutional stakeholders, like our colleagues in institutional research and our colleagues in advising. We can find moments when it would be appropriate to include student voices and student experiences in accreditation reports and in required system-level reports: alongside the mounds of data and the charts and charts and charts, a pithy and powerful quote from an undergrad about students' meaningful learning experiences in general education courses. We could partner more closely with the registrar, too. If we advocate for general education, and we should, we must identify and assuage pinch points, bottlenecks in the plan of study students struggle to move through. We can ensure that if a class is required we are offering enough classes, and that first-year students, who often are last to pick classes, can take classes that fit within their current academic, life, job schedule. We could work with advising to speak back to parents or students or politicians who are unsure why Student A, who wants to be an electrical engineer, needs to take a M/W/F 8:00 a.m. World Civ class. With our training in rhetoric, with student voices and experiences as data, we, with our local advisers, can talk back to potential dissent about general education and offer a fuller narrative of how exposure to varied curricular content can enhance disciplinary focus. Logan's case is an example: the challenges he faced in the required American Literature I course refined his passion for Army writing and helped focus his attention on what makes Army writing unique. He has a story to tell and so do our many other students who stretch themselves through general education course offerings.

Let's capture these stories in infographics, brochures, captioned videos, radio and podcast interviews. Let's tell the story of the need for general education courses by calling upon student voice and not just one-semester persistence rates.

The Classrooms: Materiality and Composition

In section 4, I engage with Logan's junior year, when he assembled for himself a little field book and worked with toy soldiers and yarn in a terrain model. Through my data collection in this section, I argued for the importance of tactical aids in the composing process. When we leave our research moments, as I am doing now with my study of Logan, I see how this finding has already impacted my work as a writing instructor and how it may impact other writing teachers who make their way through this book. To be direct: let's spend more time with the materiality of writing. Let's spend more time talking with students about how writing tools help us accomplish tasks and about which tools may be of most use to them. Here I am thinking specifically about the tools for creating text, using tangible objects to aid in the cognitive challenge of thinking through argument. How might material objects act as cognitive facilitators for final products. I am thinking of the graduate student Roozen (2009) studied. This student wrote and illustrated fan fiction to help her understand Burkean concepts. The physical act of drawing and illustrating, the materiality of the paper and pen and lines, became a cognitive facilitator for the graduate student to pass her written exams. Because I learned from Logan the importance of the little field book he assembled himself, and because I learned from him the importance of the terrain model for the collective Corps and for war gaming COAs in the MDMP, I found two ways to bring what I call *physical manipulatives*—borrowing language from my math-education colleagues—into the writing classroom. Both examples call upon material objects to serve as cognitive facilitators for writing.

For one, I have tried a paragraphing exercise in my writing classes—both in an FYC class and a 2000-level writing class. In this exercise, students bring a physical copy of their paper into class, printed just on one side. In class, they cut at each paragraph break in their paper, taping together any paragraphs that start on one page and run to the next. They throw away their name and their title; we just work with stacks of individual paragraphs. They shuffle these paragraphs and then pass them to a classmate, who assembles them. I stress that the goal is to assemble the paper in a way that makes sense to the assembler, as a reader. Students tape the paragraphs back together, forming a long scroll. We talk about transitions, and students leave with a revision plan handwritten on the back of their scroll. During the taping and reassembling process, I encourage students to relocate and find a large empty space to work—the floor, another table, down the hall, outside, wherever. *Move if you want*, I tell them, *and reassemble*. I see pedagogical benefit for the writer and the assembler. But for the assembler, it is the process of feeling and moving text I am most interested in when thinking about material objects as cognitive facilitators. The transition lesson is clear for me and the students. But what I struggle to explain aloud to the students is the importance of engaging with physical text, moving it, reassembling it. It's not better or worse than moving text on a screen, but it is an opportunity for them to see and feel what the words look like in a very different way than they do on a screen. Just as Logan and the cadets visualized a potential COA on the terrain model and moved soldiers and jeeps and sand dunes around, writing students explore how tactile text and the experience of engaging with tactile text can facilitate the cognitive challenge of authoring words. What might such an activity look like in your unique institutional context and with your unique students? General Townsend loves grid paper and a writing tool that serves at once as a pen and pencil. Lieutenant Colonel Forester loves a lime-green notebook. First Lieutenant Blackwell loves his little field book. Writers are particular about the tools they use to generate words. And our students are, too. I see my role as broadening the list of available tools for them and giving them space to see which serve them best.

The Public: Circulating Our Research Moments beyond the University

I pair curricula and classrooms with public scholarship. The three areas connect for me especially because I work at a public university. Broader decisions about the curricula and the classroom play out in the public arena. As Pew Research Center data (Brown 2018) and Gallup polls (Newport and Busteed 2017) show, public confidence in higher education, particularly among Republicans, is trending downward. State budget appropriations for higher education are also trending downward, sometimes plummeting downward, as is the unfortunate case in Alaska (Hazelrigg 2019). While I was adding missing commas to an almost finished draft of this book, a lawmaker from Tennessee mused aloud that maybe higher education should be eliminated altogether (Epstein, *Washington Post*, September 10, 2019). A response to these polls and budget numbers and misinformed musings is more direct attention to bringing what we know about writing and writing instruction to these external stakeholders. Linda Adler-Kassner's (2008) *The Activist WPA* grows timelier with each passing year (no easy task for an academic book). She outlines concrete steps for advocating for writers and writing. Alongside her work, and others within RC/WS who go public in their scholarship, I offer my exhortation here at the close of my book.

When I leave research moments, I bring my thinking and experiences to the classroom and to the public. As an employee at a public university, who typed many of the words in this book on technology purchased in part by taxpayer dollars, I believe strongly is talking about my work with those in my local community. I've talked at Rotary Club meetings and evening public-library sessions; I've written pieces for two local newspapers about my work, about the work of higher ed, about the partnership between town and school. My work with public scholarship is guided by scholarship on public engagement and by US universities and colleges with robust programs or centers for supporting public engagement in all its various guises.

An initial starting place is with terminology: *community engagement, academic service learning, community-based research, participatory action research, community-based participatory research, civic engagement, action research, public scholarship, engaged research*. An avalanche of terms with important and nuanced differences. Scholars debate these terms in journals like the *Journal of Community Engagement and Scholarship* and the *Journal of Extension*. But for my purposes here, I am thinking about how we might share findings from our research moments with the public. The Swearer Center at Brown University (2019), which oversees the only elective Carnegie Classification (the Carnegie Foundation's Classification for Community Engagement) helpfully differentiates between traditional research and engaged research by drawing on the work of Andrew Furco. For example, while traditional research "breaks new ground in a discipline," engaged research "breaks new ground in a discipline *and has direct application to broader public issues*" (emphasis in original). The Center for Community and Civic Engagement at Carleton College (2019) provides more specifics, with a helpful visual that captures eight potential outlets for public scholarship and visualizes public scholarship as the meeting point for creativity, civic responsibility, reciprocity, and public knowledge. Doing the work is not the end of the work, however. Faculty take on the additional task of representing their scholarship to internal promotion and tenure committees, and I am grateful for the programs and centers around the United States that help scholars better describe how their public scholarship can meet local promotion and tenure guidelines. For one, in *Going Public: A Guide for Social Scientists*, Arlene Stein and Jessie Daniels (2018) highlight the work of the University of Minnesota Twin Cities. In the document "Assessment of Community-Engaged Scholarship" (2019), UMN details characteristics of engaged scholarship and then provides a rubric of sorts with columns for criteria, indictors, and evaluation. Stein and Daniels (2018) also outline practical steps for writing punchy prose directed toward general readers: "Strive to be simple and direct, coherent and compelling, rather than comprehensive and complete. Use active verbs, people your prose rather than filling it with objects" (56). They also detail possible challenges, such as readers misinterpreting a complex argument a writer offers in a pithy Op-Ed and the trolling invited by digital communication.

Adrianna J. Kezar, Yianna Drivalas, and Joseph A. Kitchen's (2018) edited collection *Envisioning Public Scholarship for Our Time: Models for Higher Education Researchers* provides timely pieces that help readers think through how public scholarship should, for example, respond to the Black Lives Matter movement (Davis, Harper, and Christian 2018) and address legal (Hurtado 2018) and ethical dilemmas (Sam and Gupton 2018). The editors see public scholarship as "service to a diverse democracy and social justice, which are interconnected and necessary to build an equitable society" (4). They go so far as to argue scholars have an "ethical obligation" (Kezar, Drivalas, and Kitchen 2018, 15) to go public with their research and offer a direct question, followed by an equally powerful response: "Are we doing our job adequately if we only write journal articles and make presentations at research conferences? We say no" (16). In *Decolonizing Educational Research: From Ownership to Answerability*, Leigh Patel (2015) offers "answerability as a construct and cognitive tool" (73) and details how qualitative education researchers can enact research answerable to learning, knowledge, and context. To be fair, Patel is not thinking about public scholarship, but I place her work in conversation with the voices represented in *Envisioning Public Scholarship for Our Time* because these scholars push us to form research designs and findings that lift up communities. This is tough work. It makes me uneasy. Though I rally to their call for public scholarship that addresses social justice, diversity, and equity, and though I am on board with public scholarship as an ethical obligation (and as doing more than presenting fifteen minutes of content at an annual conference only attended by those in the know and those with a thousand bucks to offset registration, hotel, travel, and food), I know I have more work to do, that the public scholarship I undertake is not enough. Through my continued learning and trying and failing and doing, I suggest two steps for supporting public scholarship within a local context: connect to institutional history and an institutional mission statement; connect to an institutional center for teaching and learning (CTL).

For the first, I'm inspired by Ashley Holmes's (2016) *Public Pedagogy in Composition Studies*. Holmes argues for a type of service learning in general education writing courses like first-year composition. But I see her making broad arguments about public scholarship and the engaged scholar. Holmes argues we get an institutional foothold into doing this work by connecting our work with an institution's mission and history. Making this connection explicit in grant applications, annual performance reviews, promotion and tenure material, class syllabi, and various other professional documents shows how the work we wish to undertake can support the broader institutional goals. For my local context, UNG received the Carnegie Foundation's Classification for Community Engagement. The University of North Georgia articulates a vision statement (2022) alongside its mission statement. The vision statement reads: "The University of North Georgia will be a regional and national leader for academic excellence, engagement, educational opportunity, and leadership development." UNG had the same vision statement in 2014 when Logan and I worked together. I see the *engagement* in the vision statement, and I couple that with our elective classification to articulate in my annual performance review and posttenure review materials that my publications in local newspapers and my talks at the public library and the Rotary Club, and the half-day workshop I led on public scholarship, align with the focus of the institution. To bolster this argument further, as Holmes suggests, I additionally turn to speeches delivered by my university president to see how she articulates *engagement*; I look at our annually released economic-impact data; I see how the University System of Georgia thinks about the term *engagement*. Tapping into these larger institutional structures may support the public scholarship we have an ethical obligation to undertake.

We can also support this kind of work by connecting with our local CTLs. Often nested under academic affairs or an office of research and engagement, CTLs are interdisciplinary hubs of faculty innovation led by and focused on faculty. Under various titles, CTLs are among the few centers or programs not student facing or public facing; they interface with faculty and support the teaching and research of faculty through developing and implementing a variety of professional-development opportunities. They often directly support institutions during change moments like accreditation visits, the development of system-level student-success initiatives, and the revision of faculty-handbook material on promotion and tenure. CTLs support faculty who facilitate and sustain change. As C. Edward Watson (2018) writes, "The primary means through which institutions change is via the innovation, pedagogy, creativity, and scholarship of its faculty." Through my work with the UNG's Center for Teaching, Learning, and Leadership (CTLL), I have led workshops on public scholarship with our director for academic engagement and a colleague in the English department. I see CTLs as a key force in jumpstarting and sustaining conversation about public scholarship at individual institutions. CTLs are faculty-led and faculty-focused change agents.[1]

Throughout my work, I've tried to emulate the description of *scholar* articulated by Michael Day, Susan H. Delagrange, Mike Palmquist, Michael A. Pemberton, and Janice R. Walker (2013), who, in the epigraph to this conclusion, provide us with a definition of being a scholar: "Being a scholar, in short, means engaging in reflective, well-informed practices that help us accomplish the goals of advancing and sharing our knowledge of what it means to write and be a writer" (186). Sharing our work in public spaces is at the heart of scholarship.

At the close of his book on virtue ethics, John Duffy (2019) exhorts RC/WS to rally around a central purpose and to communicate that purpose to the broad public. For Duffy, that purpose is the "discourse of rhetorical virtues" (143). I'm still thinking through the second part of Duffy's statement (i.e., that we should rally around rhetorical virtues), but I am with him on the first part; we need to rally around something communally crafted and communally communicated to external stakeholders. Currently, RC/WS struggles for internal coherence and thus struggles to have a voice in important public-facing conversations about literacy, writing, reading, testing, and the broad place of US higher education in a climate of soaring student debt. As Will Kurlinkus (2018) writes, "I know of no other field that teaches students to uncover and have empathy for the full messiness of humanity better than English studies, rhetoric, composition, and literacy" (12). Then he continues with these unsettling but accurate words: "And, at the same time, I also know of few fields that have so poorly marketed their ability to concretely change the world for the better" (12). At the close of this book, my thoughts are not focused on what this study might mean for how we teach thesis statements or peer review or facilitate a workshop on comma splices. With RC/WS fractured, with the public divided on the role of higher education, with misinformed public reports on student writing skills, I cannot commit myself to reflecting on what the ninety thousand plus words in this book might mean for, say, how others could teach MLA in-text citations. My thoughts are on how I can take this knowledge I gained with Logan and speak to broader issues about the shared work of higher education and the military; about how I might influence state or federal policy on transgender cadets; about how I might write to my local and federal politicians about funding levels for USACC; about how I can better frame my upcoming talk at the YMCA based on my experience leading a workshop at a Polish military academy; about how I might write to the US president about ongoing tensions in North Korea that might lead to cadets I labor with heading overseas and into yet another endless conflict with unclear goals.

We (I!) must talk to our local community stakeholders regardless of the inevitable pitfalls that may come. To be fair, I am not sure we (the RC/WS world) have our own house in order. We can't decide whether we are a discipline, a field, or neither. Or what we should label ourselves: composition studies? writing studies? Heck, for this book, I went with neither and landed on RC/WS. But maybe by more intentionally reaching outside our journals and conference and listservs, and reaching out to the local newspapers, community organizers, politicians, and readers of local newspapers, we may, in return, start developing a more acute understanding of what we are and what we want to call ourselves and how we define what it is we do. Ultimately, I exhort longitudinal writing researchers to find public avenues for circulating their work, avenues that attend to important local promotion and tenure guidelines and avenues that will establish partnerships between town and school. Such work may get us ever closer to uniting around that which we are.

AND, FINALLY . . .

Longitudinal writing research involves getting there, staying there, and leaving there. The *there* is ever shifting. The getting, staying, and leaving is not a linear, singular process. On and on we go as we seek to better understand how writers develop. I call for emphasis on self-reflexivity throughout this journey, awareness of positionality and undue influence, and the enactment of reciprocity. I call for establishing partnerships inside and outside the institution. I eagerly await the new wave of writing researchers and students who have much to teach us about how writers develop. Is it *right* to do this work of researching writers, to return to the powerful question at the heart of Bishop's poem? I suggest we arrive at answers through how we gain access to our research moments, how we stay in our research moments, and how we leave our research moments by bringing our newly coconstructed knowledge to our classrooms, to our publics, to our many moments that collectively constitute our being.

NOTE

1. On the topic of CTLs and thinking of the RC/WS audience for this book, I highlight the work of Isis Artze-Vega, Melody Bowdon, Kimberly Emmons, Michele Eodice, Susan K. Hess, Claire Coleman Lamonica, and Gerald Nelms (2013). They note that RC/WS scholars are well placed to take on positions in CTLs because of the deep-seated commitment to teaching and learning that runs through the history of RC/WS. This discipline grew out of classroom practice, where our pedagogy led to our research. Such is not the case for other disciplines, in which research in an area led to forming undergraduate classes in that area

RETREAT
A Researcher in Poland and an Officer at Fort Stewart

I'm sitting alone at Ovo Bar and Restaurant in Wrocław, Poland. An order of herring is coming my way with a glass bottle of Coke, 250 ml. Wrocław sits on the western edge of Poland, closer to Prague in distance than to the Polish capital of Warsaw. Wrocław spreads her way around the many tributaries of the Oder River, bridges stretching and connecting, all rich with Czech and German history. Churches, four times older than the founding of the Unites States of America, stand resolutely in city squares and have stood resolutely through geopolitical turbulence that rattled the town—the First World War, the Second World War, the rise of communism, the fall of communism, the introduction into NATO, the European Union.

My server brings out two slices of bread on a plate, a dollop of cream cheese and diced tomatoes on another plate. *To start*, she tells me in smooth English.

*

I've spent the last two days running workshops with English-writing instructors at Akademia Wojsk Lądowych imienia generała Tadeusza Kościuszki. Translated? General Tadeusz Kosciuszko Military University of Land Forces (MULF), an institute of higher education tasked with training and commissioning Polish Army officers. Roughly twelve hundred cadets are enrolled at MULF, all of whom, upon completing the requirements and graduating, will commission and serve in the Polish Army for a required ten years. The university curriculum for cadets runs five years: during the first three years, cadets complete requirements for a bachelor's degree; the last two years, cadets complete requirements for a master's degree. To commission as an officer, a Polish solider needs a master's degree, unlike in the United States, where a bachelor's degree is the academic requirement. An additional requirement that stands apart from US requirements is proficiency in a foreign language, specifically English, as illustrated in passing four separate NATO-sanctioned examinations in writing, listening, speaking, and reading. All in English.

*

My Polish herring arrives. A clean slice of fresh fish sitting atop sliced apples and scattered walnuts. Dill atop the herring. The whiteness of the fish leaps out from the steel-gray bowl.

*

I'm here to lead faculty-development workshops on student writing and to interview cadets and staff with MULF. The University of North Georgia has established an international partnership with MULF. According to the official memorandum of understanding signed by the two schools, we exchange cadets for a semester at a time and exchange faculty for short research projects. Following conversations with my dean, with my chief academic research officer, with people in UNG's Office of Leadership and Global Engagement, and with Colonel Marcin Bielewicz at MULF, and, more important, with my family, I arranged a visit to MULF.

The months passed, and then I was in the airport at Wrocław, where Cadet Pochodaj was waiting to pick me up. Now, I'm dining *al fresco* in the cool Polish summer air.

The teachers I worked with at MULF teach the English-language classes all cadets take. In these classes, cadets hone proficiency in reading, writing, speaking, and listening. As I sat in a classroom waiting for the workshop to begin, I saw posters that, in bright colors and shapes, illustrated English pronouns. Another poster displayed Austria's topography; another poster offered an overview on conjugating German verbs. I have no formal training in teaching English to nonnative speakers and felt out of place, not wanting to come across as a savior from the United States here to correct the wrongs of Polish instruction.

Since 1999, Poland has been a member of the North Atlantic Treaty Organization (NATO), an intergovernmental military alliance launched in the wake of World War II and now counting twenty-nine member states. Standard agreements (STANAGs) were introduced to facilitate partnerships and coordination among these very different member states. One key STANAG established an official language for communication in writing, speaking, reading, and listening. English was designated. STANAG 6001 (Bureau for International Language 2019), "Language Proficiency Levels," outlines the importance of English as the standard language for this twenty-nine-member military alliance and offers the five areas of proficiency in English on a scale of 0 to 5:

- Level 0—No proficiency
- Level 1—Survival
- Level 2—Functional

- Level 3—Professional
- Level 4—Expert
- Level 5—Highly-articulate native

Nested under STANAG 6001, NATO's "Allied Training Publication-5" (ATRainP-5) (Bureau for International Language 2016) offers details such as a definition of language proficiency and examples of different levels of proficiency in speaking, reading, writing, and listening. It defines "language proficiency" as "an individual's unrehearsed, general language communication ability" and offers three reasons for such an agreement:

> Participating nations agree to adopt the appended table of language proficiency levels for the purpose of:
>
> a. Communicating language requirements for international staff appointments.
> b. Recording and reporting, in international correspondence, measures of language proficiency.
> c. Comparing national standards through a standardized table while preserving each nation's right to maintain its own internal proficiency standards. (1.1)

STANAG 6001 articulates, then, the target goal, and ATrainP-5 articulates important definitions and examples of the target goal. Both STANAG 6001 and ATrainP-5 are found on the website for the Bureau for International Language Coordination, a unit of NATO.

These documents drive MULF's curriculum. The teachers here, like many teachers at US public primary and secondary schools, teach for the test. At MULF, cadets must display level-2 proficiency in all four areas by the end of their second year. To commission as an officer, Polish cadets must display level-3 proficiency in reading and listening.

Back in the classroom, Colonel Bielewicz introduced me and I stood. I brought with me material from the scholarship of teaching and learning applicable to a range of disciplines. I talked assignment design, specifically principles within transparency in learning and teaching (TILT), with my Polish colleagues. We talked about the importance of clear expectations in writing assignments and communicating criteria for success to our students (Winkelmes et al. 2016). We talked about the three points of TILT (i.e., purpose, task, and criteria). I brought work on metacognition from educational psychologist Yves Karlen (2017). We talked about how we might invite cadet writers to reflect on their work before and after an assignment and how this reflection does not have to take much time but can be a quick jotting of ideas on the back of the assignment sheet. The point is to give cadets, any learner, a chance to stop, breathe, and think about how to move forward or how they moved forward. Concern was raised about the number of students assigned to a teacher, about the need to teach and prepare students for the NATO test, about finding time in a busy structured curriculum to have students reflect informally on their academic performance. All understandable concerns; all concerns also raised in US faculty-development workshops.

Without air conditioning in the classroom, I broke into a sweat. The open window brought in a breeze and the *pop* of gun fire at the shooting range. We dismissed after an hour. The instructors moved swiftly to their next classes, grabbing carbonated mineral water on the way out the door.

*

I finish my polish herring and start on my main course: baked chicken, salad, and carrots. The day turns cool as the sun falls away and the gray haze of twilight descends.

*

Day two at MULF, and the conversation turned to grading. The common challenges writing teachers face in the US, instructors in Poland face. How do I grade so many papers effectively? How do I ensure students read my comments? Shouldn't I mark everything I see? Yesterday, I covered the board in concepts and ideas. This day, I let my new colleagues drive the conversation. On the white board, we wrote ideas on what works.

The instructors were all civilians. Colonel Bielewicz stood in the doorway dressed in camo. He oversees what he calls the *language department*. The civilian instructors are his charge, cadets passing the exam his responsibility. A few months earlier, I met him in person at my university, where he was guest lecturer in a security-studies class. His round head holds his wide smile well.

After the second workshop, I sat in an office with an instructor who was lucky enough to have his own office and to have an A/C unit. The unit purred as it dropped condensation into a plastic water bottle the instructor delicately placed beneath the unit. We talked students and writing and travel. Midway through our conversation, a knock on his door. His wife, who also teaches at the school, popped in. Her office did not have A/C, and it was in the 90s Fahrenheit. She came in for the cool air. They told me of their upcoming travel to an Egyptian resort, a popular destination for Poles.

Another knock on the door, and Colonel Bielewicz entered with cadet Jacob Pochodaj in tow. Jacob had picked me up from the airport when I arrived, escorted me around Wrocław, and would drop me off at the airport. I followed Jacob to a transport van, and he flung the door open for me. I got in the backseat, Jacob in the front seat. The civilian driver took off; a cigarette wedged between two fingers, he waved at the armed guard at the gate.

*

I finish my meal, hand over my credit card to pay, and my mind wanders back to the two workshops—What I could have done better? What I could have prepped for more?— common concerns that arise after a presentation, a workshop, a teaching session. I hold these concerns; they are important. But I also place them to the side for the moment. I reflect on the shared commitment writing teachers have to creating an environment for students to succeed. The commitment to teaching and to students and to literacy connected us. I reflect on geopolitical turbulence: that despite current political instability caused by countries isolating themselves (Britain's decision to leave the EU; fringe and mainstream political movements in Italy, France, and Poland seeking to dismantle the EU from within; Trump's disparaging comments on NATO), on the be ground level, layers below the presidents and chancellors and generals and ambassadors, teachers are coming together and reflecting on their shared commitment to student learning.

I hang with these thoughts until twilight gives way to dark. I head to my room. Tomorrow, a tour of Auschwitz I and Auschwitz II. Friday, Krakow.

Then home.

AN OFFICER AT FORT STEWART

After I returned from Poland, I wrote an email to Logan. It was almost a year to the day since he had graduated and commissioned. He had completed BOLC; he was married; he was stationed at his duty base:

> Hi, Logan,
>
> I am rapidly finishing up the book. As I am working on my conclusion, I wanted to see if you would be willing to answer two questions via email:
> Describe the writing project you found most meaningful
> What made that project meaningful for you?
> If this meaningful project came from class, what class?
> Finally, had you written anything like your meaningful writing project and do you imagine writing something similar in the future?
> Odd questions, I know. I am borrowing these questions from a wonderful book The Meaningful Writing Project.
> Thanks for entertaining my questions.
>
> -Michael

Twelve days later, he wrote back:

> Dr. Rifenburg,
>
> Been out in the field for a few weeks. Will get back to you as soon as I can, sorry for delayed response
>
> Regards,
> Logan Blackwell

His full response came a few days later. With his permission, I quote in full:

> Dr. Rifenburg,
>
> It's taken me quite some time to reflect on a meaningful project as each one served some purpose in my life whether it was to inspire, heal, and sometimes soothe. However, the piece(s) that meant the most was a 3 part piece of prose I wrote to my spouse, read to her at 3 different developmental points in our relationship: The first being an invitation to enter the relationship, the second being our first celebration together (her birthday), and the last being my proposal to her. This project meaningful because in writing this, My words had meaning to someone and my words had weight. They moved her and in turn moved me. This is the pinnacle of what I want my writing to do and she took it in. It meant something to the both of us and it showed me the power of authenticity in a piece of writing. I believe I could write something like this again in the future, however the difficulty will be finding an audience to reach and discovering the message to craft. Before the "Cosmos" piece I wrote to my spouse, I had never written anything that had such powerful consequence. Let me know what else you need, I've enjoyed our chats over the years and I'm always happy to answer questions and receive feedback. Our chats have been enjoyable, almost therapeutic over the years, and your mentorship keeps writing on my mind. I can only hope one day, I'll be able to publish something we can all enjoy reading. Thanks for everything, truly. I look forward to hearing from you again soon. Please feel free to keep sending questions. I can't wait to see the final product.
>
> Regards,
> Logan Blackwell

For four years, Logan and I sat together, talked together, read together. I read his curricular and extracurricular writing. I followed him into his MILS classes and into the ballroom-dance club he founded. As I researched (with) Logan, I continued serving as director, then codirector, of the first-year composition program. In this position, I found myself called upon, time and again, to send data points on student performance up the chain of command. For example, the University System of Georgia partnered with the John N. Gardner Institute for Excellence in Undergraduate Education to redesign gateway courses in which, according to student-performance metrics, students consistently struggle. Each of the twenty-six system schools decided which specific gateway courses to redesign; my university decided on general education courses in math, history, psychology, and English. As cochair of the English Course Committee, I'm working with colleagues in our center for teaching and learning, English, and Institutional Effectiveness and specifically learning about curriculum design and spending time with quantitative data, such as one-semester persistence rates, degree-to-completion numbers, retention numbers. I can rattle off these data points for the important VPs and AVPs I come across when walking around campus.

I find great value in pausing as a university and system to check on student performance in these important courses. But the mounds of data and dashboards and Excel spreadsheets and the work with faculty on student learning but not with any direct input from the students themselves—all this wears on me. My work with course redesign landed as I was finishing up my data collection on Logan. Amid these large-scale curricular redesign projects driven by metrics, I also turned again to Eodice, Geller, and Lerner's (2016) *The Meaningful Writing Project.* As important as data points are for tracking student learning and tracking teaching effectiveness, our students are not just data points to be moved around. *Drilled to Write*, an $n=1$ study, is a complement to the Excel spreadsheets that line my office walls. Like Eodice, Geller, and Lerner, I wanted to hear from students: in my case, one student. In this final chapter, I borrow two questions from Eodice, Geller, and Lerner's study to ask Logan: In your four years of writing, what stands out? Why? These questions do not make for tidy data points on an institutional-effectiveness dashboard. But, when placed alongside persistence rates and other metrics, these questions provide greater insight into the learners with whom we labor.

Logan's response didn't surprise me. But it did strike me. It showed me school-sanctioned assignments were not the ones that stayed with Logan. The ones that stayed with Logan were the ones that formed the foundation for developments in his personal life. The "3 part piece of prose" he wrote his now-wife stayed with him because "they moved her and in turn moved me." For Logan, such a reaction was what he believed writing should accomplish: "This is the pinnacle of what I want my writing to do."

I don't want to perform a close reading of his email. I'm thinking of the Billy Collins (1996) poem in which he describes his struggles with students wanting to interpret a poem instead of enjoying it: "But all they want to do / is tie the poem to a chair with rope / and torture a confession out of it." I would like Logan's email to sit powerfully on the page and not be teased apart line by line by me. That kind of dissection can stifle prose's power by making the emotional into the analytical. But I do want to pause and notice that the pieces in his "3 part piece of prose" provided Logan a sense of agency; that these three pieces allowed him to engage with his audience, his girlfriend; that these pieces connected to "[his] passions and to future aspirations and identities" (Eodice, Geller, and Learner 2016, 4). In short, Logan's email to me outlining his most meaningful writing project aligns with the central findings from Eodice, Geller, and Lerner: writers seek agency, engagement, and connections to imagined futures. Logan found his meaningful writing project on his own.

Sure, this is an *n*=1. Logan is unique. He writes a lot. For fun. But stories that populate the pages of this book, emails like the one above, and findings from *The Meaningful Writing Project*, are what show the power and wonder of writing. Students seek outlets to express who they are, and, for many, this outlet is the written word. Sometimes I wonder whether the most effective thing I can do for the student writers on my campus is to reserve a dedicated space for them, help them get the material tools they need, and then shut up and let them write. As Logan's email illustrates, the 126 credit hours he accumulated and the study abroad and summer Army training sessions were not what ran through his head when he put his fingers to the keyboard to respond to me. Instead, he remembered that which occurred outside the tidy path of school-focused qualitative research. What he remembered was the meaningful world of self-sponsored writing. As a researcher, the questions I come to are, How might I gain access into this space? Should I? So, at the end, I come back to the start: a new research question.

Logan's email leaves me with my spirits buoyed by his passion for writing. Logan's email leaves me with unresolved questions about teaching, curriculum design, and research. And I try to embrace equally my buoyant spirit *and* these unresolved questions. For both will inevitably bring me back to continued work with our student writers and with faculty—in the United States and in Poland—who labor with our students.

I opened this book with directions from Army Training Circular (TC) 3-21.5, *Drill and Ceremonies* (US Army 2021) on conducting reveille. Now comes retreat. Section 13-2 of TC 3-21.5 offers the sequence for retreat:

> At the last note of "To the Color" or the national anthem, the adjutant faces about, commands *Order, ARMS*, and then directs TAKE CHARGE OF YOUR UNITS. Unit commanders render the *Hand Salute*. The adjutant returns all *Salutes* with one *Salute*. This terminates the retreat formation.

With the flag lowered for the day, I'll leave Logan in his office at his Army post. And I will remain here at my office in Georgia.

Tomorrow, cadets will raise the flag again, and Logan and I will get back to work. Logan is moving onto new experiences with writing, experiences for which the ROTC curriculum tried to prepare him. I'm moving onto international research on Army writing instruction, trying to make sense of what I learned in Poland. Both of us moving forward, chasing the beauty of writing and learning.

Summer is ending as I type these words. My mind and body are still jet-lagged from my time in Poland. In one month, a new semester at UNG begins. In two weeks, roughly two hundred new cadets will arrive on UNG's Dahlonega campus, move through in-processing, participate in FROG week, and then, when the fall officially begins, be taught to lead, instructed to plan, coordinated to commission.

And they will be drilled to write.

Appendix A
US ARMY ECHELONS

Field Army, 50,000 plus soldiers
  Commanded by a general

Corps, two or more divisions, roughly 20,000 to 45,000 soldiers
  Commanded by a lieutenant general

Division, three brigades, 10,000 to 15,000 soldiers
  Commanded by a major general

Brigade, three to five battalions, 2,000 to 5,000 troops
  Commanded by a brigadier general or colonel

Battalion, three to five companies, 100 to 1,000 soldiers
  Commanded by a lieutenant colonel

Company, three to four platoons, 60 to 200 soldiers
  Commanded by a captain or first lieutenant or major

Platoon, three to four squads, 18 to 50 soldiers
  Commanded by a second lieutenant

Squad, six to ten soldiers
  Commanded by a sergeant

Appendix B
US ARMY OFFICER RANKS FROM HIGHEST TO LOWEST

General
Lieutenant general
Major general
Brigadier general
Colonel
Lieutenant colonel
Major
Captain
First lieutenant
Second lieutenant

Appendix C
US ARMY CADET RANKS FROM HIGHEST TO LOWEST

Cadet officer ranks
- Cadet colonel
- Cadet lieutenant
- Cadet major
- Cadet captain
- Cadet first lieutenant
- Cadet second lieutenant

Cadet noncommissioned ranks
- Cadet command sergeant major
- Cadet sergeant major
- Cadet master sergeant
- Cadet sergeant first class
- Cadet staff sergeant
- Cadet sergeant
- Cadet private first class
- Cadet private

Appendix D
ABBREVIATIONS

AAR: after-action review
ADP: Army doctrine publication
AO: area of operation
AR: Army regulation
BAC: Basic Airborne Course
CBRN: chemical, biological, radiological, and nuclear
COA: course of action
DA: Department of the Army
FM: field manual
FRAGO: fragmentary order
FROG: Freshman Recruit Orientation Group
FT: fort
IPR: in-process review
LT: lieutenant
MDMP: military decision-making process
MLC: Military Leadership Center
MS: Military Science (used to designate a person [i.e., MS IV cadet])
NDA: National Defense Act
NCO: noncommissioned officer
NLT: no later than
OCPS: occupational camouflage pattern
OML: Order of Merit List
OPORD: operations orders
PE: practical exercise
PMS: professor of military science
ROTC: Reserve Officers' Training Corps
SMC: senior military college
TRADOC: Training and Doctrine Command
UNG: University of North Georgia
USACC: United States Army Cadet Command
WARNO: warning order

Appendix E
INTERVIEW TRANSCRIPT WITH GENERAL STEPHEN J. TOWNSEND, COMMANDER, UNITED STATES AFRICA COMMAND

I conducted this interview with General Townsend in his office at Fort Eustis, Virginia, where he served as commanding general, US Army Training and Doctrine Command. As of July 2022, he serves as commander, United States Africa Command.

RIFENBURG: Last time I heard you talk was at the American Association of Colleges and Universities' meeting Atlanta, Georgia. You opened by telling a story about your English professor. You pulled a prank on your English professor.

TOWNSEND: That backfired!

RIFENBURG: So, what kind of student were you? How did you do in your English classes?

TOWNSEND: I was a middling student overall. Mostly because I didn't care about my academics. I was solely focused on getting a commission in the infantry. That was my entire objective. I wish I had maybe had some better coaching and more thoughtful approach to my academics. But I did actually quite well in English because of that English professor Lail, Guy Lail. He and another one, Elsa Gaines, were the two that, there were others, but Lail and Gaines were much respected and feared by the student population.

And I had Lail for the time I was there, and he taught me how to write. He taught me how to write an argumentative essay designed to argue a point, convince. There was a sort of fairly simple template with your introduction and thesis. And then you gotta discredit the opposition, what the opposition is going to say. Then you get one to three points in support of your argument, and you conclude. And it was so effective that I still remember today what he taught me. That has held me in good stead throughout my Army career.

RIFENBURG: In preparation for our conversation today, I chatted with [UNG's] Professor of Military Science Colonel [Joshua] Wright. We talked a bit about the trajectory of Army writing. I sit in on military-science classes, and cadets are writing operations orders, they are doing 9 Line MEDEVAC reports, they are doing counseling forms. And

Col. Wright mentioned that as he moved into his position, and maybe this is true in your position, he is writing more memorandums, more correspondences. So, I am thinking about transitioning from operations orders to memos. Two questions: One, do you see that as a transition of cadets writing one form, supporting officers and general officers writing in a different form, and can you think of a moment where you shifted to writing more memos, more correspondences?

TOWNSEND: Hmmm. I never really thought about that transition. Those are just different purposes for the writing. The whole purpose for writing is to inform or convince, right? You either want to inform someone so that they know what you know. Or you want to convince someone to do something you want them to do. I think, really. That is what is boils down to: Why are you writing? Unless you are just writing for entertainment purposes or art purposes.

But in the military, you are trying to inform someone and convince a decision maker to decide something. I see this as a continuum of writing. I see this as a continuum. And you are up and down the continuum all the time. Today, I have reviewed memorandums, briefing slides, emails, an essay. Just today. I have reviewed these different documents and edited some of them. Just today. For me, the continuum started in college. I just got what Dr. Lail, or Mr. Lail, I can't remember if he had a PhD or not. But Professor Lail, I just got what he was trying [to teach], he communicated in such a simple way that I got it. And his point was your writing should be simple and clean, and if you follow a general organization then you will kinda get all the key points across in a style that flows logically and convincingly. That just resonated with me.

So, I started out in the Army. My next sort of transition was writing operations orders to my soldiers, my platoon, and company. And what I realized is that they if they better understood the plan, the better I wrote the operation order, the better they understood it, the better execution, the more likely I would get the outcome I wanted. I quickly realized that at that level, I wasn't writing a decision memorandum to convince bosses; I was communicating with my soldiers instructions that were coming down from higher about how we would execute our part of the operation. So, I had this moment of *a-ha*, so I gotta write really clear op orders.

Then I got to the career course lovingly known as "bonehead English," or English for infantry officers. The infantry school had undertaken a measure to try and teach captains, there was a hole in our swing, and it was obvious captains could not write well enough, cleanly enough. So, we had these two women who instructed us in what was then called Captains' Career Course, now called Advanced Course. They taught bonehead English to infantry officers. I had an easy time with bonehead English because Professor Lail had taught me how to write. So, I had no problem with bonehead English at all.

Now I moved from company operation orders to battalion S-3.[1] Now I am actually writing documents, decision papers, intended to convince. I did that for a while. Then I go off to case cube—combined armed services, staff, college, which had a strong component. The Army was doing that very deliberately, a separate course between your career course and advanced course in Command and General Staff College. There was a course that all captains went to that taught you how to write clearly and to brief. You actually learned the various types—an information paper, a decision memo, an information briefing, a decision briefing. And for nine weeks all you did was write and brief, write and brief, write and brief. All of these things stood me in good stead by the time I got to the Ranger Regiment next. And it was very rigid writing. Writing and very demanding, clean. Writing and briefing styles were critical to what we were doing.

My first assignment out of the tactical Army landed me at Pacific Command, and first I was a war planner, then later I became a country desk officer for China. Then I became the speech writer for the combatant commander. And when I was first approached them wanting to make me a speechwriter, I said, "You got the wrong guy; I have a Georgia public-school education. My writing is sort of the Army writing style, clean and simple." And they go, "Nope, that is exactly why we want you."

That stunned me. I interviewed for the job and got the job, and next thing you know I spend a year and a half as the combatant commander speechwriter. I learned a lot in that job. I learned a lot by doing and got a lot of coaching from the combatant commander and several graybeard kinda colonels on the staff who reviewed my work before the admiral got to see it. I got a lot of coaching on my writing. All of that has really played out on this continuum of things. I find that writing to inform and writing to convince—that I learned first from Professor Lail in 1979, 80—that writing has stood me in good stead, and I employ those things I learned 36, 37, 38 years ago, I employ them almost every day in this job.

RIFENBURG: One of my close friends, Major Forester, is out there at Fort Shafter. He works with General Brown, and he works as a speechwriter.

TOWNSEND: Uh-huh.

RIFENBURG: I read a recent *Army Times* article (Rempfer, January 9, 2019) about remarks you delivered at an event hosted by the Association of the United States Army. According to the article, you expressed concern about the officers and enlisted making tough choices in battle, and you described the importance of mission command to prepare troops to understand and achieve the broader purpose of a task instead of getting bogged down in paperwork and minutiae. Additionally, you stressed that mission command is helpful in case near-peer adversaries spoof the Army's C2 [command and control].[2] As I read your remarks and thought about them as a college writing teacher who works closely with cadets at my school, I am trying to teach cadets, and all writers, to adjust their writing for given situations and not stick to formulaic templates that restrict how we write. As TRADOC continues to promote mission command, what is something my colleagues and I can do to just begin planting the seeds for these young cadets to start seeing more flexibility in writing and also help TRADOC push these doctrine tenets of mission command?

TOWNSEND: Okay, there are some misconceptions out there about mission command. I think mission command applies to all facets of being a solider and of life. The whole point behind mission command is to empower disciplined initiative. And I can break that down into writing for young writers, young officers. I want you to follow the plan. I want you to follow your orders. I want you to follow the template. Until you realize they don't fit the situation you are in. There is something unique about the situation, and you need to deviate to get the mission accomplished or to get the point across. You need to deviate. So, you should basically follow the standard, the template, the doctrine, but you should apply it to the situation you are in. If it fits, use it. If it doesn't fit, don't be bound by it. That is the whole point behind mission command: to come up with what will work. If I gave you an order to follow a plan, if that works, then follow that because the whole enterprise is aligned and knows what you are doing. But if you get out there on the battlefield and realize that my orders don't actually fit what is actually happening here, I need to do something different. Then do something different.

Same thing with writing. Something I learned with the Rangers. Back then, people thought the Rangers were very rigid in their application of rules and SOP, standing operating procedures or standard operating procedures. I didn't find that to be the case at all. What the Rangers wanted you to do is to use discipline initiative. Follow your orders and follow your SOPs. But if they don't fit, I want you to win. Don't follow the plan knowing you are going to fail, right? So, what I learned in the Rangers was a saying: to deviate from the standard, to flex off the standard, you first have to learn what the standard is. We have a similar kinda approach in the Army; we have a thing called a *doctrinal template*, right? On a flat surface of the earth, knowing the enemy is going to be arrayed a certain way, here is your doctrinal solution for that. Except, you know what? The world is never flat, and the enemy never does exactly what his manual says he is going to do. So, you never actually apply the doctrinal template in real life. You take that doctrinal template and use it as a guideline and apply what we call a *situational template*. That is the doctrine applied to the situation I am in. I would tell writers to do the exact same thing I laid out here. First of all, follow your doctrinal template. It will keep you from leaving something out that is really important.

I told you already that Professor Lail gave us as a doctrinal template for an argumentative essay intended to convince or drive a decision. It was an introduction, the problem, the thesis, kinda address the opponent's argument right up front and dismisses those or mitigates those and then gives one to three points that kinda convince, supports your point and supports for those [your point] and then conclude. So, that template is so effective I still use it today. The Army taught me how to write really clean without a bunch of fancy prose; just plain English is more than good enough. So, those are doctrinal templates. Sometimes I use a different template to fit the situation. Sometimes I use less-than-clean English because I am trying to make a point here. So that is what I tell our young writers out there, our young officers: follow your orders, follow the templates, apply them to the situation you are in. Deviate if you must, have a reason for doing so, if you think it makes a more effective argument or point, clarify then deviate. By all means, deviate.

RIFENBURG: A broad historical question. As I have been researching the Reserve Officer Training Corps, I've been reading the 1916 National Defense Act. So, when Congress designated ROTC through this act. What is so unique about ROTC in my mind is civilians and soldiers coming together to train future Army officers. We have ROTC at UNG, for example, and the cadets take military-science classes, but they also take classes with people like me, with civilians. Together, we are training and preparing future Army officers. In your mind, what are some benefits of that, of working alongside civilian professors like me, like my colleagues, to prepare future supporting officers that might work under you one day?

TOWNSEND: First of all, I would say the main benefit is it mans our Army with the quality officers that we need. Our military academies are not big enough. For example, in the Army we graduate one thousand plus or minus new lieutenants each year after a four-year program. Our Army requires between six and seven thousand officers a year. So, the military academy [i.e., West Point] cannot produce all the officers we need. So, in 1916, they realized we need a large source of commissioned officers other than the military academy. ROTC was created. So, we have to have to it to augment what our military academy produces. Our ROTC program currently produces almost 70 percent of the officers our Army needs. Well over five thousand this year, and next year it is going to be around six thousand. So, pretty huge chunk.

Okay, now, what are some of the benefits? Here is where I think there are some of the unique benefits. You have already mentioned some of them. So, I take military-science classes with my fellow cadets, actually sometimes there are civilians in those classes because some universities and programs allow the civilian students to take the military-science classes for credit. Actually, we encourage that because we think it might attract some people who are not considering ROTC, a military-history course or orienteering and land navigation. Students that like to be outside and do outdoor activities, take a military-science course and next thing you know they like that, "I am going to enjoy ROTC," which is exactly what we would like to see. So, they take those courses, and then they go, like you said, and get civilian courses. So, I think they get a really broad perspective.

They almost get the best of both worlds. They get university life in America, but they also get ROTC. I would tell you that my experience at North Georgia, college then, now University of North Georgia, was fantastic preparation for the Army. My day at North Georgia was a lot like the Army. So, different than a West Point day, by the way. I would wake up at North Georgia, and in the morning, we would do one of two things. We either did inspections or we did PT [physical training]. Kinda like the Army does every morning. Then we would have breakfast. Some days we would march to breakfast together. Some days you were free to go on your own schedule. Then we went to class. And like you said, I was in an ROTC class, and in those days we didn't let civilians take an ROTC class, so I was in an ROTC class and with my fellow cadets, but I was at civilians classes all day long, and I was in uniform because at North Georgia we wore the uniform all day, all duty day, and afterwards when I was no longer on academic probation as a freshman, I got home at the end of the school day, or duty day, and took my uniform off and then I was just like every other college kid in America, except we called the dorms "barracks" instead of "dorms." But we would go back and, you know, it was a sorta quasi, like Army lifestyle. Got up in the morning and you did PT, and you had breakfast, and went to work in uniform all day long, and you got off and you mixed up with your civilian students and you did social life in the evenings.

That is kinda how the Army is and that is how life at North Georgia was. I thought it was great preparation for life in the Army. And I actually think that kind of lifestyle gives cadets who go to our senior military college a real strong advantage because in some ROTC programs, they only get a smidgen of military life every day or every week. And other places, they are completely immersed in it and that is all they do. But at North Georgia, at a place like that, it was a really good balance, I think; prepared one well for military life.

RIFENBURG: It also seems to benefit our civilian students a lot to have cadets in the class with them. To have an active military presence on the campus. There seems to be benefits for civilian students to be a part of that environment.

TOWNSEND: I would agree with that. I think that just as the values of the Corps of Cadets pick up on the values of the institution, of the community they are in, those Corps of Cadets also affect the values and the environment that they are in. As you said, the civilian students, I think, some of those good Army values rub off on the civilians. I saw that as a student there.

RIFENBURG: Kind of a different question. As a college professor, someone who researches writing and studies writing, I think a lot about the material we use to get writing done. So, are we writing by hand, are we writing on a screen, are we writing with a stylus on a tablet? The tools people use to accomplish writing. As you prepare troops for the battlefield, what are some writing tools you expect them to take with them into the field?

TOWNSEND: [laughs and reaches for his left ankle pocket] Okay, so I have been carrying this since I was a second lieutenant. A notebook. And a pen.

RIFENBURG: Always a pen?

TOWNSEND: No, actually, this is a pen and pencil all in one. So, it does both. So, when I was a young lieutenant, our battalion had a standard that every leader would carry note material and a writing instrument at all times. My father actually, who was a retired master sergeant, that was one of his points of guidance to me, that a young lieutenant would always have pen and paper on you because you might have to take a message, write notes, or write an order to send to someone. So, you should always have pen and paper and I still do.

But I am also a modern soldier [reaches for right ankle pocket once more and pulls out black iPhone], so I also have my electronic device. In fact, I have two of them. I have my personal one and I have my government-issued one here. And sometimes I take notes on this, and I write. Actually, it is easier to disseminate if I write on here [holds up his phone] than if I write on here [holds up his notepad]. But this [the iPhone] has its uses, and I never expect to find myself without it. This [the notepad] also has its uses. But there are times when I prefer this [notepad]. Between these two things, this is how I communicate. When I am in the office, I also have that [pointing to desktop computer] that desktop computer.

RIFENBURG: [noticing two monitors] Do you like the two monitors?

TOWNSEND: Actually, one of those is a VTC [video teleconferencing] screen. That is a VTC over there on the left.

RIFENBURG: Do you use a laptop at all?

TOWNSEND: That is a laptop [pointing to below the VTC]. I have gone entirely on a laptop. That laptop stays here in the office, and when I am the road, I just unplug it and it goes with me. And it plugs right back into that docking station. All my files and things are there. But between this modern communication device and this old-school communication device, it works. And I would advise any of our young officers who are starting off to adopt the same approach. But a stack of 3 × 5 cards with an alligator clip and a pen, you can never go wrong with that.

RIFENBURG: That is good advice. So, the notebook that you have in your left hand, are you particular about lined paper or not lined paper.

TOWNSEND: [laughs] Actually, I favor gridded paper. [opens notepad and flips through]. It comes lined, and it comes gridded. Actually, that is an old leftover. I don't so much need gridded anymore. But I first became exposed to notebooks with gridded paper when I was a captain. And I realized that as a captain, I found myself drawing sector sketches, range cards, operation diagrams, action-on-the-objectives sketches, and having gridded paper allowed me to not only write but also draw on it to scale with the grid. Because I could write each block equaled one meter, or something like that, and I could draw a sketch on it. Right? So, I always used gridded paper, and I have never fallen out of that even though I don't need it anymore. I don't draw very many actions-on-the-objective sketches or range cards or that kind of thing anymore. Defensive fire plans.

RIFENBURG: I appreciate you humoring me there. I ask this question to a variety of people, and I have been surprised. People are particular about the tools they use. I like blue ink; I love this pen [holding out the pen I took notes with during the interview].

TOWNSEND: I like blue ink, too!

RIFENBURG: So, I am particular about the tools I use. You mentioned earlier in our discussion that you spend a lot of time reviewing documents. When you review documents, do you prefer doing that on a screen or printing out hard copies.

TOWNSEND: My staff prefers when I do it on the screens, but I prefer the hard-copy technique. First of all, I'm not of the more modern age that actually goes to the computer first. I probably go to hard copy, pen and paper first. And it just works for me better. To me, I can think better if I can sit and read the printed word and I can write in the margins or on the back of something or line through. That works better for me. So, what my staff frequently does is, when we are on the road, frequently when I am traveling is when I am reviewing documents because that is when I have the most time to do it, sitting in transportation, whether that is a car or an airplane or something like that. I will review documents. I will mark them up. And what do they do? They take pictures of them or they scan them and turn them into digital to get back to the staff, so they can make the changes.

RIFENBURG: Can they read your handwriting?

TOWNSEND: Yeah. I try to write clearly enough. And I am not one of those guys who, if I don't like the way something is written, I will not say, unless it is really horrible, I will not say, reword or rewrite this. I will actually write in the margins what I think it should say. Then I am pretty demanding about, I don't have too many demands, but one of them is that if I take the time to write up your draft, bring it with you. Keep it. Don't throw it out. And bring it back with the last copy. I did that just this morning when I marked up a document about a plan we are publishing here. It just speeds my checking. Because I can't remember. I know I changed this but can't recall what I said. Anyway, so I am kinda demanding about that. But I think I prefer working in hard copy. It just works better for me. I can also do it anywhere. It is harder to do that if you are completely electronic. You kinda gotta be around a computer, and you can't really do that on your phone. You need a laptop or something at a minimum. But I can do the hard copy anywhere.

RIFENBURG: I have to do the same thing for my publications. When an editor suggests changes, I have to write a brief revision memo even saying on what page I made changes, and I have to accompany that with my new draft.

TOWNSEND: Right.

RIFENBURG: Just two more questions and then I will get out of here and, if possible, I would like to get a picture with you. When you think about USACC [US Army Cadet Command], about thirty thousand senior cadets operating with an over $800 million budget according to the public-affairs officer at Fort Knox, many of whom will commission as officers, what are some things that are concerning to you? What keeps you up at night as you think about these thirty thousand senior cadets?

TOWNSEND: Okay. I sleep like a baby. Almost nothing keeps me up at night. I am not one who brings the burden of command and the worries of the moment to bed with me. But when I am awake, what concerns me or worries me is, are we preparing these future officers as well as we possibly can given the time and the resources we have? Have we resourced it enough? Are the resources at an acceptable level? And then are we using those resources we got, time, personnel, money, other resources like ammunition and training aids and things? Are we maximizing the benefit to prepare these young future officers as well as we can? I think a young lieutenant, in the Army or any service in the US Armed Forces, has some of the most awesome responsibilities of any American. On the first day at their first unit, they will be given command of a platoon of soldiers that will range from sixteen to fifty, thereabouts, soldiers dependent on their leadership. Their lives, safety, health, welfare, training, readiness, mission accomplishment, depends on that young lieutenant's leadership from the first day they arrive. They got a lot of help. They got some great NCOs [noncommissioned officers] to help them, around them, beneath them, and around them. And they got some officers above them: company commanders and battalion commanders to also help them. But they are in a fairly unique responsibility, very early age in the US Armed Forces, particularly in the ground forces, Army and Marines, where we put that young lieutenant in day one in charge of forty or fifty people. That is awesome responsibility. They need to be prepared as well as they can be for that. So, we have to take every useable minute we can to prepare them well.

I was just out there at Kansas City and spoke there at the Marshall Awards. These are the best cadets from their cohort across America. We had about three hundred cadets there to include some West Point cadets. All handpicked by their programs to come to this Marshall Awards program. They got a lot of leader development. And then I spoke to them at their final dinner. And I told them about this awesome responsibility. These four years of preparation have led to this moment where they just received their branches [duty assignments]. Both at West Point and ROTC. Most of them knew where their branches were going to be, and they were excited about the future. They were all commissioning here in a matter of a few months, and they were headed out to begin their Army career. Them being as prepared as they possibly can be. Because you might have a gradual introduction to the Army, or it might be sudden and stark. You might be arriving to a unit that is going to have a very good training path for a year or two leading up to a deployment. Or you might be arriving to a unit that is deploying next week, and you are going, too. So, that is what I mean by sudden and stark to the hardest thing we might do in our Army. And they got to be ready for that. That is why I work every day to make sure our soldiers and sergeants and our officers are a trained and educated and prepared as they can be for their responsibility.

RIFENBURG: Last question: When are you going to write a book? Or a memoir?

TOWNSEND: [laughs] I don't have plans to write a book. If I do . . . I don't have time! If I was writing a book right now, I should be working harder and getting these young officers and soldiers ready.

RIFENBURG: Does that interest you when you retire?

TOWNSEND: Uh. Yeah. Sure. [laughs] Sure, Why not? Sometime down the road, I'd say there is a decent chance I'd write a book. I don't know. Never thought about it.

NOTES

1. For an explanation of "S-3," see chapter 8, note 1.
2. Near-peer adversaries are, as the term suggests, countries on a similar military and economic footing with the United States. China and Russia often fall into this category. To spoof the Army's command and control, essentially, means to hack into the Army's digital communication technologies and stall them or simply disable them.

REFERENCES

Adams, John Quincy. 2013. "She Goes Not Abroad in Search of Monsters to Destroy." *American Conservative*, July 4. https://www.theamericanconservative.com/repository/she-goes-not-abroad-in-search-of-monsters-todestroy/.
Adelman, Cliff, Peter Ewell, Paul Gaston, and Carol Geary Schneider. 2014. "Degree Qualifications Profile." Lumina Foundation, October 1. https://www.luminafoundation.org/resources/dqp.
Adler-Kassner, Linda. 2008. *The Activist WPA: Changing Stories about Writing and Writers*. Logan, UT: Utah State University Press.
Alexander, Jonathan, Karen Lunsford, and Carl Whithaus. 2020. "Toward Wayfinding: A Metaphor for Understanding Writing Experiences." *Written Communication* 37 (1): 104–131.
American Educational Research Association. 2011. "Code of Ethics." https://www.aera.net/Portals/38/docs/About_AERA/CodeOfEthics(1).pdf.
Anderson, Paul, Robert Gonyea, Chris Anson, and Charles Paine. 2015. "The Contributions of Writing to Learn: Results from a Large-Scale Multi-Institutional Study." *Research in the Teaching of English* 50 (2): 199–235.
Angeli, Elizabeth L. 2019. *Rhetorical Work in Emergency Medical Services*. New York, NY: Routledge.
Anson, Chris. 2016. "The Pop Warner Chronicles: A Case Study in Contextual Adaptation and the Transfer of Writing Ability." *College Composition and Communication* 67 (4): 518–549.
Anson, Chris, and Shawn Neely. 2010. "The Army and Academy as Textual Communities: Exploring Mismatches in the Concepts of Attribution, Appropriation, and Shared Goals." *Kairos* 14 (3). kairos.technorhetoric.net/14.3/topoi/anson-neely/index.html.
Artze-Vega, Isis, Melody Bowdon, Kimberly Emmons, Michele Eodice, Susan K. Hess, Claire Coleman Lamonica, and Gerald Nelms. 2013. "Privileging Pedagogy: Composition, Rhetoric, and Faculty Development." *College Composition and Communication* 65 (1): 162–184.
Arum, Richard, and Josipa Roksa. 2011. *Academically Adrift: Limited Learning on College Campuses*. Chicago, IL: University of Chicago Press.
Axe, David. 2007. *Army 101: Insider ROTC in a Time of War*. Columbia, SC: University of South Carolina Press.
Bakhtin, Mikhail. 1986. *Speech Genres and Other Late Essays*. Translated by Vern W. McGee. Austin, TX: University of Texas Press.
Bass, Randall. 2017. "Coda." In *Understanding Writing Transfer: Implications for Transformative Student Learning in Higher Education*, edited by Jessie L. Moore and Randall Bass, 144–154. Sterling, VA: Stylus.
Bazerman, Charles. 2004. "Speech Acts, Genres, and Activity Systems: How Texts Organize Activity and People." *What Writing Does and How It Does It: An Introduction to Analyzing Texts and Textual Practices*, edited by Charles Bazerman and Paul Prior, 309–339. London: Routledge.

Bazerman, Charles. 2009. "Genre and Cognitive Development: Beyond Writing to Learn." In *Genre in a Changing World*, edited by Charles Bazerman, Adair Bonini, and Débora Figueiredo, 279–294. West Lafayette, IN: Parlor.

Bazerman, Charles. 2011. "Standpoints: The Disciplined Interdisciplinary of Writing Studies." *Research in the Teaching of English* 46 (1): 8–21.

Bazerman, Charles. 2021. "The Puzzle of Conducting Research on Lifespan Development of Writing." In *The Expanding Universe of Writing Studies: Higher Education Writing Research*, edited by Christiane Donahue, Cynthia P. Monroe, and Kelly Blewet, 403–416. New York, NY: Peter Lang.

Bazerman, Charles, Arthur Applebee, Virginia Berninger, Deborah Brandt, Steve Graham, Paul Kei Matsuda, Sandra Murphy, Deborah Wells Rowe, and Mary Schleppegrell. 2017 "Taking the Long View on Writing Development." *Research in the Teaching of English* 51 (3): 351–360.

Bazerman, Charles, Arthur Applebee, Virginia Berninger, Deborah Brandt, Steve Graham, Paul Kei Matsuda, Sandra Murphy, Deborah Wells Rowe, and Mary Schleppegrell. 2018. *The Lifespan Development of Writing*. Urbana, IL: NCTE.

Beaufort, Anne. 2007. *College Writing and Beyond: A New Framework for University Writing Instruction*. Logan, UT: Utah State University Press.

Behm, Nicholas, Sherry Rankins-Robertson, and Duane Roen, eds. 2017. *The Framework for Success in Postsecondary Writing: Scholarship and Applications*. Anderson, SC: Parlor Press.

Bergmann, Linda, and Janet Zepernick. 2007. "Disciplinarity and Transfer: Students' Perceptions of Learning to Write." *WPA: Writing Program Administration* 31 (1/2): 124–149.

Bishop, Elizabeth. 1979. "Questions of Travel." *The Complete Poems, 1927–1979*. New York: Farrar, Strauss & Giroux.

Bivens, Kristin Marie. 2018. "Rhetorically Listening for Microwithdrawals of Consent in Research Practice." In *Methodologies for the Rhetoric of Health and Medicine*, edited by Lisa Melonçon and J. Blake Scott, 138–157. New York, NY: Routledge.

Bizzell, Patricia. 2014. "We Want to Know Who Our Students Are." *PMLA* 129 (3): 442–447.

Blaauw-Hara, Mark. 2021. *From Military to Academy: The Writing and Learning Transitions of Student-Veterans*. Logan, UT: Utah State University Press.

Blackwell, Logan. 2015a. "I am My Sister's Keeper." *Odyssey* (blog). Oct 19. https://www.theodysseyonline.com/sisters-keeper.

Blackwell, Logan. 2015b. "The 7 Professors You Meet at UNG." *Odyssey* (blog). Sept. 28. https://www.theodysseyonline.com/the-7-professors-you-meet-ung.

Blackwell, Logan. 2015c. "7 Students You See at UNG." *Odyssey* (blog). Aug. 24. https://www.theodysseyonline.com/7-students-you-see-at-ung.

Boyer, Ernest L. 1998. *Reinventing Undergraduate Education: A Blueprint for America's Research Universities*. Stony Brook, NY. Boyer Commission on Educating Undergraduates in the Research University.

Braziller, Amy, and Elizabeth Kleinfeld. 2020. *The Bedford Book of Genres*. 3rd ed. Boston, MA: Bedford.

Brown, Anna. 2018. "Most Americans Say Higher Education Is Heading in the Wrong Direction, But Partisans Disagree on Why." Pew Research Center, July 26. https://www.pewresearch.org/fact-tank/2018/07/26/most-americans-say-higher-ed-is-heading-in-wrong-direction-but-partisans-disagree-on-why/.

Brown, David West, and Laura L. Aull. 2017. "Elaborated Specificity versus Emphatic Generality: A Corpus-Based Comparison of Higher- and Lower-Scoring Advanced Placement Exams in English." *Research in the Teaching of English* 51 (4): 394–417.

Brown University, Swearer Center. 2019. "Engaged Scholarship." https://www.brown.edu/academics/college/swearer/engaged-research.

Brubacher, John. S., and Willis Rudy. 1968. *Higher Education in Transition: An American History, 1636–1956*. New York, NY: Harper.

Bureau for International Language Coordination. 2016. "NATO Standard ATrain-5. Standard Proficiency Levels, Ed. A. Version 2." https://www.natobilc.org/files/ATrainP-5%20EDA%20V2%20E.pdf.

Bureau for International Language Coordination. 2019. "STANAG 6001, Ed 5: Overview of Language Proficiency Levels." https://www.natobilc.org/documents/TrainingResources/STANAG%206001%20Overview%20Feb%202019.pdf.

Calhoon-Dillahunt, Carolyn. 2012. "Important Focus, Limited Perspective." *College Composition and Communication* 63 (3): 495–499.

Carroll, Lee Ann. 2002. *Rehearsing New Roles: How College Students Develop as Writers.* Carbondale, IL: Southern Illinois University Press.

Carleton College Center for Community and Civic Engagement. 2019. "What Is Public Scholarship?" https://apps.carleton.edu/ccce/scholarship/what_is/.

Center for Plain Language. 2018. "2018 Report Card." https://centerforplainlanguage.org/reports/federal-report-card/2018-report-card/.

Chiseri-Strater, Elizabeth. 1991. *Academic Literacies: The Public and Private Discourse of University Students.* Portsmouth, NH: Boynton/Cook.

Clark, Christopher. 2014. *The Sleepwalkers: How Europe Went to War in 1914.* New York, NY: Harper.

Collins, Billy. 1996. "Introduction to Poetry." *The Apple That Astonished Paris.* Fayetteville, AR: University of Arkansas Press.

Conference on College Composition and Communication. 2015a. "CCCC Guidelines for the Ethical Conduct of Research in Composition Studies." https://cccc.ncte.org/cccc/resources/positions/ethicalconduct.

Conference on College Composition and Communication. 2015b. "Student Veterans in the Classroom: Realizing Their Strengths and Assessing Their Needs." https://cccc.ncte.org/cccc/resources/positions/student-veterans/summary.

Cook-Sather, Alison, Catherine Bovill, and Peter Felten. 2014. *Engaging Students as Partners in Learning and Teaching: A Guide for Faculty.* San Francisco, CA: Jossey-Bass.

Council of Writing Program Administrators. 2014. WPA Outcomes Statement for First-Year Composition (3.0). http://wpacouncil.org/positions/outcomes.html.

Council of Writing Program Administrators, National Council for Teachers of English, and National Writing Project. 2012. *Framework for Success in Postsecondary Writing.* http://wpacouncil.org/aws/CWPA/asset_manager/get_file/350201?ver=7548.

Davis, Charles H. F., III, Shaun R. Harper, and Wilmon A. Christian, III. 2018. "Black Data Matter: Connecting Education Research to the Movement for Black Lives." In *Envisioning Public Scholarship for Our Time: Models of Higher Education*, edited by Adrianna Kezar, Yianna Drivalas, and Joseph A. Kitchen, 53–65. Sterling, VA: Stylus.

Day, Michael, Susan H. Delagrange, Mike Palmquist, Michael A. Pemberton, and Janice R. Walker. 2013. "What We Really Value: Redefining Scholarly Engagement in Tenure and Promotion Protocols." *College Composition and Communication* 65 (1): 185–208.

DePalma, Michael-John. 2015. "Tracing Transfer across Media: Investigating Writers' Perceptions of Cross-Textual and Rhetorical Reshaping in Processes of Remediation." *College Composition and Communication* 66 (4): 615–642.

Department of Health and Human Services. 2016. *Code of Federal Regulations*, Title 45, Part 46: Protection of Human Subjects, Section 116. https://www.govinfo.gov/content/pkg/CFR-2016-title45-vol1/pdf/CFR-2016-title45-vol1-part46.pdf.

Dias, Patrick, Aviva Freedman, Peter Medway, and Anthony Paré. 2013. *Worlds Apart: Acting and Writing in Academic and Workplace Contexts.* New York, NY: Routledge.

Dippre, Ryan J., and Talinn Phillips, eds. 2020. *Approaches to Lifespan Writing Research: Generating an Actionable Coherence.* Perspectives on Writing. Fort Collins, CO: WAC Clearinghouse. https://wac.colostate.edu/books/perspectives/lifespan/.

Downs, Donald, and Ilia Murtazashvili. 2012. *Arms and the University: Military Presence and the Civic Education of Non-military Students*. Cambridge, MA: Cambridge University Press.

Driscoll, Dana Lynn, and Jennifer Wells. 2012. "Beyond Knowledge and Skills: Writing Transfer and the Role of Student Dispositions." *Composition Forum* 26. https://compositionforum.com/issue/26/beyond-knowledge-skills.php.

Dryer, Dylan. 2019. "Divided by Primes: Competing Meanings among Writing Studies' Keywords." *College English* 81 (3): 214–255.

Duffy, John. 2019. *Provocations of Virtue: Rhetoric, Ethics, and the Teaching of Writing*. Logan, UT: Utah State University Press.

Edwards, Mike, and D. Alexis Hart, eds. 2010. "Rhetoric, Technology, and the Military." Special issue, *Kairos: A Journal of Rhetoric, Technology* 14 (3). http://kairos.technorhetoric.net/14.3/.

Elon University of Center for Engaged Learning. 2014. "Elon Statement on Writing Transfer." https://www.centerforengagedlearning.org/elon-statement-on-writing-transfer/.

Eodice, Michele, Anne Ellen Geller, and Neal Learner. 2016. *The Meaningful Writing Project: Learning, Teaching, and Writing in Higher Education*. Logan, UT: Utah State University Press.

Fishman, Jenn, Andrea Lunsford, Beth McGregor, and Mark Otuteye. 2005. "Performing Writing, Performing Literacy." *College Composition and Communication* 57 (2): 224–252.

Flint, Abbi, and Hannah Goddard. 2020. "Power, Partnership, and Representation: A Dialogue Exploring Student Academic Representation Systems as a Form of Partnership." In *The Power of Partnership: Students, Staff, and Faculty Revolutionizing Higher Education*, edited by Lucy Mercer-Mapstone and Sophia Abbot, 73–87. Elon University Center for Engaged Learning Open Access Book Series. https://www.centerforengagedlearning.org/books/power-of-partnership/chapter-4/.

Gere, Anne Ruggles, ed. 2019. *Developing Writers in Higher Education: A Longitudinal Study*. Ann Arbor, MI: University of Michigan Press.

Gere, Anne Ruggles, Anne Curzan, J. W. Hammond, Sarah Hughes, Ruth Li, Andrew Moos, Kendon Smith, Kathryn Van Zanen, Keely L. Wheeler, and Crystal J. Zanders. 2021. "Communal Justicing: Writing Assessment, Disciplinary Infrastructure, and the Case for Critical Language Awareness." *College Composition and Communication* 72 (3): 384–412.

Goldberg, Jeffrey. 2016. "The Obama Doctrine." *Atlantic*, April. https://www.theatlantic.com/magazine/archive/2016/04/the-obama-doctrine/471525/.

Goggin, Maureen Daly, and Peter N. Goggin, eds. 2018. *Serendipity in Rhetoric, Writing, and Literacy Research*. Logan, UT: Utah State University Press.

Gonzalez v. Raich. 2005. 545 U.S. 1.

Gorzelsky, Gwen, Carol Hayes, Ed Jones, and Dana Lynn Driscoll. 2017. "Cueing and Adapting First-Year Writing Knowledge: Support for Transfer into Disciplinary Writing." In *Understanding Writing Transfer: Implications for Transformative Student Learning in Higher Education*, edited by Jessie L. Moore and Randall Bass, 113–121. Sterling, VA: Stylus.

Hansen, Kristine. 2012. "The 'Framework for Success in Postsecondary Writing': Better than the Competition, Still Not All We Need." *College English* 74 (6): 540–543.

Halley, Brittany. 2021. "Materiality Matters: How Human Bodies and Writing Technologies Impact the Composing Process." *Young Scholars in Writing* 18. https://youngscholarsinwriting.org/index.php/ysiw/article/view/326.

Hart, D. Alexis, and Roger Thompson, eds. 2016a. "Round Table: Veterans' Voices." Special issue, *Pedagogy: Critical Approaches to Teaching Literature, Language, Composition, and Culture* 16 (3): 511–517.

Hart, D. Alexis, and Roger Thompson. 2016b. "Veterans in the Writing Classroom: Three Programmatic Approaches to Facilitate the Transition from the Military to Higher Education." *College Composition and Communication* 68 (2): 345–371.

Hart, D. Alexis, and Roger Thompson. 2020. *Writing Programs, Veteran Studies, and the Post 9/11 University: A Field Guide*. Studies in Writing and Rhetoric. Urbana, IL: NCTE.

Haswell, Richard H. 1991. *Gaining Ground in College Writing: Tales of Development and Interpretation*. Dallas, TX: Southern Methodist University Press.

Haswell, Richard H. 2012. "Methodologically Adrift." *College Composition and Communication* 63 (3): 487–491.

Hazelrigg, Nick. 2019. "'Shocking' Cut May Force Layoffs in Alaska's Universities." *Insider Higher Ed*, July 1. https://www.insidehighered.com/news/2019/07/01/imminent-massive-cuts-could-force-faculty-staff-layoffs-university-alaska-system.

Herrington, Anne J., and Marcia Curtis. 2000. *Persons in Process: Four Stories of Writing and Personal Development*. Urbana, IL: NCTE.

Holmes, Ashley. 2016. *Public Pedagogy in Composition Studies*. Urbana, IL: NCTE.

Hurst v. Florida. 2016. 577 U.S.___.

Hurtado, Sylvia. 2018. "Legal Arenas and Public Scholarship." In *Envisioning Public Scholarship for Our Time: Models of Higher Education*, edited by Adrianna Kezar, Yianna Drivalas, and Joseph A. Kitchen, 53–65. Sterling, VA: Stylus.

Hutchins, Edwin. 1995. *Cognition in the Wild*. Cambridge, MA: MIT Press.

Inoue, Asao. 2015. *Antiracist Writing Assessment Ecologies: Teaching and Assessing Writing for a Socially Just Future*. Perspectives on Writing. Fort Collins, CO: WAC Clearinghouse. https://wac.colostate.edu/books/perspectives/inoue.

Inoue, Asao. 2019. "How Do We Language So People Stop Killing Each Other, or What Do We Do about White Language Supremacy." *College Composition and Communication* 71 (2): 352–369.

Ivanič, Roz. 1998. *Writing and Identity: The Discourse Construction of Identity in Academic Writing*. Philadelphia, PA: John Benjamins.

Johnson, Kristine. 2019. "Topics and Networks: Mapping Forty Years of Scholarly Inquiry." *WPA: Writing Program Administration* 42 (3): 44–58.

Jones, Susan R., Vasti Torres, and Jan Arminio. 2014. *Negotiating the Complexities of Qualitative Research in Higher Education*. 2nd ed. New York, NY: Routledge.

Kalish, Kate, Holly Hassel, Cassandra Phillips, Jennifer Heinert, and Joanne Baird Giordano. 2019. "Inequitable Austerity: Pedagogies of Resilience and Resistance in Composition." *Pedagogy: Critical Approaches to Teaching Literature, Language, Composition, and Culture* 19 (2): 261–281.

Kaomea, Julie. 2001. "Dilemmas of an Indigenous Academic: A Native Hawaiian Story." *Contemporary Issues in Early Childhood* 2 (1): 67–82.

Kaplan, Fred. 2016. "Obama's Way: The President in Practice." *Foreign Affairs*, January/February. https://www.foreignaffairs.com/articles/2015-12-07/obamas-way.

Karlen, Yves. 2017. "The Development of a New Instrument to Assess Metacognitive Strategy Knowledge about Academic Writing and Its Relation to Self-Regulated Writing and Writing Performance." *Journal of Writing Research* 9 (1): 61–86.

Kelly, Bridget Turner, and Carrie A. Kortegast, eds. 2017. *Engaging Images for Research, Pedagogy, and Practice*. Sterling, VA: Stylus.

Kennesaw State University. 2020. "First-Year Studies, MS." http://catalog.kennesaw.edu/preview_program.php?catoid=30&poid=3684&returnto=24.

Kezar, Adrianna, Yianna Drivalas, and Joseph A. Kitchen, eds. 2018. *Envisioning Public Scholarship for Our Time: Models of Higher Education*. Sterling VA: Stylus.

Kitzhaber, Albert. 1963. *Themes, Theories, and Therapy: The Teaching of Writing in College*. New York, NY: McGraw-Hill.

Kuh, George D. 2008. *High-Impact Educational Practices: What They Are, Who Has Access to Them, and Why They Matter*. Washington, DC: American Association of Colleges and Universities.

Kurlinkus, William C. 2018. *Nostalgic Design: Rhetoric, Memory, and Democratizing Technology*. Pittsburgh, PA: University of Pittsburgh Press.

Latour, Bruno. 1990. "Drawing Things Together." In *Representation in Scientific Practice*, edited by Michael Lynch and Steve Woolgar, 19–68. Cambridge, MA: MIT Press.

Law, John. 2014. *After Method: Mess in Social Science Research.* New York, NY: Routledge.

Lerner, Neal, and Mya Poe. 2014. "Writing and Becoming a Scientist: A Longitudinal Qualitative Study of Three Science Undergraduates." In *Applied Linguistics and Literacies for STEM: Founding Concepts, Methodologies and Research Projects*, edited by Mary Jane Curry and David I. Hanauer, 43–63. Philadelphia, PA: John Benjamins.

Levine, David O. 1988. *The American College and the Culture of Aspiration, 1915–1940.* Ithaca, NY: Cornell University Press.

Lillis, Theresa. 2008. "Ethnography as Method, Methodology, and 'Deep Theorizing': Closing the Gap between Text and Context in Academic Writing Research." *Written Communication* 25 (3): 353–388.

Lynch, Paul. 2013. *After Pedagogy: The Experience of Teaching.* Studies in Writing and Rhetoric. Urbana. IL: NCTE.

Malafouris, Lambros. 2013. *How Things Shape the Mind: A Theory of Material Engagement.* Cambridge, MA: MIT Press.

Malenczyk, Rita, Neal Lerner, and Elizabeth H. Boquet. 2018. "Learning from Bruffee: Collaboration, Students, and the Making of Knowledge in Writing Administration." In *Composition, Rhetoric, and Disciplinarity*, edited by Rita Malenczyk, Susan Miller-Cochran, Elizabeth Wardle, and Kathleen Blake Yancey, 70–87. Logan, UT: Utah State University Press.

McComiskey, Bruce. 2012. "Bridging the Divide: The (Puzzling) *Framework* and the Transition from K–12 to College Writing Instruction." *College English* 74 (6): 537–543.

McCullough, David. 2001. *John Adams.* New York, NY: Simon & Schuster.

Miller, Benjamin. 2014. "Mapping the Methods of Composition/Rhetoric Dissertations: A 'Landscape Plotted and Pieced.'" *College Composition and Communication* 66 (1): 145–176.

Miller, Carolyn. 1984. "Genre as a Social Action." *Quarterly Journal of Speech* 70 (2): 151–167.

Miller, Susan. 2002. "Writing Studies as a Mode of Inquiry." In *Rhetoric and Composition as Intellectual Work*, edited by Gary Olson, 41–54. Carbondale, IL: Southern Illinois University Press.

Millett, Allan R., Peter Maslowski, and William B. Feis. 2012. *For the Common Defense: A Military History of the United States from 1607 to 2012.* 3rd ed. New York, NY: Free Press.

Modern Language Association. 2004. "Statement of Professional Ethics." https://www.mla.org/Resources/Research/Surveys-Reports-and-Other-Documents/Staffing-Salaries-and-Other-Professional-Issues/Statement-of-Professional-Ethics/Read-the-Statement-Online.

Moore, Jessie L., and Randall Bass, eds. 2017. *Understanding Writing Transfer: Implications for Transformative Student Learning in Higher Education.* Sterling, VA: Stylus.

Mueller, Derek. 2017. *Network Sense: Methods for Visualizing a Discipline.* Fort Collins, CO: WAC Clearinghouse. https://wac.colostate.edu/books/writing/network/.

National Center for Education Statistics. 2012. "The Nation's Report Card: Writing 2011." https://nces.ed.gov/nationsreportcard/pubs/main2011/2012470.asp. National Center for Education Statistics. 2019. "Classification of Instructional Programs." https://nces.ed.gov/ipeds/cipcode/Default.aspx?y=56.

National Defense Act of 1916. 1916. Pub. L. NO. 64-85, 39 Stat 166. https://artsandculture.google.com/entity/national-defense-act-of-1916/m02pngll?hl=en.

Navajo Division of Health, Navajo Human Research Review Board. 2018. *IRB Research Protocol Application* https://www.nnhrrb.navajo-nsn.gov/pdf/2021/Rvised%203-6-18NNHRRB%20IRB%20application_2_10_2021.pdf.

National Endowment for the Humanities. 2014. "NEH Launches New *Standing Together* Initiative." https://www.neh.gov/news/press-release/2014-04-02.

National Writing Project. 2003. "The Neglected 'R': The Need for a Writing Revolution." https://www.nwp.org/cs/public/print/resource/2523.

Neiberg, Michael. 2000. *Making Citizen-Soldiers: ROTC and the Ideology of American Military Service*. Cambridge, MA: Harvard University Press.

Newport, Frank, and Brandon Busteed. 2017. "Why Are Republicans Down on Higher Ed?" Gallup, August 16. https://news.gallup.com/poll/216278/why-republicans-down-higher.aspx.

Obama, Barack. 2009a. "Nobel Lecture: A Just and Lasting Peace." Nobel Prize. https://www.nobelprize.org/prizes/peace/2009/obama/lecture/.

Obama, Barack. 2009b. "Transparency and Open Government: Memorandum for the Heads of Executive Departments and Agencies." White House, January 21. https://obamawhitehouse.archives.gov/the-press-office/transparency-and-open-government.

O'Neill, Peggy, Linda Adler-Kassner, Cathy Fleischer, and Anne-Marie Hall. 2012. "Creating the 'Framework for Success in Postsecondary Writing.'" *College English* 74 (6): 520–524.

Palmquist, Mike, and Barbara Wallraff. 2020. *Joining the Conversation: A Guide and Handbook for Writers*. 4th ed. Boston, MA: Bedford.

Patel, Leigh. 2015. *Decolonizing Educational Research: From Ownership to Answerability*. New York, NY: Routledge.

Patel, Leigh. 2019. "Turning Away from Logarithms to Return to Story." *Research in the Teaching of English* 53 (3): 270–275.

Perl, Sondra. 1979. "The Composing Processes of Unskilled College Writers." *Research in the Teaching of English* 13 (4): 317–336.

Perryman-Clark, Staci M., and Colin Craig. 2019. "Black Student Success Models: Institutional Profiles of Writing Programs." *Black Perspectives in Writing Program Administration: From the Margins to the Center*, edited by Staci M. Perryman-Clark and Colin Craig, 101–114. Urbana, IL: NCTE.

Pintrich, Paul R. 2000. "The Role of Goal Orientation in Self-Regulated Learning." *Handbook of Self-Regulation*, edited by Monique Boekaerts, Paul R. Pintrich, and Moshe Zeidner, 451–502. San Diego, CA: Academic Press.

Portanova, Patricia, Michael Rifenburg, and Duane Roen, eds. 2017. *Contemporary Perspectives on Cognition and Writing*. Perspectives on Writing. Fort Collins, CO: WAC Clearinghouse. https://wac.colostate.edu/books/perspectives/cognition/.

Prior, Paul. 2017. "Setting a Research Agenda for Lifespan Writing Development: The Long View from Where?" *Research in the Teaching of English* 52 (2): 211–219.

Prior, Paul. 2018. "How Do Moments Add Up to Lives? Trajectories of Semiotic Becoming vs. Tales of School Learning in Four Modes." In *Making Future Matters*, edited by Rick Wysocki and Mary P. Sheridan. Logan, UT: Computers and Composition Digital Press. https://ccdigitalpress.org/book/makingfuturematters/prior-part-3.html#content-top.

Prior, Paul, and Jody Shipka. 2003. "Chronotopic Lamination: Tracing the Contours of Literate Activity." In *Writing Selves/Writing Societies: Research from Activity Perspectives*, edited by Charles Bazerman and David R. Russell, 180–238. Fort Collins, CO: WAC Clearinghouse. https://wac.colostate.edu/books/perspectives/selves-societies/.

Reiff, Mary Jo, and Anis Bawarshi. 2011. "Tracing Discursive Resources: How Students Use Prior Genre Knowledge to Negotiate New Writing Contexts in First-Year Composition." *Written Communication* 28 (3): 312–337.

Rifenburg, J. Michael. 2019. "To Ensure Warfighting Function: Writing Inside a U.S. Army Brigade Headquarters." *Composition Studies* 47 (1): 116–135.

Rifenburg, J. Michael. 2020. "Chasing the Team: Participant Recruitment Strategies for Qualitative Research into Student-Athlete Writers." In *Navigating the Challenges in Qualitative Educational Research: Research, Interrupted*, edited by Todd Ruecker and Vanessa Svihla, 39–51. New York, NY: Routledge.

Rifenburg, J. Michael, and Brian G. Forester. 2018. "First-Year Cadets' Conceptions of General Education Writing at a Senior Military College." *Teaching & Learning Inquiry* 6 (1): 52–66.

Rogers, Paul. 2010. "The Contributions of North American Longitudinal Studies of Writing In Higher Education to Our Understanding of Writing Development." In *Traditions of Writing Research*, edited by Charles Bazerman, Robert Krut, Karen Lunsford, Sue McLeod, Suzie Null, Paul Rogers, and Amanda Stansell, 365–377. New York, NY: Routledge.

Roozen Kevin. 2008. "Journalism, Poetry, Stand-Up Comedy, and Academic Literacy: Mapping the Interplay of Curricular and Extracurricular Literate Activities." *Journal of Basic Writing* 27 (1): 5–34.

Roozen, Kevin. 2009. "'Fan Fic-ing' English Studies: A Case Study Exploring the Interplay of Vernacular Literacies and Disciplinary Engagement." *Research in the Teaching of English* 44 (2): 136–169.

Roozen, Kevin. 2010. "Trajectories of Practice: Repurposing in One Student's Developing Disciplinary Writing Process." *Written Communication* 27 (3): 318–354.

Roozen, Kevin. 2020. "Addressing the Futurity of Literate Action: Tracing the Enduring Consequences of Acting with Inscriptions throughout the Lifeworld." In *Approaches to Lifespan Writing Research: Generating an Actionable Coherence*, edited by Ryan J. Dippre and Talinn Phillips, 227–248. Perspectives on Writing. Fort Collins, CO: WAC Clearinghouse. https://wac.colostate.edu/docs/books/lifespan/chapter14.pdf.

Roozen, Kevin, and Joe Erickson. 2017. *Expanding Literate Landscapes: Persons, Practices, and Sociohistoric Perspectives of Disciplinary Development*. Logan, UT: Computers and Composition Digital Press. https://ccdigitalpress.org/expanding.

Ruecker, Todd, and Vanessa Svihla, eds. 2020. *Navigating the Challenges in Qualitative Educational Research: Research, Interrupted*. New York, NY: Routledge.

Rule, Hannah J. 2018. "Writing's Rooms." *College Composition and Communication* 69 (3): 402–432.

Russell, David, and Arturo Yañez. 2003. "'Big Picture People Rarely Become Historians:' Genre Systems and the Contradictions of General Education." In *Writing Selves/Writing Societies: Research from Activity Perspectives*, edited by Charles Bazerman and David Russell, 331–362. Fort Collins, CO: WAC Clearinghouse. https://wac.colostate.edu/books/perspectives/selves_societies/.

Sam, Cecile H., and Jarrett T. Gupton. 2018. "Cultivating Ethical Mindfulness: Using Activity Theory Framework to Address Ethical Dilemmas in Public Scholarship." In *Envisioning Public Scholarship for Our Time: Models of Higher Education*, edited by Adrianna Kezar, Yianna Drivalas, and Joseph A. Kitchen, 38–53. Sterling, VA: Stylus.

Sanchez, James Chase. 2021. "Towards Reconciliation: Composing Racial Literacy with Autoethnography." In *Race, Rhetoric, and Research Methods*, edited by Alexandria Lockett, Iris D. Ruiz, James Chase Sanchez, and Christopher Carter, 91–117. Perspectives on Writing. Fort Collins, CO: WAC Clearinghouse. https://wac.colostate.edu/books/perspectives/race/.

Schultz, Katherine, and Glynda Hull. 2002. "Locating Literacy Theory in Out-of-School Contexts." In *School's Out!: Bridging Out-of-School Literacies with Classroom Practice*, edited by Glynda Hull and Katherine Schultz, 11–31. New York, NY: Teachers College Press.

Scott, Tony, and Nancy Welch, eds. 2016. *Composition in the Age of Austerity*. Logan, UT: Utah State University Press.

Scott, Marc. 2017. "Big Data and Writing Program Retention Assessment: What We Need to Know." In *Retention, Persistence, and Writing Programs*, edited by Todd Ruecker, Dawn Shepherd, Heidi Estrem, and Beth Brunk-Chavez, 56–74. Logan, UT: Utah State University Press.

Severino, Carol. 2012. "The Problem of Articulation: Uncovering More of the Composition Curriculum." *College English* 74 (6): 533–536.

Shotton, Heather J., Amanda R. Tachine, Christine A. Nelson, Robin Zape-tah-hol-ah Minthorn, and Stephanie J. Waterman. 2017. "Living Our Research Through Indigenous Scholar Sisterhood Practices." *Qualitative Inquiry* 24 (9): 636–645.

Smith, Linda Tuhiwai. 2012. *Decolonizing Methodologies: Research and Indigenous Peoples*. 2nd ed. London: Zed Books.
Stein, Arlene, and Jessie Daniels. 2018. *Going Public: A Guide for Social Scientists*. Chicago, IL: Chicago University Press.
Sternglass, Marilyn. 1997. *Time to Know Them: A Longitudinal Study of Writing and Learning at the College Level*. Mahwah, NJ: Lawrence Erlbaum.
Stornaiuolo, Amy, Gerald Campano, and Ebony Elizabeth Thomas. 2019. "Editor's Introduction: Toward Methodological Pluralism: The Geopolitics of Knowing." *Research in the Teaching of English* 53 (3): 193–196.
Stornaiuolo, Amy, Anna Smith, and Nathan Phillips. 2017. "Developing a Transliteracies Framework for a Connected World." *Journal of Literacy Research* 49 (1): 68–91.
Sullivan, Patrick. 2012. "Essential Habits of Mind for College Readiness." *College English* 74 (6): 547–553.
Summerfield, Judith, and Philip M. Anderson. 2012 "A Framework Adrift." *College English* 74 (6): 544–547.
Syverson, Margaret. 1999. *The Wealth of Reality: An Ecology of Composition*. Carbondale, IL: Southern Illinois University Press.
Thaiss, Chris, and Terry Myer Zawacki. 2006. *Engaged Writers and Dynamic Disciplines: Research on the Academic Writing Life*. Portsmouth, NH: Boynton/Cook.
Thelin, John R. 2004. *A History of American Higher Education*. Baltimore, MD: Johns Hopkins University Press.
Tinberg, Howard, and Patrick Sullivan, eds. 2006. *What Is "College-Level" Writing?* Urbana, IL: NCTE.
Tuck, Eve, and K. Wayne Yang. 2012. "Decolonization Is Not a Metaphor." *Decolonization: Indigeneity, Education & Society* 1 (1): 1–40.
Tuck, Eve, and K. Wayne Yang. 2014. "R-Words: Refusing Research." In *Humanizing Research: Decolonizing Qualitative Inquiry for Youth and Communities*, edited by Django Paris and Maisha T. Winn, 223–247. Los Angeles, CA: Sage.
Tukufu, Zuberi, and Eduardo Bonilla-Silva, eds. 2008. *White Logic, White Methods: Racism and Methodology*. Lanham, MD: Rowman & Littlefield.
US Army. 1999. *Oath of Office-Military Personnel*, Form 71. https://armypubs.army.mil/pub/eforms/DR_a/pdf/A71.pdf.
US Army. 1986. *Effective Writing for Army Leaders*, Pamphlet 600-67. https://www.lsu.edu/hss/milsci/resources/dapam600_67.pdf.
US Army. 2010. Army Demographics, FY 10 Army Profile. https://www.armyg1.army.mil/hr/docs/demographics/FY10_Army_Profile.pdf.
US Army. 2014a. *Developmental Counseling Form*, Form 4856. https://www.hrc.army.mil/asset/20923.
US Army. 2014b. *Operations Security*. Regulation 530-1. https://armypubs.army.mil/ProductMaps/PubForm/Details.aspx?PUB_ID=3324.
US Army. 2016. *Cadet Command Reserve Officers' Training Corps Branching, Commissioning, and Accessioning Regulation*, Regulation 145-9. https://www.cadetcommand.army.mil/res/files/forms_policies/regulations/USACC%20Regulation%20145-9.pdf.
US Army. 2017. *Recommendation for Award*, Form 638. https://armypubs.army.mil/pub/eforms/DR_a/ARN32485-DA_FORM_638-003-EFILE-4.pdf.
US Army. 2018. *Reserve Officers' Training Corps Accessions Fiscal Year 2019*, Circular 601-19-1. https://www.cadetcommand.army.mil/res/files/forms_policies/circulars/USACC%20Circular%20601-19-1%20Reserve%20Officers%27%20Training%20Corps%20Accessions%20Fiscal%20Year%202018%2006-21-2018.pdf.
US Army. 2019a. "Basic Pay: Active Duty Soldiers." https://www.goarmy.com/benefits/money/basic-pay-active-duty-soldiers.html.
US Army. 2019b. *Army Awards*, Regulation 600-8-22. https://armypubs.army.mil/epubs/DR_pubs/DR_a/pdf/web/ARN18147_R600_8_22_admin2_FINAL.pdf.

US Army. 2019c. *The Operations Process*, Army Doctrine Publication 5-0. https://armypubs.army.mil/epubs/DR_pubs/DR_a/ARN18126-ADP_5-0-000-WEB-3.pdf.

US Army. 2019d. *The Army Body Composition Program*, Regulation 600-9. https://www.armyg1.army.mil/hr/bodyComposition/docs/AR600_9_28-June-2013.pdf.

US Army. 2020a. "Action Plan to Prioritize People and Teams." Oct. 13. https://www.army.mil/article/239837/action_plan_to_prioritize_people_and_teams.

US Army. 2020b. FY20 Army Profile. https://api.army.mil/e2/c/downloads/2021/02/01/aa8adcbb/army-profiles-fy20-tri-fold.pdf.

US Army. 2020c. *Preparing and Managing Correspondence*, Regulation 25-50. https://armypubs.army.mil/Search/CRRDPub.aspx?pnum=AR%2025-50.

US Army. 2020d. *Military Symbols*, Field Manual 1-02.2. https://armypubs.army.mil/epubs/DR_pubs/DR_a/ARN31121-FM_1-02.2-000-WEB-1.pdf.

US Army. 2021. *Drill and Ceremonies*, Training Circular 3-21.5. https://armypubs.army.mil/epubs/DR_pubs/DR_a/ARN32297-TC_3-21.5-000-WEB-1.pdf.

US Army. 2022. *Planning and Orders Production*, Field Manual 5-0. https://armypubs.army.mil/epubs/DR_pubs/DR_a/ARN35403-FM_5-0-000-WEB-1.pdf.

US Army Cadet Command. 2021. "Advanced Camp." https://www.cadetcommand.army.mil/advanced.aspx.

US Congress. 2010. Plain Writing Act. Pub. L. No. 111-274, 124 Stat 2861. https://www.congress.gov/111/plaws/publ274/PLAW-111publ274.pdf.

US Congress. 2018. National Defense Authorization Act for Fiscal Year 2018. Pub. L. No. 115-91. https://www.congress.gov/bill/115th-congress/house-bill/2810.

US Department of Defense. 2008. "Political Activities by Members of the Armed Forces," Directive 1344.10. https://www.esd.whs.mil/Portals/54/Documents/DD/issuances/dodd/134410p.pdf.

US Department of Defense. 2018. *Summary of the 2018 National Defense Strategy: Sharpening the American Military Competitive Edge*. https://dod.defense.gov/Portals/1/Documents/pubs/2018-National-Defense-Strategy-Summary.pdf.

University of Minnesota Twin Cities. 2019. "Assessment of Community-Engaged Scholarship." https://engagement.umn.edu/sites/engagement.umn.edu/files/UMN%20PES%20Criteria%20%20%28Final.2.19.19%29%20%281%29.pdf.

University of North Georgia. 2022. "Mission, Vision & Values." https://ung.edu/about/mission-vision-values.php.

Wardle, Elizabeth, and Doug Downs, eds. 2014. *Writing about Writing: A College Reader*. 2nd ed. Boston, MA: Bedford.

Washington Headquarters Services. n.d. "Plain Language." https://www.esd.whs.mil/dd/plainlanguage/.

Watson, C. Edward. 2018. "Centers for Teaching and Learning, Academic Change, and the Institutional Zeitgeist." *Liberal Education*. https://www.aacu.org/article/centers-for-teaching-and-learning-academic-change-and-the-institutional-zeitgeist.

Weisser, Christian, Michelle Ballif, Alexis Hart, and Roger Thompson, eds. 2013. "Veterans and Writing." Special issue, *Composition Forum* 28. http://compositionforum.com/issue/28/.

White, Edward M., Norbert Elliot, and Irvin Peckham. 2015. *Very Like a Whale: The Assessment of Writing Programs*. Logan, UT: Utah State University Press.

Winalski, Amanda. 2006. "Bam." In *What Is "College-Level" Writing?*, edited by Howard Tinberg and Patrick Sullivan, 302–311. Urbana, IL: NCTE.

Winkelmes, Mary-Ann, Matthew Bernacki, Jeffrey Butler, Michelle Zochowski, Jennifer Golanics, and Kathryn Harriss Weavil. 2016. "A Teaching Intervention That Increases Underserved College Students' Success." *Peer Review* 18 (1/2): 31–36.

Yagelski, Robert. 2015. *Writing Ten Core Concepts*. Stamford, CT: Cengage.

Yancey, Kathleen Blake. 2008. "2008 NCTE Presidential Address: The Impulse to Compose and The Age of Composition." *Research in the Teaching of English* 43 (3): 316–338.

Yancey, Kathleen Blake. 2017. "Writing, Transfer, and ePortfolios: A Possible Trifecta in Supporting Student Learning." In *Understanding Writing Transfer: Implications for Transformative Student Learning in Higher Education*, edited by Jessie L. Moore and Randall Bass, 39–48. Sterling, VA: Stylus.

Yancey, Kathleen Blake, Liane Robertson, and Kara Taczak. 2014. *Writing across Contexts: Transfer, Composition, and Sites of Writing*. Logan, UT: Utah State University Press.

Zuberi, Tukufu. 2001. *Thicker Than Blood: How Racial Statistics Lie*. Minneapolis, MN: University of Minnesota Press.

INDEX

Page numbers followed by *f* indicate figures.

A&M (agricultural and mechanical) college and universities, 29
AAC&U. *See* American Association of Colleges and Universities
Academic Literacies: The Public and Private Discourse of University Students, 40
academic literacy, 40
academic performance, cadets, 177–178, 212, 214–215; degree-to-completion numbers, 215; first-year college students, 87; gateway courses, 215; general education coursework, 87; one-semester persistence rates, 215; retention numbers, 87, 88, 91, 215
Academically Adrift: Limited Learning on College Campuses, 17, 88–89, 107*n1*
access to research subjects, 75, 77, 78
accessions, Army, 11, 30, 31, 177–178
active duty, cadets, 176–178, 186; officers, 30; political activity, 164; enlisted, 1, 9
The Activist WPA, 203
activity theory, 49, 51, 105
Adler-Kassner, Linda, 203
Advanced Camp, Fort Knox, 9, 31; ROTC requirement, 9, 30, 31, 183–184; training, 175–176
Advanced Placement test scores, 18
after-action reviews, 101
agricultural and mechanical (A&M) college and universities, 29
Air Force Academy, 22*n2*
Alexander, Jonathan, 42
Alien and Sedition Acts, 96–97
American Association of Colleges and Universities (AAC&U), 1–3, 87, 90, 91
American Educational Research Association's *Code of Ethics*, 73
American Literature I (ENGL 2131) coursework, 85, 102–107, 124, 133, 200
analytical writing, 51
Angeli, Elizabeth L., 9, 141
Anson, Chris, 14, 37, 47, 56–57
Applebee, Arthur, 43
Applied Leadership in Small Unit Operations (MILS 3100), 153–158

Approaches to Lifespan Writing Research: Generating an Actionable Coherence, 58*n2*
argumentative essay, 3
armed forces: all-voluntary military system, 34; citizenship obligations, 164; geopolitical changes, 160; modernization, 7; political activity, 164 presidential elections, 160; publications, 159*n2*; staffing increase during Trump Administration, 12; strength, 165
Arms and the University: Military Presence and the Civic Education of Non-military Students, 11
Army (US), accessions, 11, 30, 31, 177–178; active-duty soldiers, 1; branches, 176, 188; doctrinal publications, 14; FY 20 Army Profile report, 30; installations, 107*n2*; modernization, 7; national-guard soldiers, 1; Oath of Commissioned Officers, 98, 194, 195*f*, 196; officers, 30; promotions, 31; ranks, 7; regulations, 7, 9, 11, 23*n3*, 30, 54; relationship with higher education, 2; reserve soldiers, 1; S-3 designation, 119, 126*n1*
Army Action Officer: Staff Writing Guide, 56
Army Awards, 187–188
Army Cadet Command Regulation 145-9, 11, 30, 113
Army genres. *See* Army writing standards
Army Morale, Welfare, and Recreation (MWR) Program, 57
Army Reserve, 30
Army Talent Alignment Process, 12
Army Times, 163
Army Training Circular (TC 3-21.5), 5, 13, 216
Army writing standards, 2, 5–7; after-action reviews, 101; Army Regulation 25-50, 7, 54; business communication skills, 120–122, 132; counseling forms, 54; coursework, 15, 108–110; critical-thinking skills, 173, 178–180; curriculum design, 198; effectiveness, 71; future goals, 20–21; genres, 47–48; leadership skills,

INDEX

153–158; learning resources, 8; Military Decision-Making Process (MDMP), 173, 178–180; not-talk writing, 84; operations orders (OPORDs), 7, 51–53, 100, 101, 111–112, 144–149; orality, 100–101; plagiarism, 56–57; Plain Writing Act, 54, 55; publications, 5, 6, 51, 159*n1*; research, 8, 10; Reserve Officers' Training Corps (ROTC), 86; unclassified, 145*f*; terrain models, 139, 141, 150–152, 151*f*, 173; writing development, 20, 83, 84
Artze-Vega, Isis, 208*n1*
Arum, Richard, 17, 88–89
assignment design, teaching methodology, 211
Astronomy of the Solar System (ASTR 1010), second-year cadets, 126
audience, writing development, 99, 131
Aull, Laura, 18
authorial attribution, military writing, 37, 99, 130, 131
autoethnography, 21, 94–95
awards recipients, Department of Army Form 638 (US Army 2017), 15
Axe, David, 33–34

Bakhtin, Mikhail, 47
Ballif, Michelle, 35–36
Basic Airborne Course, 119
Basic Officer Leader Course (BOLC), 188–189, 191, 213
Bass, Randall, 48
Bawarshi, Anis, 50, 84, 86
Bazerman, Charles, 43, 49, 51, 43, 58*n2*, 58*n3*, 72
Beaufort, Anne, 40–42, 49
Bedford Book of Genres, The, 51
Beginning College Survey of Student Engagement (BCSSE), 88
Benning, Henry L., 107*n2*
Bergmann, Linda, 84
Berninger, Virginia, 43
big data analytics, 17, 18, 197, 199
Bishop, Elizabeth, 73–74
Bizzell, Patricia, 13, 72
Blaauw-Hara, Mark, 36
Black Lives Matter, 204
blogs, writing development, 117–118, 126, 129–132, 143, 185
BOLC (Basic Office Leader Course), 188–189, 191, 213
Bonilla-Silva, Eduardo, 22, 76
Boquet, Elizabeth H., 72, 198
Bovill, Cathy, 18–19
Bowdon, Melody, 208*n1*

Boyer report, 87
branches: accessions, 177; Army, 176; cadets, 188; combat arms, 31; National Order of Merit (OML) list, 83
Brandt, Deborah, 43
Braziller, Amy, 51
brigade headquarters, active-duty soldiers, 9
Brown, David West, 18
Brubacher, John S., 29
Bryant, William Jennings, 28
budget for Reserve Officers' Training Corps (ROTC), 7
Bureau for International Language Coordination, 211
Business Communication (BUSA 2108), 120–122, 132
Bush, George W., 32, 97, 160, 163
business communication skills, 120–122, 124–125, 132

Cadet Command Reserve Officers' Training Corps Branching, Commissioning, and Accessioning Regulation, 11, 30, 113
cadets: Advanced Camp, 9, 30–31, 175–176, 183–184; branches, 188; civilian to military life, 39; commissioning, 9, 14, 15, 20, 29, 30; Corps of Cadets, 14, 70; decision-making; processes, 179–180; deployment, 186; education-abroad opportunities, 143–144; enrollment in civilian classes, 11, 34, 102; evaluation, 179; extracurricular activities, 185; high-school writing to college-level writing, 39; learning resources, 8; legal-writing skills, 124–125; literacy development, 15, 94; memorandum of understanding with faculty, 17; military experience, 39; platoon sergeant, 142; post-graduation life, 191; reflection on writing assignments, 211–212; social media, 9; training, 9, 13*f*, 179; university curriculum, 209; US Army Cadet Command Regulation 145-9, 11, 30, 113. *See also* first-year cadets; fourth-year cadets; second-year cadets; third-year cadets
Calhoon-Dillahunt, Carolyn, 107*n1*
Campano, Gerald, 21–22, 74–76, 135, 136
campus support services for veterans, 36
Carnegie Foundation's Classification for Community Engagement, 202, 205
Carroll, Lee Ann, 40, 41, 61, 134
casualties, 9 Line BEDVAC reports, 53
CBRN (chemical, biological, radiological, and nuclear) weapons, 189, 191

CCCC Guidelines for the Ethical Conduct of Research in Composition Studies, 73, 91
Center for Community and Civic Engagement (Carleton College), 203
Center for Plain Language, 56
Center for Postsecondary Research (University of Indiana), 18
centers for teaching and learning (CTLs), 205–206, 208n1
chemical, biological, radiological, and nuclear (CBRN) weapons, 189, 191
Chemical Corps, 188–189
Chestatee Review, 95, 96f
Chiseri-Strater, Elizabeth, 40, 42, 134
chronotopic laminations of literacy development, 117–118, 168
CIP (Classification of Instructional Programs), 23n
Citadel, The (The Military College of South Carolina), 6, 65
citizenship, 34, 164
citizen-soldier ideal, 11, 19, 29, 33–35
civilian education: cadet enrollment, 102, 11, 67–68, 75; officers' training, 34; teachers, 11
Clark, Christopher, 27
Classification of Instructional Programs (CIP), 23n4
classroom practice, teaching methodology, 197
COA. *See* course of action
Coast Guard Academy, 22n2
Code of Ethics (American Educational Research Association), 73
cognitive facilitators, writing development, 139–141, 201–202
Coleman Lamonica, Claire, 208n1
college graduation rates, 87, 88, 91, 200, 215
College Writing and Beyond: A New Framework for University Writing Instruction, 41, 42
Colonel Raymond C. Hamilton Rifle Range, 108
combat branches, 31
command and control, operations orders (OPORDS), 52
commander's intent, operations orders (OPORDs), 149
command signal, operations orders (OPORDs), 146, 148
commissioning to officer, Advanced Camp, 176; branches, 188; literacy development, 14, 20, 94; Oath of Commissioned Officers, 98, 194, 195f;

196; Order of Merit List, 83; 177; postgraduation, 7, 9, 29–30, 191; requirements, 165
communication skills, 120–122, 132
Complete College America, 17
complex reasoning, first-year students, 88–89
Composition 1 (English Honors), 91
composition courses, 36, 90–91
Composition Forum, 36
Composition Risk Management, 179
compulsory military training units in land-grant institutions, 29, 34
Conference on College Composition and Communication (CCCC), 12–13, 36, 37, 91
conventional warfare, 185
Cook-Sather, Allison, 18–19
copy editing, writing development, 130–131
cordon and search techniques, 14–15, 154–156
Corps. *See* Reserve Officers' Training Corps (ROTC)
Corps of Cadets, 14, 70, 112–113
correspondence, Army, 54
Council of Writing Program Administrators (CWPA), 51
counseling forms, 14, 54
counterinsurgency techniques, leadership skills, 154–156
course of action (COA), Military Decision-Making Process (MDMP), 173, 182–184
coursework, first-year students, 90–91; third-year cadets, 153
creative writing, 61–62, 85, 93, 166–168
creative-thinking skills, operations orders (OPORDs), 53
credibility, general education coursework, 101
criteria, transparency in learning and teaching (TILT), 211
critical-thinking skills: Army writing standards, 173, 178–180; first-year students, 88–89; literacy development, 19; Military Decision-Making Process (MDMP), 173, 178–180; Mission Command and the Army Profession (MILS 4000), 187–188; operations orders (OPORDs), 52–53; writing instruction, 41
CTLs (centers for teaching and learning), 205–206, 208n1
cultural needs, writing curriculum, 17
curiosity, habit of mind, 85
curriculum design: Army writing standards, 197–198; cultural needs, 17; federally established military science, 13;

gateway courses, 215; general education coursework, 87–88, 199–201; knowledge transfer, 47; literacy, 40; Reserve Officers' Training Corps (ROTC), 15, 86; student input, 198–200; teaching methodology, 197; teaching-for-transfer, 42; universities, 209; writing experiences, 19, 93–94; writing transfer, 48
Council of Writing Program Administrators (CWPA), 51

DA Form 4856 (US Army 2014a), 54, 57
Daniels, Jessie, 204
DA-PAM 600-67 (US Army 1986), 54–55
data analysis, first-year students, 88; graduation rates, 87; research, 10, 134–135, 197
data collection, research, 10, 21, 15–17, 135, 136$n1$, 191–193
Day, Michael, 206
decision-making process, Military Decision-Making Process (MDMP): COA analysis, 179–184
decline in writing skills in middle- and high-school education, 89
Decolonizing Educational Research: From Ownership to Answerability, 204
Defense, Department of, 37$n1$
Degrees Qualifications Profile, 87–88
degree-to-completion rates, 17, 215
Delagrange, Susan H., 206
Department of Army Form 638 (US Army 2017), 15
deployments, cadets, 153, 158, 161, 185, 186
Developing Writers in Higher Education: A Longitudinal Study, 58$n1$
development in writing style, 11, 41; proficiency in genres, 50–51; proficiency, 83–84
developmental counseling forms, Army genres, 54
DFWI rates, 17, 88
Dippre, Ryan J., 11
directives. *See* operations orders (OPORDs)
disability studies, student veterans, 36
disciplinary descriptive, rhetoric and composition/writing studies (RC/WS), 23$n4$
discipline-specific instruction, 84, 105
discourse-community knowledge, 42, 49, 85
Distinguished Military Graduate (DMG), 178
distributed cognition, 140–141
diversity, equity, and inclusion, 76–78, 88
doctrinal templates, 226

Downs, Donald, 11, 34
Downs, Doug, 11, 14, 60–61
drawing, metacognition, 191–193; research method, 191–193, 196$n1$; writing space, 192f, 193
Drills and Ceremonies, Army Training Circular (TC), 5, 6
Driscoll, Dana Lynn, 50, 85, 86
Drivalas, Yianna, 204
Dryer, Dylan, 18
Duffy, John, 206
duty components, 30–31, 37$n2$
duty slots, 31, 176–177

education-abroad opportunities, 143–144
educational researchers. *See* research methods
Edwards, Mike, 36
effectiveness of Army writing standards, 71
Elliot, Norbert, 23$n4$
Elon's Center for Engaged Learning, 43
Embodiment, writing development, 44, 112
Emmons, Kimberly, 208$n1$
engaged research, 85, 202–203, 205–207
Engaging Images for Research, Pedagogy, and Practice, 197$n1$
English Composition 1 (Honors), 91
English-language proficiency levels, 210–211
English studies, critical thinking skills, 19
enlisted personnel, 30
enrollment in civilian classes, 102
Envisioning Public Scholarship for Our Time: Models for Higher Education Researchers, 204
Eodice, Michele, 17–18, 42, 89, 208$n1$, 215
Erickson, Joe, 11, 94
essay-writing contests, 95–96
ethical-dilemma writing, 108–110
ethics in research, 73–74, 91–92, 198, 204, 206
ethnography, 40, 134
evaluation, underclass cadets, 179
evaluative writing, 51
execution, operations orders (OPORDs), 52, 146, 147–148
external writing tools, cognitive writing challenges, 139–141
extracurricular activities: blog writing, 129; creating writing, 166–168; fraternities, 132; literacy development, 40, 128; non-school writing projects, 93–94, 97, 128–129; 198; Order of Merit List (OML), 117–118; second-year cadets, 185; self-sponsored writing, 170; style development, 19–21, 130–133

faculty: centers for teaching and learning (CTLs), 205–206; Green Zone training, 35; memorandum of understanding with cadets, 17; professional development opportunities, 205; workshops, 210–213
failed operations documentation, operations orders (OPORDs), 146, 148
federal agencies, plain writing, 55–57
federal government, land-grant colleges, 29
federally-established military science writing curriculum, 13
Feis, William, 7
Felten, Peter, 18–19, 43
field army, 219
field books, operations orders (OPORDs), 139–140, 145–146
field manuals, 37
findings, research methodology, 19–20
First Battalion, 507th Parachute Infantry Regiment, 119
first-year cadets: academic performance, 87; Army writing standards, 86; autoethnography assignment, 94–95; cadres, 67; complex reasoning, 88–89; coursework, 90–91, 102, 107–112; critical thinking, 88–89; extracurricular activities, 64; failed initiation into discourse communities, 85; fraternities, 113; Freshman Recruit Orientation Group (FROG) week, 10, 66–68; goals, 64; grade-school writing experiences, 62–64; higher education, 59; literacy development, 61, 92–93, 104; meaningful writing projects, 89; quantitative data analysis, 88; writing development, 60–65, 83, 84, 93, 98, 99. *See also* cadets; fourth-year cadets; second-year cadets; third-year cadets
Fishman, Jenn, 127
fitness, cadet, 177–178, 184
five knowledge domains, 41–42
five-paragraph structure, operations orders (OPORDs), 52, 146
flash-fiction writing contests, 95–96
flexibility, habit of mind, 85
Flint, Abbi, 19
flipped-classroom teaching method, 120–122
FM 1-02, 159n2
FM 5-0, Military Decision-Making Process (MDMP), 173, 179–181, 182–184
for office use only (FOUO), 145f
foreign policy, 32–33, 161
Forester, Brian, 126n1, 140, 145f, 202
Fort Benning, 107n2

Fort Eustis, Virginia, 1
Fort Knox, Reserve Officers' Training Corps, 9, 31, 175–176, 183–184
FOUO. *See* for office use only
fourth-year cadets: academic performance, 177–178, 212, 214–215; accessions, 11, 30, 31, 177–178; active duty, 176–178, 186; critical-thinking skills, 187–188; fitness, 177–178; leadership skills, 175–178; mentoring, 179; Mission Command and the Army Profession (MILS 4000), 178–180; Order of Merit List, 83, 177–178. *See also* cadets; first-year cadets; second-year cadets; third-year cadets
fragmentary orders (FRAGOs), 14, 49, 52
Framework for Success in Postsecondary Writing (Council of Writing Program Administrators, National Council 2012), 85–86
fraternities, 113, 132, 170, 177, 185
Freshman Recruit Orientation Group (FROG) week: first-year cadets, 10, 66–68; in-processing, 66; Morrell, Robert "Trent," 68–70; smoking, 68–69
From Military to Academy: The Writing and Learning Transitions of Student-Veterans, 36
Furco, Andrew, 202

gaining access to research subjects, 78
Galton, Francis, 76
Gardner, John, 88, 215
Gatekeepers, gaining access to research subjects, 75, 78
gateway courses, 88, 218
Gateways to Completion, 88
Geller, Anne Ellen, 17–18, 42, 89, 90, 215
general education courses: academic performance, 87; activity theory, 105; American Literature I, 102–107, clarity, 101; credibility, 101; curriculum design, 87–88, 199–201, 215; first-year students, 108–112; genre pathways, 105; Honors English Composition I, 91; North American genre theory, 105; orality, 101; student veterans, 36; writing instruction, 84, 101
General Tadeusz Kosciuszko Military University of Land Forces (MULF), 17, 209–210
Geneva Protocol, 189
genres: activity theory, 49; Army writing standards, 15, 47, 86; knowledge, 42, 49–51; literary analysis, 105; orality, 100–101, 152; pathways, 105; proficiency, 50; writing development, 124

geopolitical changes, armed forces, 160
Gere, Anne Ruggles, 58, 58*n1*
Giordano, Joanne Baird, 85
Goddard, Hannah, 19
Going Public: A Guide for Social Scientists, 204
Goldberg, Jeffrey, 162–163
Gorzelsky, Gwen, 50
grading, 212, 214–215
graduation rates, data analysis, 87, 88, 91, 200, 215
Graham, Steve, 43
grammar, writing development, 130
graphic control measures. *See* symbols, military
Green Zone training, higher education, 35
grid paper, 2, 4
Guantanamo Bay, 161
guard-duty component, 31

habits of mind, 85
Hart, D. Alexis, 36
Hassel, Holly, 85
Haswell, Richard H., 58*n1*, 107*n1*
Hayes, Carol, 50
heat maps, research methods, 18
Heinert, Jennifer, 85
Herrington, Anne J., 58*n1*, 134
Hess, Susan K., 208*n1*
heuristic process. *See* critical-thinking skills; Military Decision-Making Process (MDMP)
higher education: American Literature I, 102–107; commissioning from cadet to Army officer, 29; curriculum design, 48, 87–88; first-year experience, 59, 87, 88, 91, 215; fraternities, 113; Green Zone training, 35; Honors English Composition I, 91; hybrid with military training, 35; military training units, 29–30; on-campus military training programs, 33; public confidence, 202; relationship with military, 2, 19; socio-economic factors, 41; state budget appropriations, 202; student voice representation, 19, 35; veterans, 35–36
Holmes, Ashley, 205
Hull, Glynda, 127
human-research subjects, ethics, 73–74, 91–92, 198
Hutchins, Edwin, 140

implicit racial bias in writing instruction, 85–86
inclusivity, longitudinal research, 13, 76–78
Indovina, Colonel Michael, 2, 5

informative writing, 51
Innovative Team Leadership (MILS 2000), 122–124
Inoue, Asao, 76–77, 85–86
in-processing, Freshman Recruit Orientation Group (FROG) week, 66, 67*f*
inquiry stance, 79, 135, 136
inscriptions, writing development, 44, 46
institutional effectiveness, 18, 87, 215
interdisciplinary writing, 35, 105
interventionist foreign policy, 32–33
IRB application, 136
Isolationist foreign policy, 32

Jacobson, Brad, 136*n1*
Jefferson, Thomas, 32, 96–97
John N. Gardner Institute of Excellence in Undergraduate Education, 88, 215
"Johnny Can't Write," 89
Johnson, Kristine, 18
Johnson, Lyndon B., 160
Joining the Conversation, 51
Jones, Ed, 50
Journal of the First-Year Experience and Students in Transition, 88
Journal of Veteran Studies, 35
just-in-school writing, 44–45, 47, 93–94, 128

Kairos: A Journal of Rhetoric, Technology, 36
Kalish, Katie, 85
Kaomea, Julie, 78
Kaplan, Fred, 162
Karlen, Yves, 211
Kelly, Bridget Turner, 197*n1*
Kelly, John, 186
Kezar, Adrianna J., 204
Kitchen, Joseph A., 204
Kitzhaber, Albert, 58*n1*
Kleinfeld, Elizabeth, 51
knowledge domains, 41; discourse-community, 42, 49; genre knowledge, 42, 49–51; rhetorical knowledge, 42, 49; subject-matter knowledge, 42, 49; writing-process, 42, 49
knowledge producers, human-subject research, 198
knowledge transfer, 47
knowledge-makers, 72
Kortegast, Carrie A., 197*n1*
Kuh, George D., 87, 90
Kurlinkus, Will, 206

Lail, Guy, 3, 4, 223
laminations of literacy development, 117–118, 127, 133, 168

Index 251

land-grant colleges, military education requirements, 29
language proficiency levels, 210–211
Latour, Bruno, 46, 150
Leadership and Personal Development (MILS 1000), 91, 109
leadership skills, Army writing standards, 153–158; Basic Officer Leader Course (BOLC) training, 188–189; cadets, 177–178; Corps of Cadets, 112–113; Innovative Team Leadership (Military Science 2000), 122–124; Reserve Officers' Training Corps (ROTC), 9, 30, 31, 175–176, 183–184, 193–194
Lee, Weston C. (U.S. Army 1st Lt.), 158
Legal Environment of Business (BUSA 2810), 124–125
Lerner, Neal, 17–18, 42, 72, 84–85, 89, 198, 215
Levine, David O., 37–38n3
lieutenant, rank of, 29–31, 66, 94, 131, 140, 159
Lifespan Writing Development Group (LWDG), 43–47, 128
Lillis, Theresa, 15
literacy development, 61; 86; academics, 40; audience, 131; cadets, 15, 92–94; chronotopic laminations, 117–118, 168; creative barriers, 61–62; critical-thinking skills, 19; deficient students, 18; first-year students, 92–93; longitudinal research, 40–43; modeling, 112; non-school writing, 94, 97; rhetoric and composition/writing studies (RC/WS) scholarship, 127; self-sponsored writing, 168–169; tasks, 61; voice, 131; writing-definition assignment, 101
literary analysis, 104–105
Literary, Scientific, and Military Academy. *See* Norwich University
literate becoming, 43–45, 118, 133
literature general education coursework, 102–107
location disclosure regulations, Army operations, 9, 23n
longitudinal research, 136n1; cognitive facilitators, 201–202; curriculum, 199–201; engaged research, 202–203; ethics, 73–74; first-year students, 88–89; gatekeepers, 75; participants, 72; positionality, 76–78; public scholarship, 202–207; qualitative research design, 73; racism, 76–78; researchers, 72; rhetoric and composition/writing studies (RC/WS), 40–43, 206; self-reflexivity, 74–78; Stanford Study of Writing (SSW), 127; student writing, 88–89, 198–207; students' perspectives, 198; traditional research, 202; writing development, 40; writing transfer, 57
Lumina Foundation and the National Institute for Learning Outcomes Assessment (NILOA), 87–88
Lunsford, Andrea, 127
Lunsford, Karen, 42

Making Citizen-Soldiers: ROTC and the Ideology of American Military Service, 11
Malenczyk, Rita, 72, 140, 198
mapping exercises, writing development, 191–193
masculine pronouns, 5
Maslowski, Peter, 7
materiality, writing development, 201–202
Matsuda, Paul Kei, 43
Mattis, James, 108, 164, 185
McCullough, David, 97
McGregor, Beth, 127
MDMP. *See* Military Decision-Making Process
Meaningful Writing Project, The, 17–18, 42, 89, 213, 215
meaning-making outputs, 44, 45, 128
medals, 187–188
medivac reports, 14, 49, 53f, 101, 131, 146, 223
memorandum, Army correspondence, 14, 54
mentoring underclass cadets, 179
Merchants Marine Academy, 22n
message, Army correspondence, 54
metacognition teaching methodology, 85, 191–193, 211
middle school education, writing skills, 89
Military Decision-Making Process (MDMP), 173, 178–179, 199; analysis, 180–182, 184; approval, 183; comparison, 182; development, 182; mission statements, 181; orders production, dissemination, and transition, 183; receipt of mission, 180
Military Leadership Center (MLC), 108, 183
military operations, 51–53
Military Symbols, 156–157, 159n2
military training units, 7, 19, 29–30, 35, 39
military writing style, 14, 37
Miller, Benjamin, 18
Miller, Carolyn, 48–49
Miller, Susan, 71–72
Millett, Allen, 7
Minthorn, Robin Zape-tah-hol-ah, 79

Mission Command and the Army Profession (MILS 4000), 178–179, 187–188
missions, operations orders (OPORDs), 52, 146, 147
MLC (Military Leadership Center), 108, 183
Modeling, literacy development, 112
Modern Language Association Statement of Professional Ethics, 73
Modernization, armed forces, 7
Moore, Jessie L., 43, 48
morale of cadets, 56, 122–124
Morrell, Robert "Trent," 10, 16, 68–70, 89–90
Morrill Act (1862), 29
Morrill, Justin, 29
Mountain Order of Colombo, 67
multiculturalism, 41, 134
Multi-Service Tactics, Techniques, and Procedures for Cordon and Search Operations (ATP 3-06.29), 155
Murphy, Sandra, 43
Murtazashvili, Ilia, 11, 34
Myers-Briggs personality test, 121

n of 1 research methodology, 17
Naming Commission, 107*n*2
narrative summation, writing development, 106
National Assessment of Educational Progress, 89
National Center for Education Statistics, 23n
National Commission on Writing in America's Schools and Colleges, 89
National Defense Authorization Act, 6–7, 12, 28–29, 107*n*2
National Guard, 30
National Order of Merit list. *See* Order of Merit List
National Resource Center (NRC) for the First-Year Experience and Students in Transition, 88
national-guard soldiers, 1
NATO (North Atlantic Treaty Organization), 210–211
Naval Academy, 22*n*2
Naval Act of 1916, 7
Navy Junior Reserve Officers Training Corps (NJROTC), 64
Neely, Shawn, 14, 37, 56–57
Neiberg, Michael, 11, 33
Nelms, Gerald, 208*n*1
Nelson, Christine A., 79
Nestor, Colonel Adam, 2, 3, 4
9 Line MEDEVAC reports, 14, 49, 53*f*, 131, 146, 223

1916 National Defense Act, 11
Nobel Peace Prize, 161–162
noncommissioned officers (NCOs), 30–31, 112
non-MILS coursework, 142
non-school writing, 94, 97, 117–118, 127–128
North American genre theory, 105
North Atlantic Treaty Organization (NATO), 210–211
Norwich University, 6, 29
not-talk writing, 50, 84, 86

Oath of Commissioned Officers, 98, 194, 195*f*, 196
Oath of Enlistment, 194
Obama, Barack, 9, 32–33, 56, 160, 162–163
occupational camouflage pattern (OCPs), 2
Odyssey blog, 117–118, 126, 129–132, 143, 185
officers, 13, 29–31, 188–189, 220, 221
OML List. *See* Order of Merit List
on-campus military training programs, higher education, 33
one-semester persistence rates, 17, 18, 215
openness, habit of mind, 85
operation orders (OPORDs), 7, 100, 198; Army genres, 51–53; chain of command, 144; command and control, 52; command signal, 146, 148; commander's intent, 149; cordon and search techniques, 14–15; critical-thinking skills, 52–53; execution, 52, 146, 147–148; external tools, 145–146; failed operations documentation, 146, 148; field book, 139–140, 145–146; five-paragraph version, 51–53, 146; form, 51*f*; Military Science 1000 assignments, 111–112; mission, 52, 146, 147; orality, 101, 151–152; service and support, 146, 148; situation, 146–147; supervise and refine, 149; sustainment, 52; terrain models, 139, 141, 150, 151*f*, 152, 173; third-year cadets, 144; troop-leading procedures, 149; unclassified, 145*f*
The Operations Process (US Army 2019c), 51
Operations Security (2014b), 9, 23*n*3
OPORDs. *See* operations orders
oral delivery, writing development, 62–64, 93, 94, 100–101, 151–152
Order of Merit List (OML), 31; accessions, 177; extracurricular activities, 117–118; fraternity membership, 113, 175; Distinguished Military Graduate (DMG), 178; Outcome Metrics Score (OMS), 177–178

Index 253

orders production, dissemination, and transition, 183
orientation. *See* FROG week
Otuteye, Mark, 127
Outcome Metrics Score (OMS), OML Model, 177–178

Palmquist, Mike, 51, 206
paragraphing exercises, 201–202
participants in research, 72, 198, 134, 135
Partridge, Alden, 29
passive voice, 5
Patel, Leigh, 21, 79, 136n2, 134, 204
Peckham, Irvin, 23n4
pedagogical issues, centers for teaching and learning (CTLs);: engagement, 205, 208n1; genres, 48–51; paragraphing exercises, 201–202; positionality, 21–22, 76–78, 135, 207; research process, 22, student veterans, 37
Pedagogy: Critical Approaches to Teaching Literature, Language, Composition, and Culture, 36
Pemberton, Michael A., 206
Perl, Sondra, 94–95
persistence, habit of mind, 85
Phillips, Cassandra, 85
Phillips, Nathan, 79, 135
physical tools for writing development, 201–202
physical-fitness labs, 7
physical-readiness (PR) training, 91, 102, 119, 124, 142, 153
Pintrich, Paul, 191–192
plagiarism, Army writing standards, 56–57
Plain Writing Act of 2010, 54–57
Planning and Orders Production (US Army 2022), 179
platoon sergeant, 142
Poe, Mya, 11, 84–85, 198
poetry readings, writing development, 127, 128
Polish Army, commissioning army officers, 209
political activity, armed forces, 164
positionality, data collection, 21–22; ethics, 135; longitudinal research, 76–78; self-reflexivity, 207
post-graduation life, cadets, 191
PowerPoint presentations, 14, 49, 58, 140, 153–155
PR (physical-readiness training), 91, 102, 119, 124, 142, 153
precamp, ROTC, 183, 184f
Preparing and Managing Correspondence, 7, 11, 54

President of the United States of America, ROTC establishment and maintenance, 28
primary sources, research methodology, 10–11
Prior, Paul, 43–44, 117, 133, 168, 191–193
privatization, academic services, 17
Proclamation of Neutrality in 1793, 32
professional-development opportunities, faculty, 205
professor of military science (PMS), 75
proficiency, writing development, 83–84
pronouns, masculine, 5
Public Pedagogy in Composition Studies, 205
public scholarship: Black Lives Matter, 204; Carnegie Classification, 202; centers for teaching and learning (CTLs), 205–206; connection with institutional history, 205; engaged research, 202–203; ethics, 204; rhetoric and composition/writing studies (RC/WS), 206–207; student input, 198; teaching methodology, 197
public speaking, 62–64, 93, 94
purpose, transparency in learning and teaching (TILT), 211

qualitative case studies, limitations of, 42
qualitative data research, 10, 41–42, 73–74, 87–88, 92, 134

racial bias/racism in research, 76, 85–86
RC/WS. *See* rhetoric and composition/writing studies
reading comprehension skills, 126
receipt of mission, Military Decision-Making Process (MDMP), 180
reciprocity, research methodology, 198
recommendations for awards forms, 14
recruiting research participants, 91–92
regulations, Army operations location disclosure, 9, 23n3
Rehearsing New Roles: How College Students Develop as Writers, 41
Reiff, Mary Jo, 50, 51, 84, 86
Research in the Teaching of English, 74–75
research methods: Advanced Placement test scores, 18; autoethnography, 21; big data analytics, 10, 17, 197; Center for Postsecondary Research, 18; curricular writing experiences, 19, 93; data collection, 10–11, 15, 17, 21, 134–135; diversity, 76–78, 134; drawing, 191–193; engaged research, 202–203; ethics, 91–92, 198; ethnography, 40, 134; findings, 19–20; gatekeepers, 75, 78; heat

maps, 18; lifespan-writing, 43; longitudinal research, 72, 198–207; modeling, 112; *n of 1*, 17; positionality, 21; primary sources, 10–11; public scholarship, 202, 204, 207; qualitative data, 10, 41–42, 73, 92; racial bias/racism, 76; reciprocity, 134–135, 198; rhetoric and composition/writing studies (RC/WS), 206–207; secondary sources, 10–11; self-reflexivity, 74–75, 198; student voice; representation, 18–19, 197; traditional research, 202; writing development, 127

research moments, conclusion, 201–204; data analysis, 134, 201; gatekeepers, 75; inquiry stance, 79; research process, 22, 73; research subjects' access, 78

research participants, extracurricular writing, 127; mapping exercises, 191–193; recruiting, 91–92

Reserve Officers' Training Corps (ROTC): Advanced Camp at Fort Knox, 9, 30, 31, 175–176, 183–184; *Army Awards*, 187–188; Army writing standards, 47, 86; civil education institutions, 28; commissioning from cadet to Army officer, 28–30; compulsory military training, 29, 34; coursework, 48, 75, 86; establishment through Title 10 2111a(f), 6; higher education, 34; leadership training, 7, 193–194; National Defense Act of 1926, 28; number of cadets, 7; officer training, 31; Order of Merit List (OML), 113, 117–118, 175, 178; physical-fitness labs, 7; precamp, 183, 184*f*; S-3 designation, 119, 126*n1*; terrain models, 139, 141, 151*f*, 173; World War I, 37–38*n3*; writing curriculum and cadet literacy development, 15, 47

reserve-duty component, 31

responsibility, habit of mind, 85

Retreat ceremony, 216

Reveille, Drills and Ceremonies, 5, 6, 13

rhetoric and composition/writing studies (RC/WS), centers for teaching and learning (CTLs), 208*n1*; disciplinary descriptive, 23*n4*; drawing research tool, 191–193; engaged research, 206–207; genre studies, 48–49; knowledge transfer, 47; legal writing, 125; lifespan-writing, 43–47; longitudinal studies, 40–43, 134; modeling research tool, 112; public speaking, 62, 93, 94; research methodology, 11; rhetorical knowledge, 14, 42, 49; scholarship, 18, 127, 206; student engagement, 72, 90;

veterans, 12–13, 35–36; writing development, 118

Rhodes, Benjamin, 161

ribbons, 187–188

Rifenburg, J. Michael, 10, 15, 72, 75, 166

Rite in the Rain paper, 139, 146

Robertson, Liane, 42

Rogers, Paul, 58*n1*

Roksa, Josipa, 17, 88–89

Roozen, Kevin, 11, 21, 79*n3*, 94, 127–128, 201

ROTC. *See* Reserve Officers' Training Corps

Rowe, Deborah Wells, 43

Rudy, Willis, 29

Ruecker, Todd, 79*n2*

Rule, Hannah, 136, 192

Russell, David R., 105

S-3 designation, ROTC, 119, 126*n1*, 183, 190, 224

salary, Army, 30–31

Schleppegrell, Mary, 43

Scholarship of Teaching of Learning (SoTL), 19

school-sponsored writing, literacy development, 61–62

Schultz, Katherine, 127, 128

screen-based writing, 98–100, 230

second lieutenant, 29–31, 66, 94, 131, 140, 159

secondary sources, research methodology, 10–11

second-year cadets: Astronomy of the Solar System (ASTR 1010), 126; Business Communication (BUSA 2108), 120–122, 132; coursework, 119–120; extracurricular activities, 127–133, 185; Legal Environment of Business (BUSA 2810), 124–125; literacy development, 117–118; Military Science 2000: Innovative Team Leadership, 122–124; morale, 120–122. *See also* cadets; first-year cadets; fourth-year cadets; third-year cadets

secretary of defense, 8, 30, 107*n2*, 108, 153, 164, 185

Seidman, Irving, 75

self-reflexivity in research, 74–78, 198, 207

self-sponsored writing activities, 61–62, 117–118, 166–168, 170

seminars, first-year writing coursework, 90

semiotics in research, 44–47, 128

senior military colleges (SMCs), 6, 29, 34

service academies, 22–23*n2*

service and support, operations orders (OPORDs), 146, 148

Shipka, Jody, 117, 133, 168, 191–193
Shotton, Heather J., 79
situation, operations orders (OPORDs), 52, 146–147
situational templates, 226
The Sleepwalkers: How Europe Went to War in 1914, 27
SMCs (senior military colleges), 6, 29, 34
Smith, Anna, 79, 135
Smith, Linda Tuhiwai, 79
smoking, Freshman Recruit Orientation (FROG) week, 68–69
social media, cadet training, 9
socioeconomic factors, access to higher education, 41
"A Soldier's Will," 62*f*, 63*f*
source attribution, Army writing standards, 56–57
space for writing, 192*f*, 193
special branches, 31
standard agreements (STANAGs), NATO members, 210
standard operating procedures, 37
stand-up comedy, writing development, 128
Stanford Study of Writing (SSW), 127
state budget appropriations for higher education, 202
Stein, Arlene, 203
Sternglass, Marilyn, 40–41, 134
Stornaiuolo, Amy, 21, 74–76, 79, 135, 136
storying research, 135, 136*n1*
Student Army Training Corps (SATC), 38*n3*
students: academic performance, 214–215; degree-to-completion numbers, 215; disability studies, 36; engagement, 90; failed initiation into discourse communities, 85; general studies, 36; genre knowledge, 49–51; individual dispositions, 85–86; input, 72, 85, 90, 198, 200; military experience, 35, 37; multiculturalism, 41; perception of academic environment, 40–41; perspectives, 198; research methodology, 18–19, 197; retention, colleges and universities, 87, 88, 91, 215; student/teacher ratio, 212; success initiatives, 198; veterans, 13, 36; wayfinding, 42; Writing Transfer Project, 50
subject-matter knowledge, 42, 49
Sullivan, Patrick, 39, 86*n1*
Summary of the 2018 National Defense Strategy, 11
supervise and refine, operations orders (OPORDs), 149
support services for veterans, 36
sustainment, operations orders (OPORDs), 52
Svihla, Vanessa, 79*n2*
Swearer Center at Brown University, 202
symbols, military, 156–157, 159*n2*
synchronization matrices, 14

Tachine, Amanda R., 79
Taczak, Kara, 42
TC 3-21.5 (Army Training Circular), 5, 13, 216
teaching: business communication, 120–122, 132; critical thinking skills, 41; discipline-specific, 84, 105; general education, 84; influence of Beaufort's research, 41; meaningful projects, 89; racial bias, 85–86; seminars, 90; student input, 90, 198, 200; transfer of learning, 42; university-level, 42
teaching methodologies: assignment design, 211; curriculum design, 197; flipped-classroom approach, 120–122, 132; interdisciplinary, 35; metacognition, 211; postsecondary writing, 85–86; public scholarship, 197; student/teacher ratio, 212; transparency in learning and teaching (TILT), 211
team leadership skills Military Science 2000: Innovative Team Leadership, 122–124
Terms and Military Symbols, 159*n2*
terrain models, OPORDs, 139, 141, 144, 150, 151*f*, 152, 173
Texas A&M, 6
textbooks, genres, 51
textual production, 133
Thaiss, Chris, 58*n1*
theater performance, writing development, 127
Thelin, John R., 29
Thicker Than Blood: How Racial Statistics Lie, 76
think-aloud writing assignment, 94–95
third-year cadets: Applied Leadership in Small Unit Operations (MILS 3100), 153–158; coursework, 153, 169; creative writing, 166–168; education-abroad opportunities, 143–144; literacy development, 168–169; non-MILS coursework, 142; operations orders (OPORDs), 139–140, 144–149, 151–152; platoon sergeant, 142; terrain models, 139, 141, 150–152, 151*f*, 173; unclassified writing, 145*f*
Thomas, Ebony Elizabeth, 21, 74–76, 136

Thompson, Roger, 36
TILT (transparency in learning and teaching), 211
Time to Know Them: A Longitudinal Study of Writing and Learning at the College Level, 40
Tinberg, Howard, 39
tools for writing development, 50, 201–202
Torres, Vasti, 75
Townsend, General Stephen, 1–5, 16, 140, commissioning, 223; doctrinal templates, 226; personnel resources, 231–232; Reserve Officers' Training Corps, 227; screen-based writing, 230; situational templates, 226; writing tools, 228–229
traditional first-year compositional courses, 14
traditional research, 202
TRADOC (Training and Doctrine Command), 159*n1*
training cadets, 9, 13*f*, 193–194
Training Management, 179
transfer, writing, curriculum design, 47–48
transparency in learning and teaching (TILT), 211
triangulation, data collection, 17
troop-leading procedures, operations orders (OPORDs), 149
Trump, Donald, 12, 163–165, 186, 213
Tuck, Eve, 78
Twitter, cadet training, 9

unclassified OPORDs, 145*f*
United States Military Academy. *See* West Point
University of North Georgia (UNG): active-duty components, 30; cadets, 7; Center for Teaching, Learning, and Leadership (CTLL), 206; civilian teachers, 75; civilian students, 34, 67–68; compulsory composition courses, 90; drill field, 13*f*; engaged research, 205; Freshman Recruit Orientation Group (FROG) week, 66–70; memorandum of understanding, 17; Military Leadership Center (MLC), 108; military students, 34; mission statement, 205; Morrell, Robert "Trent," 68–70; Order of Merit List (OML), 31; partnership with General Tadeusz Kosciuszko Military University of Land Forces (MULF), 210; vision statement, 205; Reveille, 6
United States foreign policy, 32–33
university curriculum, general education coursework, 199–201, 209

University of Indiana, Center for Postsecondary Research, 18
University of Michigan, English and Education PhD program, 18
urban student population, 41
US Army Cadet Command (USACC), 1, 11, 16, 30, 113, 177
US Army Regulation 530-1, *Operations Security* (2014b), 23*n3*
US Army Training and Doctrine Command (TRADOC), motto, 1, 16
US Army. *See* Army
US Department of Defense, 11

veterans, higher education, 35–37
Virginia Tech, 6, 35, 65
vision statement of University of North Georgia (UNG), 205
Virginia Military Institute (VMI), 6, 34
voice in writing development, 5, 19, 131
voluntary military system, 34

Walker, Janice R., 206
Wallraff, Barbara, 51
War Department. *See* Defense, Department of
war gaming. *See* course of action
Wardle, Elizabeth, 14, 60–61
warning orders (WARNOs), 14, 49, 52, 150, 180, 181
warrant officers, 37*n2*
Waterman, Stephanie J., 79
Watson, C. Edward, 206
wayfinding, 42
Weisser, Christian, 35–36
Wells, Deborah Rowe, 43
Wells, Jennifer, 85
West Point (United States Military Academy), 22, 23*n1*, 31, 66, 79*n1*
What Is "College-Level" Writing?, 39
White Logic, White Methods: Racism and Methodology, 76
White, Edward, 23*n4*
Whithaus, Carl, 42
Wickham, Army Chief of Staff John A., Jr., 54–55
Winalski, Amanda, 39
World War I, 27, 31, 32, 37, 37–38*n3*, 189
Worlds Apart: Acting and Writing in Academic and Workplace Contexts, 46
writing: definition of, 14; purpose of, 4, 46
Writing about Writing (2014), 14, 60–61, 92, 94, 98
Writing across Contexts, 42
Writing Beyond the University research seminar, 43

writing development: Army standards, 83, 84; audience, 99, 131; blogs, 117–118, 126, 129–132, 143, 185; cognitive facilitators, 139–141, 201–202; copy editing, 130–131; creative writing, 85, 93, 166–168; curiosity, 85; curricular activities, 40, 93–94; discourse communities, 85; effectiveness, 71; embodiment, 44; engagement, 85; essay contests, 95–96; extracurricular activities, 40, 93–94, 97, 128–129; first-year cadets, 88–90, 99; flash-fiction contests, 95–96; flexibility, 85; grammar, 130; habits of mind, 85; individual dispositions, 85–86; inscriptions, 44; interdisciplinary, 105; just-in-school, 44–45, 47, 93–94, 128; lifespan, 43–47, 128; literacy tasks, 61–62; materiality, 201–202; metacognition, 85; modeling, 112; narrative summation, 106; not-talk writing, 84, 86; openness, 85; oral delivery, 62–64, 93, 94, 100–101, 152; perceptions of academic environment, 40; persistence, 85; poetry readings, 127, 128; proficiency in genres, 50–51; proficiency, 83–84; responsibility, 85; rhetorical purposes, 118; self-sponsored, 117–118; semiotic becoming, 44–45; stand-up comedy, 128; Stanford Study of Writing (SSW), 127; studies, 40–42; theater performance, 127; undergraduate studies, 57; voice, 5, 131
writing knowledge transfer, 47, 49, 50

Writing Program Administration, 18
Writing Programs, Veteran Studies, and the Post 9/11 University, A Field Guide, 36
writing space, 13, 136, 192f, 193
writing studies, purpose of, 71–72
writing style: Army standards, 13–14, 20–21; college-level knowledge and skills, 14; cordon and search techniques operation order (OPORD), 14–15; critical thinking skills, 19; extracurricular, 20–21, 93–94, 97; general education coursework, 199–201; genres, 49–50, 105, 124, 139–141; high school–level to college-level, 39; literacy development, 61–62; oral delivery, 62–64, 93, 94, 152; rhetorical power, 14; societal factors, 42; traditional first-year courses, 14; transferring across domains, 47
Writing Ten Core Concepts, 51
writing transfer, 41, 47–51, 57
writing-definition assignment, 100
writing-process knowledge, 42, 49

Yagelski, Robert, 51
Yancey, Kathleen Blake, 42, 47–48, 169, 170
Yañez, Arturo, 105
Yang, K. Wayne, 79
YouTube, cadet promotional videos, 9

Zawacki, Terry Myers, 58n1
Zepernick, Janet, 84
Zuberi, Tukufu, 21, 76–77

ABOUT THE AUTHOR

J. Michael Rifenburg is an associate professor of English at the University of North Georgia, one of six senior military colleges in the United States. He also serves as codirector of first-year composition and senior faculty fellow for scholarly writing with UNG's Center for Teaching, Learning, and Leadership. He authored *The Embodied Playbook: Writing Practices of Student-Athletes* (Utah State University Press, 2018) and coedited *Contemporary Perspectives on Cognition and Writing* (WAC Clearinghouse, 2017).

www.ingramcontent.com/pod-product-compliance
Lightning Source LLC
Chambersburg PA
CBHW020521080526
44583CB00013B/687